A SOLDIER'S DREAM

A SOLDIER'S DREAM

✯

CAPTAIN TRAVIS PATRIQUIN
AND THE AWAKENING OF IRAQ

WILLIAM DOYLE

NAL
CALIBER

NAL Caliber
Published by New American Library, a division of Penguin Group (USA) Inc., 375 Hudson
Street, New York, New York 10014, USA • Penguin Group (Canada), 90 Eglinton Avenue
East, Suite 700, Toronto, Ontario M4P 2Y3, Canada (a division of Pearson Penguin Canada
Inc.) • Penguin Books Ltd., 80 Strand, London WC2R 0RL, England • Penguin Ireland,
25 St. Stephen's Green, Dublin 2, Ireland (a division of Penguin Books Ltd.) • Penguin Group
(Australia), 250 Camberwell Road, Camberwell, Victoria 3124, Australia (a division of Pearson
Australia Group Pty. Ltd.) • Penguin Books India Pvt. Ltd., 11 Community Centre, Panch-
sheel Park, New Delhi - 110 017, India • Penguin Group (NZ), 67 Apollo Drive, Rosedale,
Auckland 0632, New Zealand (a division of Pearson New Zealand Ltd.) • Penguin Books
(South Africa) (Pty.) Ltd., 24 Sturdee Avenue, Rosebank, Johannesburg 2196, South Africa

Penguin Books Ltd., Registered Offices:
80 Strand, London WC2R 0RL, England

First published by NAL Caliber, an imprint of New American Library,
a division of Penguin Group (USA) Inc.

First Printing, June 2011
1   3   5   7   9   10   8   6   4   2

Copyright © William Doyle, 2011
Maps copyright © Jeffrey L. Ward, 2011
All rights reserved

NAL CALIBER and the "C" logo are trademarks of Penguin Group (USA) Inc.

LIBRARY OF CONGRESS CATALOGING-IN-PUBLICATION DATA:

Doyle, William, 1957–

A soldier's dream: Captain Travis Patriquin and the awakening of Iraq/William Doyle.
p. cm.
Includes bibliographical references and index.
ISBN 978-0-451-23000-3

1. Patriquin, Travis, 1974–2006.   2. Iraq War, 2003—Biography.   3. United States.
Army—Biography.   4. Iraq War, 2003—Campaigns—Iraq—Anbar (Province)
5. Counterinsurgency—Iraq—Anbar (Province)   I. Title.
DS79.766.P37D69 2011
956.7044'342092—dc22   2011003175
[B]

Set in Fairfield • Designed by Elke Sigal

Printed in the United States of America

To my son, Brendan, and my wife, Naomi

★

To the family of Travis Patriquin, and to all military families

CONTENTS

Author's Note   *ix*

Prologue   The Banks of the Euphrates   *1*

Chapter 1   The Gate of the Himalayas   *17*

Chapter 2   The Edge of the Arabian Desert   *45*

Chapter 3   The City of Death   *61*

Chapter 4   The Earth Was on Fire   *87*

Chapter 5   A Time to Strike   *103*

Chapter 6   Before the Dawn   *119*

Chapter 7   A Baptism in Blood   *137*

Chapter 8   The Awakening of Iraq   *149*

Chapter 9   The Men on the Wall   *167*

Chapter 10   A Cocky Son of a Bitch   *189*

CONTENTS

Chapter 11   The Turning Point   *211*

Chapter 12   A Soldier's Dream   239

Epilogue   A Soldier's Legacy   263

Source Notes   287

Acknowledgments   308

Index   309

AUTHOR'S NOTE

For six months in 2006, a charismatic young American military officer and Afghanisthan war veteran with a passion for Arabic culture helped his colleagues and the tribes of Iraq's Anbar province achieve a historic victory against al-Qaeda and engineer a major turning point in the Iraq War.

This book is my attempt to tell his story, largely through his own words and the memories of the people who knew and loved him.

I first learned of Captain Travis Patriquin in August 2007, when I read an article by Martin Fletcher in the *Times* (of London) about a U.S. Army soldier and Arabic linguist who was being hailed as a martyr by Iraqis. In the history of the Iraq War, I'd never heard of such a thing. *An American soldier was being publicly hailed as a martyr by Iraqis.* I had to find out more about who this man was.

Fletcher's story told of the late Captain Travis Patriquin's key role in the American military effort to help Iraqis launch the Anbar

Awakening, a tribal revolt against al-Qaeda in Iraq that directly led to sharply lower levels of violence in the former center of the insurgency, Anbar province, and elsewhere in Iraq, and had major ripple effects that shaped the course of the Iraq War.

I was amazed by Patriquin's story, and as I interviewed scores of his American and Iraqi colleagues, I came to realize that Patriquin's journey is critical to understanding America's experience in the Middle East and perhaps to understanding America's future on the world stage.

This is not a book mainly about combat, though there is combat in it. It is not a book about an author's experience with troops at war. There are many good books about that, and this isn't one of them. This is not a book about generals, or power struggles in the corridors of the White House, the Pentagon, and Washington think tanks. It is not a micro-history of the Iraq War, or counter-insurgency policy, or the famous "surge," or combat operations in Anbar province, or, for that matter, the Awakening. Lots of good books have been written, or will be, about all that, too, hopefully many of them by Iraqis.

And this is not intended to be a work of hagiography that exaggerates the contribution of one man to the course of the Iraq War. Tens of thousands of Iraqis, Americans, and others have died in the struggle to bring stability to that tormented land, and in the scheme of things each of those sacrifices is equally infinite to those who have died and to their loved ones.

As for the hundreds of thousands of Americans who have served in Iraq, I think Patriquin's colleague Lieutenant Colonel Vincent Tedesco said it well when he told me: "Travis was a unique individual who made a very significant contribution. But there are thousands of men and women who fought in Iraq in a variety of different units before and after our time, who did great and glorious things for their nation, stories that will never be told. If in honoring Travis we can in some way illuminate the contributions and sacrifices of the common soldier, then I'm all in favor of it. He was exceptional but he was also representative of the quality of the individuals that are the strength of our military."

This book explores the experience of one soldier who served in Afghanistan, and then Iraq, who played a crucial role in shaping events there in a pivotal place and moment of the war, and was killed. This is a view of the Iraq War from a very narrow focus—that of a single American soldier, who happened to help shape a turning point in the conflict.

This book is based largely on hundreds of interviews I conducted with about one hundred and fifty of Travis Patriquin's family, friends, military colleagues, and Iraqis who worked with him closely, and on Patriquin's own personal and professional writings.

It is also based on thousands of pages of documents obtained by the author from various sources inside and outside the U.S. military. These documents, many of them not previously available to the public, include U.S. military meeting reports, situation reports, memos, e-mails, after-action reports, data sheets, maps, PowerPoint presentations, and intelligence briefings. Some documents and interviews were given to me anonymously or not for attribution.

And this book is based on the memories and journals of four people who worked with Patriquin on a daily basis as Arabic interpreters and cultural advisors in Iraq: a Syrian-born American named Majd Alghabra; a Syrian-educated American, Sterling Jensen; and two native-born Iraqis, Atheer Agoubi and Sa'ad Mohammed, the latter of which is a pseudonym.

American politicians, pundits, and generals have stumbled over one another to take credit for reductions in violence and improved conditions in Iraq, claiming they resulted from their support of the American troop surge beginning in early 2007. But the success of the surge was largely made possible by the Awakening. And the Awakening may not have succeeded as it did without the crucial early efforts in 2006 of a very small group of American army and marine officers to support it, and particularly the work of one American soldier, Captain Travis Patriquin. Patriquin was loved by Iraqis as a brother and formed one of the closest connections with the Iraqi people ever achieved by an American soldier.

When I first met Patriquin's wife, Amy, she said she thought her late husband would have loved the idea of someone writing a book about him. She said she had only one thing to ask of me—"tell the truth."

That's what I've tried to do.

This is the story of a man who helped the Iraqis engineer a turning point in the Iraq War.

It is the story of one of the over 4,400 American military men and women who have died in that conflict, a war that so far has killed almost 100,000 Iraqi civilian men, women, and children. They were two body counts that Travis Patriquin dreamed of stopping.

This is the story of how sometimes, one soldier can help change the course of a war.

Get to know their families, clans and tribes, friends and enemies, wells, hills and roads. . . . If you succeed, you will have hundreds of miles of country and thousands of men under your orders.

—T. E. LAWRENCE, IN THE *ARAB BULLETIN*, 1917

★

I support world peace! One carefully placed round at a time.

—SIGN ON TRAVIS PATRIQUIN'S DESK, 2006

★

God's plan is unknown to us, but there is a plan,
I believe that with all my being, and we're all a part of it.

—CAPTAIN TRAVIS PATRIQUIN

Much have I seen and known; cities of men
And manners, climates, councils, governments,
Myself not least, but honour'd of them all;
And drunk delight of battle with my peers,
Far on the ringing plains of windy Troy.
I am a part of all that I have met;
Yet all experience is an arch wherethro'
Gleams that untravell'd world whose margin fades
For ever and forever when I move.

—ALFRED LORD TENNYSON,

"ULYSSES"

★

Whenever I describe Travis to someone, it sounds like a movie.
But the thing is, some movies are true.

—STAFF SERGEANT KEN BAKER,

U.S. ARMY SPECIAL FORCES (RET.)

A SOLDIER'S DREAM

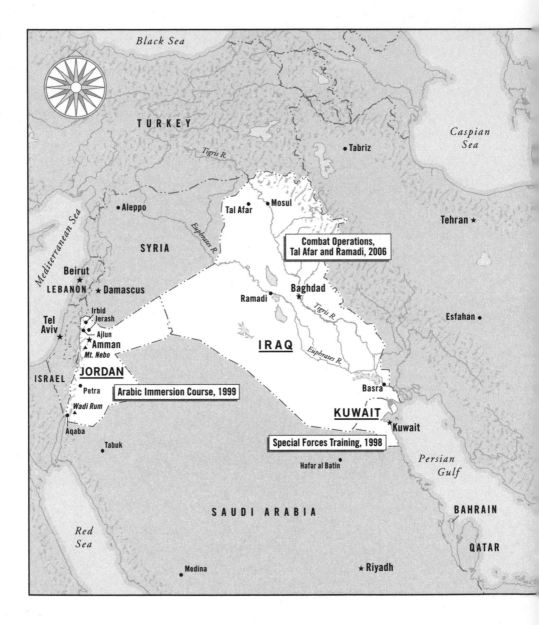

Black Sea

Caspian Sea

TURKEY

Tigris R.

• Tabriz

• Aleppo

Tal Afar • • Mosul

Tehran ★

SYRIA

Euphrates R.

Combat Operations,
Tal Afar and Ramadi, 2006

Mediterranean Sea

Beirut
★
LEBANON   ★ Damascus

Ramadi •

Baghdad
★

Tigris R.

Esfahan •

Irbid •
Jerash •

Tel
Aviv ★

Ajlun ★
★ Amman
Mt. Nebo ▲

IRAQ

Euphrates R.

JORDAN

ISRAEL

• Petra

Arabic Immersion Course, 1999

Basra •

▲ Wadi Rum

KUWAIT

Aqaba •

• Tabuk

★ Kuwait

Special Forces Training, 1998

Persian
Gulf

• Hafar al Batin

SAUDI ARABIA

BAHRAIN

Red
Sea

QATAR

Medina •

★ Riyadh

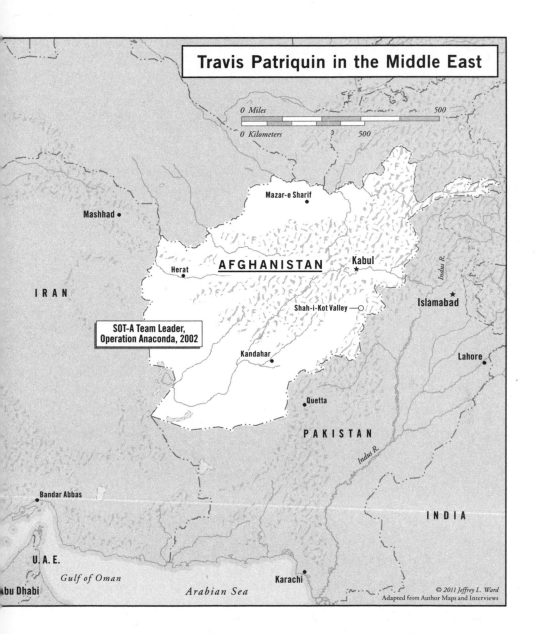

Travis Patriquin in the Middle East

0 Miles   500

0 Kilometers   500

Mazar-e Sharif

Mashhad

AFGHANISTAN   Kabul

Herat

Indus R.

IRAN

Shah-i-Kot Valley

Islamabad

SOT-A Team Leader,
Operation Anaconda, 2002

Kandahar

Lahore

Quetta

PAKISTAN

Indus R.

Bandar Abbas

INDIA

U. A. E.

bu Dhabi   Gulf of Oman

Karachi

Arabian Sea

© 2011 Jeffrey L. Ward
Adapted from Author Maps and Interviews

PROLOGUE

★

THE BANKS OF THE EUPHRATES

Captain Travis Patriquin was about to meet a man who some Americans believed was the Tony Soprano of western Iraq, and he seemed worried that if the meeting got screwed up, his new mission would be in jeopardy before it even started.

Sheik Sattar abu Risha was believed by some American military and intelligence officials to be an upstart mobster and the boss of a vicious gang of kidnappers, carjackers, highway robbers, and smugglers of oil, sheep, electronic goods, and stolen vehicles. He was also thought to be a pretty good contractor, for basic jobs like rubble removal and roadwork.

Captain Patriquin was sure that the last big battle of the Iraq War was about to unfold, in this city, Ramadi, and at this time, the summer of 2006, and he knew the Americans needed Sheik Sattar's help.

Inside the Humvee, as Patriquin's convoy bounced across Highway 1 toward Sattar's compound, one of Patriquin's Iraqi interpreters sensed the young officer's anxiety and tried to reassure him. "Don't worry, Captain Patriquin. He's a simple man with two hands and two feet."

"But will he work with us?" Patriquin mused.

That was all that mattered to the soldier, who was the tribal and civil affairs officer for the U.S. Army's First Brigade, First Armored Division, and was responsible for coordinating brigade-level contacts and outreach to Sunni tribal sheiks in bloody Ramadi. Ramadi, the capital of al Anbar province, was the worst deathtrap for American soldiers in the Iraq War, the site of some 30 percent of their fatalities.

Most of the sheiks in the area were either intimidated by insurgents or active supporters of insurgents engaged in shooting, rocketing, mortaring, and blowing up American soldiers. Some sheiks, like the volatile Sattar, were thought to be open to selling their services to the highest bidder, be it al-Qaeda or the Americans. Along with his brother, Ahmed, Sattar was co-leader of the Abu Risha clan, a small, obscure rural offshoot of the largest tribal group in Anbar province, the Dulaimi Confederation.

Sattar was also a man who some U.S. experts thought had potential to help the American mission in Anbar province, mainly by providing information on insurgents. But if Sattar turned against the Americans, the balance of power might shift dramatically in favor of the insurgents in the area. The previous and current battalion commanders responsible for this slice of Iraqi "battle space," Lieutenant Colonels Mark Lovejoy and Tony Deane, both urged Patriquin's brigade to cultivate Sattar as a friendly player, as they'd been doing.

Patriquin wanted nothing to go wrong at this encounter.

He brought along his boss, Lieutenant Colonel Jim Lechner, the deputy commander of Patriquin's brigade and a veteran of the Battle of Mogadishu in 1993. As recounted in the combat classic *Black Hawk Down*, Lechner, then serving with the Third Ranger

Battalion, suffered a horrific gunshot injury to his leg during a firefight with Somali militia. Patriquin had an admiration for the thirty-nine-year-old Lechner that one observer said "bordered on hero worship." Lechner recalls, "Travis and I were both Infantry officers. We were both prior enlisted and he was a little older and closer to my age than most captains. Travis had a great personality and we clicked on a number of levels. I think we both respected each other as soldiers and warriors."

Patriquin knew that the presence at this meeting of Jim Lechner, the personification of the forward-leaning, hard-charging American warrior and the brigade's number-two officer, would be a show of respect for Sattar.

Patriquin brought along two Baghdad-born Arabic interpreters to back him up, so he wouldn't miss a single nuance or phrase. He peppered them with questions on protocol and atmosphere. And for days he had been devouring every scrap of information he could find on the sheik.

The man Patriquin was about to meet, thirty-five-year-old Sheik Sattar, was a smoldering, swashbuckling enigma who to some Americans evoked a Hollywood fantasy of a charismatic Arab warrior-prince. One Arab interpreter for the Americans, however, who spent years living with Bedouin tribes in the Gulf States and met his share of powerful sheiks, took one look at Sattar and his then relatively modest dwelling space and scoffed in disappointment. "I know sheiks," he thought. "This guy isn't a sheik. The Americans don't know any better."

Sattar's grandfather was a powerful Anbar sheik who did business with British forces who occupied Iraq, then called Mesopotamia, in the early 1920s after the defeat of the Ottomans in World War I, and then fought in the nationalist revolution against the same British authorities.

Sattar's diminutive frame was typically adorned in a gold-trimmed headdress, a neatly trimmed mustache and goatee, pristine white robes from head to toe, cowboy boots, and either an ivory-handled Texas Sesquicentennial Colt .45 revolver or .44 Magnum pistol holstered on his waist over his garment. He smoked Cuban cigars, was fond of fine Arabian horses, sprinkled himself with expensive aftershave, and enjoyed nightclubbing in Dubai when his business schedule allowed.

CIA operatives had been courting Sheik Sattar as a source of information ever since the earliest days of the war, as had U.S. Special Operations officers and various other military and intelligence people. But Sattar's motivations and dealings often seemed murky or impenetrable to the Americans, who argued with each other over whether to play ball with Sattar or throw him in jail.

Sattar and his family members periodically performed legitimate construction and road repair work for American forces, but Sattar himself was also thought to be an oil, sheep, and car smuggler, a kidnapper for profit and erstwhile business partner with various insurgent factions. One American officer recalls, "We thought of him as a little Mafia guy, he had a large portion of the U.S. military contracts going on."

One U.S. Marine Corps intelligence analyst who served in Anbar province, Major Ben Connable, said of Sattar, "He had insurgent credentials, he had smuggling credentials, and he was kind of a criminal vagabond, these kinds of suave criminals that became so popular in western Iraq during the sanctions period." Another American military official, army tribal expert Lieutenant Colonel Richard D. Welch, said Sattar made a fortune "running a band of thieves who kidnapped and stopped and robbed people on the road between Baghdad and Jordan," the major east-west highway that passed near his house. Some other sheiks in Anbar province claimed that Sattar fed false intelligence to the Americans to get rid of his competitors. One American officer described Sattar as "more diabolical than Tony Soprano."

None of these allegations had been proven in any courts of law, which for years had ceased to function in Iraq anyway, and in the brutal landscape of Saddam-era and occupation-era Iraq, many sheiks resorted to these kinds of enterprises. Sattar later described himself as being in the construction and import-export businesses.

Late in 2003, U.S. intelligence intercepts picked up indications that Sattar might be planning to orchestrate the assassination of the American battalion commander then responsible for the area, Lieutenant Colonel Tom Hollis of the army's 1-16 Iron Rangers, apparently because Hollis's troops were conducting so many checkpoints and vehicle searches that Sattar's smuggling operations were crippled. Hollis was supposedly to be ambushed right after a scheduled meeting with Sattar.

Armed with advance warning of the possible attack, Hollis mounted up a strike team, surrounded Sattar's compound with American troops, weapons, and vehicles in an early-morning show of firepower, knocked on the front door, and elliptically told a disheveled Sattar that he expected the two men to "work together and look out for each other." He added, "We're here to help you and protect you. We're all friends of Anbar province. Let's put our differences aside."

Sattar evidently got the message and no harm came to Hollis. The following year, Sattar's suspected smuggling activities were getting so flagrant that, fearing they were feeding into insurgent activities, U.S. Special Forces operatives reportedly forced their way into the sheik's compound, arrested him, and detained him for several days. Sattar submitted an invoice to the Americans for property damages incurred during the raid, and he was reimbursed.

Rumors circulated in the U.S. military that Sattar had done

business with hyper-radical foreign-led insurgents in Iraq when they fled the U.S. onslaught on Fallujah in 2004 and muscled their way into the provincial capital of Ramadi. But as many as ten of Sattar's relatives, including his father and at least three brothers, were executed by the insurgents, who began interfering with the business operations of Sattar and other sheiks. Apparently, all of this led Sattar to increasingly consider open cooperation with the Americans.

Sattar and his older brother, Ahmed, held influence over the rural district that abutted what had been Patriquin's home for the last several weeks, the American military base at Camp Ramadi, not far from the edge of the desolate desert that stretched out to Saudi Arabia and Jordan. The brothers had good control of their area, and in American military parlance, it had been a "white zone" for many months, mostly free of IEDs and mortar attacks.

But Patriquin worried that if Sattar's vision didn't overlap with the plans of the new American brigade in Ramadi, real trouble could occur. Sattar was believed to have sway with rural tribes around Ramadi, and influence over at least several hundred young Sunni "military-aged males," or MAMs in military parlance. They were the seeds of a private army that could be turned against al-Qaeda, or against the Americans or the Iraqi government. Sattar had offered to field some of these men in combat patrols with the Americans. But U.S. military officials rebuffed him, afraid of launching a tribal militia they worried could destabilize their as yet largely ineffectual efforts to stand up a legitimate Iraqi government and security forces run from Baghdad.

Sattar was said to be disgruntled that the U.S. Army National Guard unit that preceded Patriquin's brigade had only achieved a defensive stalemate with al-Qaeda and other insurgents. Insurgents were roaming and striking at will throughout Anbar and most of the rest of Iraq south of Kurdistan, and Sattar seemed to be losing faith in the American military to ever defeat the insurgency, which appeared to be gaining power with each passing day of carnage across the country. The insurgents were riding a wave of terror that might be unstoppable. Sattar might be about to give up on the Americans.

But Travis Patriquin had at least four weapons he was ready to unleash on Sattar.

The first weapon was his personality. Though only thirty-one years old, he had amassed enough star-caliber charisma, confidence, and simultaneous humility to go head-to-head with Sattar or pretty much anyone else in a duel of personalities. "He was a charmer," said Captain Jon-Paul Hart, a roommate of Patriquin's in Iraq, "and he loved to charm people." Another close colleague, Captain Chad Pillai, described Patriquin as "a free-spirited goofball" with "tremendous personal magnetism," and a "very free spirit who was very independent, and did not fit the traditional mold of most army officers."

The second weapon was his brain. Patriquin was a polymathic, autodidactic, omnivorous consumer of books, Web pages, pop culture, and human conversation who inhaled mountains of information on a universe of topics and traveled to war zones with the Koran and Caesar's writings shoved in his duffel bag.

His brigade commander, Colonel Sean MacFarland, thought Patriquin might have some kind of attention-deficit disorder, though overall a productive one. Since his childhood, Patriquin seemed to be on an intellectual rampage through the collected written works of mankind, and he wanted to write a book of his own someday, though he hadn't figured out what it would be about yet.

"Travis was a Renaissance Man," says his friend Captain Andrew Duprey, who shifts into the jarringly epic language occasionally used by colleagues when they recall Patriquin. "You read about Leonardo da Vinci and the giants of the Renaissance or the Great Awakening, times when people were skilled not only in language, but in the arts. People were deep thinkers, they conceived new and esoteric ideas and expanded them beyond the realm of anyone's comprehension. Travis was that guy. He was a modern-day da Vinci. I seriously believe that. He had a love for people, for language, for music, for history—he had a love for life in everything he did."

Patriquin's third weapon was his experience. He'd been a soldier for over ten years. As a communications specialist, paratrooper, and support soldier in the army's 5th and 7th Special Forces Groups, he'd tramped through rain forests in South America during drug wars, jumped out of airplanes in the dead of night from ten thousand feet over Fort Bragg wearing 120 pounds of combat gear, and won a Bronze Star for leading troops in combat with al-Qaeda forces in the Battle of Shah-i-Kot Valley in Afghanistan in 2002.

When it came to weapons and war, he'd seen it all.

And Patriquin's final weapon was his voice.

Unlike the vast majority of American military officers, Patriquin actually spoke Arabic, the primary language of the nation America was still trying to stabilize three years after invading it. He spent over a year in intensive Arabic-language instruction at the military's Defense Language Institute in Monterey, California; he journeyed to Kuwait twice on Special Forces exercises; and in 1999, he traveled to the Holy Land for an Arabic immersion course at Jordan's Yarmouk University. He spoke Arabic with a distinct American accent, but this was obscured by the fearlessness and gusto with which he plunged into Arabic dialogue.

Unlike the relative handful of his military colleagues who

only studied formal Modern Standard Arabic and could easily get lost in a real-world street conversation, Patriquin was a connoisseur of Arabic slang and Iraqi colloquialisms, a talent he'd picked up by spending huge amounts of time learning and practicing with every Iraqi interpreter and merchant he could talk to during his brigade's recent four-month stint in the northern Iraqi city of Tal Afar.

But while Patriquin was skilled and conversant in Arabic, he was not technically fluent to the extent of being able to speak in long exchanges without help. There was a wide margin for gaps, errors, and getting lost, and he knew it. So he brought along interpreters to his meetings with key Iraqis.

In the Humvee, he told his two interpreters of his plan for the meeting with Sattar. "I'm going to talk with him face-to-face," he announced. "I'm going to try to speak as much Arabic with him as I can, but just in case, you guys have to back me up. You guys stand behind me. If I don't understand a phrase, I'm just going to turn my face to you, and you translate it, okay?"

The American vehicles swept up to the mansion, and Sattar greeted them at the entrance to his diwan, or living room and meeting area.

Sattar and Patriquin shook hands for the first time, offering each other the standard Arabic greetings of *as-salamu alaykum* and *alaykum as-salam*, or "peace be upon you," "and also with you."

As Patriquin introduced the members of his group in conversational Arabic, Sattar looked puzzled.

"Where are you from?" Sattar asked Patriquin.

"I'm American," replied the captain.

"Yes, but are you from an Arab country?" asked Sattar. "Are you from Iraq, from the north or from the south?"

One of the Iraqi interpreters realized that the sheik was

evidently mistaking Patriquin for an Arab-born national who moved to the United States, perhaps in childhood, became an American citizen, and now had returned to Iraq with the American military.

"No," repeated Patriquin, "I'm American!" At this, reports one of the interpreters present, Patriquin broke into "the biggest smile I've ever seen on an American officer."

Sattar looked startled.

"Are you a translator?" pressed Sattar.

"No, I'm a captain."

"Well then," said the Iraqi, "you deserve your rank."

"Yes, I think so too!" Patriquin said with a grin.

At this, Sattar laughed. "I'm so surprised! This is the first time I've met an American who can speak the Iraqi dialect so clearly. But how did you learn the language?"

"I am very interested in Arab culture," explained Patriquin. "That's why I learned the language. And that's why I came here to Iraq. I want to help bring peace to Iraq."

In Iraqi and other Arab cultures, there can be a good deal of cheek kissing and hand-holding among men, and for the past few months Patriquin had been cultivating a facial feature that he quipped was his "man-kiss curb-feeler"—a thick black mustache.

For most Iraqi men, wearing a mustache was automatic, a badge of manhood. An extreme insult was "a curse be upon your mustache." Iraqis literally swore by their facial hair, and to compliment a man they said, "An eagle could land on his mustache."

With a few exceptions, like some Special Forces soldiers, civilian contractors, and marines in units who deployed earlier in the war, Americans with mustaches were rarely seen in Iraq, especially regular army officers. For them, a mustache was a quaint throwback to the disco era or *Magnum, P.I.* reruns. Career-conscious army soldiers, especially officers in the "high and tight" physical mode of West Point graduates, just didn't wear them.

For Patriquin, the decision to grow a mustache was a sign of respect for Arab culture. He knew it would help him blend in with Iraqis and make them more comfortable with him. On top of this, he was letting his jet-black hair grow distinctly shaggier than regulation length, adding another cosmetic distinction that surprised Iraqis.

"You look like an Iraqi," observed an intrigued Sheik Sattar. "You've got dark skin and a thick mustache."

"Well, I like my mustache," replied Patriquin, "and I like the way the Iraqi people look and how they dress."

To this, Sattar observed, "Your brigade shows respect by sending me someone who speaks Arabic, and can speak to me directly without using a translator."

"I'm trying to learn more about Iraqi culture," Patriquin continued, in Arabic. "I would like to learn it from you."

Still laughing, Sattar declared, "All right, then, have a seat. You are welcome in my house."

Glancing over at his boss, Lieutenant Colonel Lechner, Patriquin said, "I cannot sit while my colonel is here."

Sattar replied, "Okay, tell your colonel to sit, but we have a long conversation we have to go through, you and me. He can't speak Arabic and he can't understand me."

When the group sat down, Sattar fired off a round of questions, "Why did your brigade come to Ramadi? What are you going to do? What is your plan? How are you going to get us security in the area?"

"We had a successful mission in Tal Afar," Patriquin responded, "which is why we were sent here. This is one of the worst spots in Iraq. Our mission is to get this area secure before we leave.

But let me ask you, how can we see things from your perspective? What do you think is the best thing we should do to get security to Ramadi?"

"If things were in my hands," Sattar said, "there would be success."

"What idea do you have that will help us succeed?" asked the American.

"The thing we have to do is build a new military force."

"What do you mean, build a military force?"

"Let me use my own fighters," said the Iraqi.

Patriquin was open to this idea, in theory. But it was just what most of the top American generals and civilian officials in Iraq did not want to hear. They were there to suppress militias, not raise them. From the first days of the invasion, irregular militias outside the control of the Iraqi government and coalition military were usually considered forbidden, a destabilizing threat in an already hopelessly chaotic landscape.

"We need to get our own people to fight the insurgents," declared Sattar. "We need to have our own people fight for the city.

"Americans will never have success if they have their own soldiers fighting for the city," the sheik explained. "The local people have more information than American intelligence. The insurgents wear civilian clothes. How will the Americans ever know who's an insurgent? But the local people can tell who the insurgents are, because they can tell who's not from the area."

Patriquin knew there were a few barely functioning Iraqi police and Iraqi army units in Anbar province, but the handful of police were largely terrorized, stayed at home, or were confined to their stations, and the army was far from combat-effective, and was comprised largely of Shiite conscripts from outside Anbar who were little trusted by local Sunnis.

"We tried to have Iraqi police, but the Star Colonel was killed," said Sattar. "You need to send us a man like the Star Colonel."

Star Colonel? Patriquin didn't understand this reference. He looked at his translators for help with a quick discussion to the side. He switched to English and asked them, "Star Colonel? Who's that?"

"Lieutenant Colonel Mike McLaughlin," an interpreter responded. "He was killed earlier this year."

"But why is he calling him Star Colonel? Our generals have stars, but not the colonels."

"He had your job for the 2/28 [the Second Brigade, Twenty-eighth Infantry Division, Pennsylvania Army National Guard, Patriquin's predecessors]. He tried to recruit Iraqis into the police."

Patriquin still didn't get the reference. "Why Star Colonel?"

The explanation: "All the sheiks loved him. They called him Gold Colonel, or Star Colonel, and the Star of Ramadi. He died in the explosion at the police recruiting event at the glass factory in January."

Sattar returned to his main point of the day: "I don't care if you have helicopters, aircraft, and spies, you'll never know more than the local people. Americans don't speak the language.

"If the local people don't fight against al-Qaeda, you'll never win," he continued. "There's no way you're going to make this city secure. You guys are going to destroy the city and make it just like Fallujah.

"You should let me use my own fighters," he concluded.

Patriquin nodded and said, "Okay, I can't promise you anything, but I'm going to tell my bosses about your idea. I agree with you. But I have to write a report and submit it to my colonel."

Sattar beckoned the delegation to his dining hall, invited Patriquin to sit beside him, and soon plates stuffed with food appeared.

"Where are the spoons?" asked another American who was present at the meeting.

"There are none," Patriquin said and smiled. Like many Arab meals, this was a fingers-only setup, a culinary approach that perplexed some Americans but delighted Patriquin.

"Captain Patriquin," announced the host, "I want you to put your hand on the food first."

"No, no, you are the sheik," Patriquin demurred, "you have to put your hand on the food first."

Laughing, Sattar suggested, "Why don't we put them together, as a sign of our peace?"

In a compound near the banks of the Euphrates River, as pet camels, falcons, and deer cavorted nearby, two Arabic-speaking guys with mustaches dug into big plates of rice, bread, and roast lamb.

Soon, the two men would help unleash forces that changed the course of the war in Anbar province, and all of Iraq.

CHAPTER 1

★

THE GATE OF THE HIMALAYAS

★

Patriquin braced himself against a boulder on a mountain in eastern Afghanistan, peered through his gun sight, and lined up the shot.

He had trained nine years for this one moment, on military firing ranges in Georgia, Kentucky, Germany, Uzbekistan, and the Amazon rain forest.

He joined the army on the same day he graduated from high school in 1993, and now beneath an electric blue sky in the seventy-five-mile-square Shah-i-Kot Valley on March 2, 2002, First Lieutenant Travis Patriquin was experiencing the first hours of combat in his life, in an area where Alexander the Great and his army marched in 330 BC, as did the British in the nineteenth century, and the Soviet army in the 1980s, when they tried and failed to capture and hold the valley.

Patriquin squeezed the trigger and the bullet hit the al-Qaeda fighter's upper body a moment later, dropping him on the cold ground of the mountainside.

"Holy shit, you got him!" cheered a nearby soldier, amazed at the feat's degree of difficulty.

Patriquin had scored a hit while shooting downhill from almost seven hundred meters, at the outside edge of the normal effective range of his weapon, and he did it in the unstable environment of cold crosswinds and oxygen-starved thin air of a remote valley in the foothills of the Himalayan Mountains.

After "walking in" a few rounds toward his target, Patriquin had corrected his aim like a golf pro shooting long drives on a gusty day. "It's called Tennessee elevation and Kentucky windage," he later explained. "It's how you adjust the impact of a round by lifting the barrel or moving it left to right, depending on the wind. A bullet can go farther."

For this group of forty-two soldiers hunkered down around Patriquin, after a morning of frustration and harassing sniper and small-arms fire, Patriquin's shot was one of the first times they could reach out and strike back at the enemy. The al-Qaeda fighter had been moving up toward the Americans in a methodical, determined advance that revealed good training and discipline. He seemed to have an almost Caucasian appearance—perhaps he was a Chechen or Uzbek volunteer—and as he climbed he carried his weapon under his arm with a soldier's demeanor.

If the target was lucky, he was quickly falling unconscious from shock and multiple internal injuries after Patriquin's bullet penetrated his soft tissue and fragmented in his body. A more unfortunate scenario would be a clean impact that severed blood vessels but avoided major organs, causing him to bleed out slowly in the morning sun.

Earlier this morning, when his group came under fire soon after being dropped off at the landing zone by helicopter, a strange thought crossed Patriquin's mind: "Why is he shooting at me? I never did anything to him."

Wait a minute.

The guy was moving.

From Patriquin's perch, it looked like the al-Qaeda casualty was kneeling toward the southwest and praying. He was facing in the general direction of Mecca, apparently praying to Allah. Then he picked up his rifle, slowly rose, and resumed his climb up the slope toward the American position.

Surprised, the burly, bearded Patriquin squinted through his gun sight and lined up another shot. He pulled the trigger again, and again he saw the al-Qaeda fighter drop down, apparently pray for a few moments, and struggle back up on his feet again to resume his ascent.

Incredible. Patriquin was sure he'd hit the guy twice now. Either something strange was happening with the bullets at this altitude, or this was one highly motivated, durable terrorist.

Patriquin fired once more. Again the shot struck.

This time the target stayed down for good. "Their resiliency is amazing," Patriquin later recalled of the enemy. "You shoot them, they fall down on their knees, pray to Allah, and they get back up. I shot that guy three times. Then he died."

This was the highest-altitude battle in American history: the base of the valley was at an altitude of eighty-five hundred feet, and the adjacent peaks swept up to over ten thousand feet. It was also the U.S. military's first winter combat since the Korean War, its biggest light infantry battle since Vietnam, and its first major ground combat since the Gulf War in 1991.

The sky over the Shah-i-Kot Valley was a symphony of allied AH-64 Apache gunships, B-2 and B-52 bombers, F-16 and F-18 fighter-bombers, AC-130 attack aircraft, A-10 tank-killing aircraft, and Predator unmanned aircraft, and the valley echoed with strafings, missiles exploding, and two-thousand-pound bomb detonations on suspected enemy positions.

A few months earlier, on September 11, 2001, Patriquin was stuck in an office job in the 82nd Airborne Division at Fort Bragg, North Carolina, hopping around on a knee brace. "The 82nd doesn't want me anymore," he lamented to a friend, "because I've got a bum knee and I can't jump out of airplanes." He'd torn his knee ligaments while jumping through an obstacle course in his second failed attempt to make it through the physically punishing Ranger School course at Fort Benning, Georgia. Earning a Ranger tab was considered almost essential for any army officer who wanted a successful career, and it looked like Patriquin's hopes of earning one were dashed.

This was a real career hurdle, explained Dave Osborne, Patriquin's former commander at Officer Candidate School. "If you're in the infantry and you're an officer and you don't have a Ranger tab, the first thing people will do is wonder, 'What happened?' It is almost nonoptional to go to Ranger School. Everybody goes. Not everybody finishes. It's very tough to complete, only about a fifty percent graduation rate. But in the infantry, you'd better get a Ranger tab by the time you're captain, because you'll almost certainly not make it to major without one."

Patriquin was disappointed, but resigned to this turn of fate. "There's not much more I can do," he told a friend. "I know I'm a capable leader. I know that physically I could have completed the course. I can lead patrols. There's no reason I shouldn't graduate from Ranger School. But for some reason, every time I go, something happens. Maybe this is just part of the plan. Maybe I'm just not supposed to make it through Ranger School."

In the weeks that followed, the 82nd Airborne was sidelined from the upcoming American assault on Afghanistan, and Patriquin was eager to somehow get into the fight. He knew that Afghanistan was where history and careers could be made.

So he decided to hustle his way onto the battlefield.

Patriquin was blessed with a strong talent for picking up foreign languages, and within a matter of weeks he pulled off the impressive trick of teaching himself passable Pashto in his spare time by scouring the Internet for online lessons. He threw himself into a program of intense physical therapy to try to get his bum knee back in shape. He contacted former colleagues from his old units in the Special Forces, where he served in the 1990s as a support soldier, to pull strings for him to get back into Special Forces, at least temporarily, since it looked like they were going to be the superstars in this new war.

His pitch to officers of the Afghanistan-bound 5th Group stationed at Fort Campbell, Kentucky, was simple, a claim few other Americans could make: He said he could speak Pashto, the language of the majority of Afghans and their overthrown Taliban leaders, and that he also spoke Arabic, the language of many of the Taliban's al-Qaeda allies. He practically demanded to be deployed to Afghanistan. The 5th Group grabbed him and in a few weeks he was off, first to the coalition staging base in Uzbekistan, then down to Bagram Air Base north of Kabul.

Today, Patriquin was leading a three-man Special Operations Team Alpha, or "SOT-A," a signals intelligence collection team attached to a group of forty regular army 10th Mountain Division light infantry soldiers. Using a heavy pack of radio interception equipment, Patriquin's team would listen in on enemy transmissions, translate, and identify threats for officers of the Tenth Mountain Division and for other American units dropped into the valley.

Patriquin's two team members were both 5th Special Forces Group staff sergeants, Rory Mauldin, who could translate Urdu, and Jeremy Sandor, who, like Patriquin, could translate Arabic. Like many Special Forces soldiers, all three men wore beards and no uniforms, relying on mostly mix-and-match civilian survival gear they put together themselves. To conform to Geneva Convention rules, each wore at least one piece of official U.S. military gear, to identify themselves as combatants. Patriquin was wearing performance flannel and fleece clothing his mother-in-law ordered for him online from L.L.Bean and Lands' End.

It was freezing, and Patriquin was happy he remembered to bring along thick furry headgear. "Nothing beats a mushroom hat in the winter," he recalled later, as this was "as cold and shitty and bad terrainy as an op gets nowadays."

Patriquin's group was part of an allied ground force of more than fourteen hundred men, drawn mostly from the army's 10th Mountain and 101st Airborne divisions, which also included Special Forces troops from allied nations. The task force's job was to destroy what was thought to be the last pockets of al-Qaeda and their hard-line Taliban allies left in Afghanistan after the disaster of the Battle of Tora Bora, the airstrike-heavy attack ten weeks earlier that allowed Osama bin Laden and his deputies a wide-open door to escape eastward to freedom in the wild tribal areas of Pakistan.

Battles are often the story of plans quickly falling apart and everything going wrong, and the Battle of the Shah-i-Kot Valley was such a saga, despite the brief advantage of surprise. "Things weren't just not going according to plan," remembers one American officer who entered the valley that day, "they were going bad—it was bad news all around." The *Financial Times* military correspondent Peter Spiegel later called it "a horribly planned mess of an operation in which commanders sent U.S. troops into a battle they had not been prepared for, against enemies they did not know existed, without the weapons they needed."

In fact, al-Qaeda had spring-loaded the entire valley into a gigantic booby trap to ambush the incoming Americans and their allies. When the Chinook CH-47 helicopters dropped them off at dawn that morning, all nine of the landing zones were "hot," sucking in mortar and small-arms fire. "I looked to the north, and I saw our adjacent unit from the 101st Airborne Division," recalls Patriquin's colleague Lieutenant Anthony Passero of the 10th Mountain Division. "They were more than two kilometers away, but I could see them running around their position while rocket-propelled grenades exploded around them." The troops dropped off at the landing zone immediately to Patriquin's south were trapped in a continuous gun battle for eighteen hours.

The loads of U.S. troops dropped off in separate spots in the valley were so small, and so spread out over such rugged terrain, that their combat power on the ground was badly fragmented. "Nothing was mutually supporting," recalls Captain Roger Crombie, commanding the forty-three soldiers in Patriquin's group. "Once we got on the ground, it became very apparent that nobody was in a mutually supporting position, and it would have taken hours to move across that terrain to help anybody."

U.S. military intelligence analysts had figured there should only be a few hundred enemy fighters holed up in a handful of tiny villages on the valley floor. Instead, the villages were largely empty and there were up to a thousand al-Qaeda and Taliban lying in wait, many of them not down below but dug into the cliffs around and above the Americans, in heavily camouflaged and entrenched firing positions. The enemy had bracketed the valley with heavy machine guns and 82mm mortars that the U.S. intelligence planners assumed they didn't have in any strength. "Mortars were a good tactical move by the enemy, because with the high angle of fire, they can shoot over ridges and hills," said one army officer. "It also is difficult for the other side to determine location."

The U.S. plan called for a seventy-two-hour operation. Instead, it would last for the next eighteen days.

The valley was in such a remote place that the Americans could not easily bring in vehicles, tanks, or heavy artillery. Their aerial resupply with paradrops was crippled by altitude, distance, and frequent bad weather; and their rotary-wing aircraft could not easily hover and engage targets at standoff ranges. The extreme altitude was a brutal enemy for ground troops. "We weren't conditioned for the mountains even though we were the 10th Mountain Division," recalls Lieutenant Passero. "We had a half hour of mountain training."

The plan assumed that Lieutenant Patriquin and the other troops would have to physically separate hordes of civilian refugees streaming out of the valley from al-Qaeda and Taliban fighters, so they brought along stacks of flex-cuffs, and interpreters like Patriquin to interrogate suspects. Patriquin was especially excited about this aspect of the operation, because he hoped that by interacting with large groups of Afghan civilians he could project to them an image of an American soldier that would be so positive and friendly that they would be impressed and even inspired by the United States. In his opinion, this was one of the most critical jobs of the U.S. military, especially Special Forces troops—if the military was going to be an instrument of foreign policy, it had a perfect opportunity to improve America's image in the countries where it operated. But there were no Afghan civilians for Patriquin to meet—they'd all fled the area.

The original plan called for a thousand-man allied Afghan

militia force commanded by General Zia Gulbuddin, and led by U.S. Special Forces teams, to push into the valley from the north and west, and "hammer" enemy troops into the "anvil" of Travis Patriquin and the other coalition troops stationed on the valley's eastern ridgeline overlooking the probable escape passes. The Afghans were supposed to be the main attack element and Patriquin and his colleagues the supporting force.

But early that morning, at "D-hour," as the Afghans approached the target area, an air force AC-130 mistakenly opened fire on their convoy, killing several Afghan soldiers and one U.S. Special Forces advisor. The Afghans turned around and headed home. Half the plan was out the window—and what was intended to be the supporting force now comprised the main attack force on the ground. "The mission completely fell apart within moments after infil," recalls Patriquin's colleague Staff Sergeant Mauldin.

Patriquin and his group came under fire as soon as they landed that morning. "We were supposed to land at HLZ [Helicopter Landing Zone] Five, which was right near our battle position on high ground," remembered his commander, Captain Crombie of the 10th Mountain Division. "As we came in to land, though, the CH-47 kept drifting, and drifting, so we finally landed right down in Route Chevy, which is what we were going to block [and watch over]. Now we're down in the valley, we get off the helicopter, it flies away, and there are some guys with an AK-47 and an RPG-1 one hundred meters in front of us. And they were young, probably fourteen years old. If they were older guys we probably would have had some big problems on the LZ, but they were probably scared out of their wits. That was their first contact. We fired some 40-millimeter rounds at them and that was it."

Patriquin and the other troops made a backbreaking two-hour climb up a sheer cliff wall dotted with juniper trees to occupy a small bowl-shaped hilltop dubbed "Blocking Position Eve." It was located on the north flank of Takur Ghar mountain, and was one of nine such positions overlooking the Shah-i-Kot Valley. The thin air made every uphill step an ordeal, and with 110 pounds in their rucksacks and another 40 pounds of heavy body armor, water, and ammunition strapped to their bodies, some soldiers thought they would explode from exertion before getting to the top.

A detachment of about fifteen enemy soldiers was hiding behind a hill some nine hundred meters away from the Americans, just outside the maximum range of their rifles. The logical response was blasting them with indirect fire using the battalion's 60mm mortar team. But the soldiers had to bump the mortar team from the helicopter to make room for Patriquin's team and their gear. Not only were they without heavy mortars, but their artillery had been scrapped, with close air support (CAS) as a replacement. Unfortunately, problems at the next landing zone to the south were sucking up all the CAS missions.

One by one, enemy fighters came out from behind the hill and advanced into the open, and one by one the Americans shot them when they came within range. "They were trying to rescue their fallen comrades," recalled Lieutenant Anthony Passero, who thought this was both admirable and stupid.

"The first one came out low crawling," reported Passero, who noticed a very long sniper rifle slung over the enemy fighter's back. "We fired some M203 [grenade] rounds at him, because I knew we needed to save our machine-gun ammunition for later on in the operation. Sergeant Mojica hit him, and the man got up and staggered down the road. He found the only tree out there and sat right beside it. He did not move for the rest of the day. I wanted to save ammunition, so if we hurt someone bad enough, my order was always to let them bleed out. Besides, the more wounded enemy soldiers we had out there, the more people would come out from the hill. Three more men came out from behind the hill throughout the day, and we handled them in the same manner. We had six bodies lying out there by the end of the day."

Staff Sergeant Rory Mauldin describes an exhilarated Patriquin as "totally positive" and "so super-happy, he was giggling" as he worked the radios, interacted with other army troops and air force ground radio controllers, and consolidated their position. He seemed to be having the time of his life, to the point of being goofy.

"Bullets were cracking over our head all morning, all day," remembers Mauldin. "We were hearing radio reports that were among the scariest things I've ever heard in fourteen years in the U.S. military. Two of the other blocking positions were getting hammered, suffering sixty percent casualties. There was no air support for our unit." Mauldin looked over at Patriquin and figured he was probably thinking the same thing he was: "This is not going well. Our little Special Forces SOT-A teams always get in these crazy situations in the nastiest places. They never send us anywhere normal. We always end up in insane places with shit falling apart. Well, things could always get worse!"

Patriquin sketched the scene in the after-action report he wrote soon after the battle: "As soon as we opened fire, heavy fire was returned from the ridgeline. Having just climbed back up the mountainside, I was exposed to the enemy fire. So I low-crawled approximately 200 meters under fire to co-locate with a 249/203 [grenade launcher] position so I could spot for them with my ACOG [advanced combat optical gun sight]. The entire element would continue to receive fire from this ridgeline for the remainder of the day. Staff Sergeant Sandor, SSG Mauldin and I got our radio equipment up and running, and immediately DF'd [direction-found] and intercepted voice with lines of bearing to the towns of Marzak, Kale and Serkhankel. SSG Sandor, SSG Mauldin and I conducted site improvement, building a rock wall around a rock ledge, taking turns on the system, and crawling up to the hilltop to observe enemy movements. Our intercept antenna was at the highest point occupied by friendly troops in the AO [area of operations]."

By afternoon it was obvious there would be no exodus of civilians or enemy fighters from there or anywhere else in the valley toward Patriquin's position. In fact, the soldiers in his formation had no reason to be there. At four thirty p.m., the order came over the radio to collapse and abandon Blocking Position Eve. The battalion was being extracted from the valley. They had taken casualties at other locations and had to go back to Bagram Air Base to refit and rearm, and get new orders.

"The mission got scrapped and it became a survival scenario," explains Mauldin. Now, the assignment for Patriquin's team and the 10th Mountain Division troops was simply to stay alive until they could reach the "exfil point" on foot and board evacuation helicopters. They had to pack up and march through high ground and fierce alpine conditions to a landing zone seven kilometers north to be evacuated.

Their packs were much too heavy for the march. Patriquin was carrying nearly 150 pounds in his backpack, including food, ammunition, translation books, a portable stove, cold-weather gear, plus his SOT-A team's four-piece, 43-pound radio interception gear, or Man-Portable Signal Intelligence System, which cost American taxpayers $750,000.

In desperation, the group decided to dump everything that wasn't "mission-critical" out of their rucksacks into a pile, including a good deal of their food, plus Patriquin's translation books and his cherished portable stove, and rig the pile of gear to be blown up with grenades.

As twilight approached, forty-three American soldiers set off on a long, excruciating night march over horrendous terrain infested with al-Qaeda and Taliban forces a few hundred meters away.

"We decided to move through the high ground instead of through the valley floor," recalls Lieutenant Passero, who marched with Patriquin. "The movement was treacherous because of the combination of our heavy loads and the thin air at that altitude. We had to take a thirty-minute break at the top of every hill in order to catch our breath and consolidate the platoon together. The snow made movement even harder. It was up to our knees, so that made movements uphill difficult. Movement downhill was tricky because we were so heavy, the snow was deep, and the mountains were steep."

"It was ungodly," reports Captain Roger Crombie. "Regardless of the slope of the terrain, there was not a flat place to put your foot—and trying to move on that at night while wearing night vision goggles was slow." They had to move over ground that was often nothing but boulders and rocks.

Patriquin was soon marching in knee-deep snow on a bad knee while carrying nearly 150 pounds on his back. "Fuck! Shit!" He tossed off the oaths as he slipped and slid in pitch-black down the rocky, snow-packed slopes and the ground rocked with the detonations of air-dropped ordnance. Patriquin recalled in his after-action report, "I was very tired and was hallucinating a little bit, and my knee kept popping out of place. I told SSG Sandor to watch me and let me know if I did anything too weird, or passed out."

The ground was taking such a beating and shaking so much that Mauldin was finding it hard to walk, and he felt like a drunk.

He kept falling over and couldn't see what he was falling into. It seemed every time he put his foot down, the ground shook. He recalls that "in the distance we could see snow-covered hillsides that were glowing. At first we weren't sure what we were seeing. It was white phosphorus being dropped for the gun runs, and we were laughing in amazement at the light show."

At one point the Americans spotted an enemy position so close they could see figures huddled around a fire. "Should we attack it?" asked an officer. Patriquin shook his head. They were in no shape to attack anything at the moment. Everyone agreed.

By midnight most of the soldiers were about to collapse, so they set up camp at the wall of a ravine and huddled together for a few hours' sleep. They'd been up for twenty-two hours. "We had traveled a total of six hundred meters in six hours," reported Captain Passero. "We walked forever and didn't get anywhere. I think we were walking in circles."

As he lay on the rough ground trying somehow to sleep, Patriquin was colder than he had ever felt in his life. The water was frozen in his camelback canteen. He and Mauldin slept with their hands shoved in each other's armpits to try to stay warm. Another soldier's teeth chattered so violently through the night that they hurt for the next three weeks.

Mauldin was impressed by how happy and positive Patriquin stayed through the whole ordeal. As a new SOT-A team member on his first mission, he remembered the mantras Patriquin emphasized to him during the train-up for the assault into the Shah-i-Kot Valley, mantras that reflected both the secret nature of their profession and the prevalence of what Patriquin called "suck," or obstacles and physical pain.

"Part of our job in this gray zone we work in is to enjoy suffering," Patriquin explained to Mauldin. "You have to enjoy the suck, or it will drive you nuts. If you don't learn to enjoy the suck it will eat you alive." Years earlier, at Fort Bragg, Patriquin offered a similar tip when he came upon a drenched soldier standing his post on sentry duty in a blinding rainstorm. "This really sucks," noted the soldier. "Sure does," agreed Patriquin, "but remember—suck builds the team, bro!" The soldier laughed and said, "Well, if this is the suck, I guess we're one hell of a team!"

When Patriquin and his fellow troops woke up around five a.m. on a mountainside in Afghanistan on the morning of March 3, 2002, their commander, Captain Crombie, realized they'd never get anywhere if they kept trying to march through the impossibly rugged high ground.

Crombie decided the only way the formation could make it to the evacuation point was to do exactly what they had been taught never to do: walk through the low ground, which was all out in the open. "The bottom line was that we had to make it to the 101st Airborne evacuation point as soon as possible," recalled Lieutenant Passero. "We would use speed as our defense."

They got moving at five thirty a.m. and made steady progress through the morning, linking up at about nine a.m. with troops of a rifle platoon from their battalion who were also trying to make it to friendly lines. They were almost out of food and water. They reached a creek, popped iodine tablets into their canteens and camelbacks, and refilled them.

Captain Crombie had a funny feeling about the ravine they were heading into. He got on the radio and reminded everyone what happened in the book *We Were Soldiers Once . . . and Young* at Landing Zone Albany during the Vietnam battle of Ia Drang in 1965, when a unit was ambushed and decimated. Many of the squad leaders had read the book at Bagram, and they immediately got the point.

The sun was up, it was nine thirty a.m., and the temperature had already gone from zero degrees to about sixty-five degrees Fahrenheit.

"Hey, Travis, why in the hell am I seeing a flash over there?" Mauldin asked Patriquin.

"That's not good," noted Patriquin.

He later wrote in his after-action report: "SSG Mauldin observed enemy moving on a ridgeline several kilometers away, and gave enough early warning for me to be able to order everyone around me into a nearby gully. Seconds later, a mortar round impacted directly where we had previously been. The far ambush was executed with mortar fire from the west and small-arms fire from the east. Later there was mortar fire from the east as well."

"Suddenly a mortar round came out of nowhere," recalled Lieutenant Passero. "It landed about a hundred feet from me, and sent shrapnel flying through the air around us."

"React to indirect fire," Captain Crombie shouted. "Twelve o'clock, three hundred meters."

"Drop your fucking rucksacks!" someone called out.

The soldiers followed the "react to contact" battle drill: drop to the ground; try to identify where the enemy is firing from; return fire.

Forty-three American soldiers scrambled to find cover.

Many of the troops threw down their heavy packs before landing facedown in the dirt or behind rocks.

Patriquin described the scene in his report: "The mortars were bracketing us and we were in direct fire with small arms. Most of the company dropped their rucksacks. While exposed and under direct fire, Staff Sergeant Mauldin dropped his rucksack [containing sensitive radio interception equipment] and emptied a magazine of 5.56 [ammunition cartridges] into it. This selfless act ensured not only the destruction of his equipment, but that it wouldn't fall into the hands of the enemy. I kept my rucksack on for another 500 meters. Keeping command and control of my element and evading fire while carrying the rucksack was extremely difficult, the infantrymen kept urging me to drop it. When I told them that I had sensitive equip and intel [including the radio's computer "brain"] in it, they nodded and began protecting me in addition to our fire and maneuver, at great risk to themselves."

Their machine gunners scrambled to set up firing posts and began sending suppressive rounds into the cliffs. Fire rained down on the U.S. troops from the high ground on at least two sides, from the rising sun in the east, and from AK-47s, a .50-caliber machine gun, mortars, and something that sounded like an old D-30 Soviet artillery piece in the west.

They were pinned down in mostly open terrain, running, shooting, and scooting, leapfrogging forward in short three- to five-second sprints, then jumping into the dirt. "Everybody was engaging the enemy, including me," remembers Captain Passero. "When your platoon leader is firing his rifle, then you know you're in trouble."

It was a well-coordinated ambush; machine-gun rounds were hitting the ground four and five inches from their feet. "Bullets were flying everywhere; they were hitting the dirt right in front of us," says Passero. "One private put his hand down to move himself over; when he picked his hand up, a bullet landed right where his hand was. We knew that we had .50-caliber machine-gun rounds flying through the air at us. We could also make out at least three riflemen with AK-47s. Mortar rounds continued to come in, and it would have been mass confusion without the heroic actions of everyone in the platoon."

There was tenacity and skill on the part of al-Qaeda and the

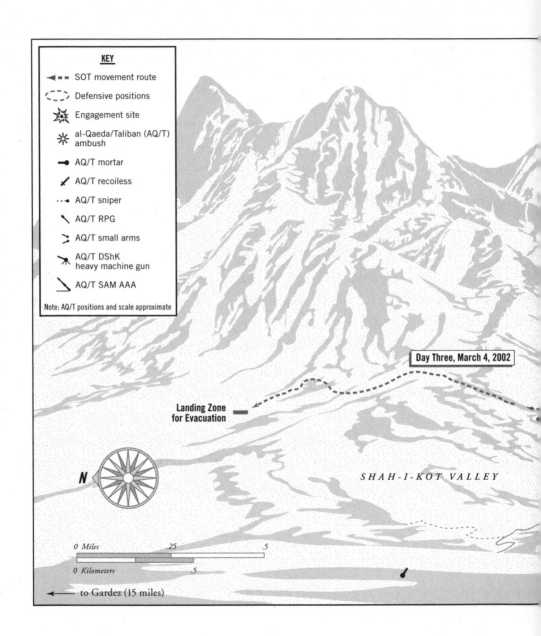

KEY

SOT movement route

Defensive positions

Engagement site

al-Qaeda/Taliban (AQ/T) ambush

AQ/T mortar

AQ/T recoiless

AQ/T sniper

AQ/T RPG

AQ/T small arms

AQ/T DShK heavy machine gun

AQ/T SAM AAA

Note: AQ/T positions and scale approximate

Day Three, March 4, 2002

Landing Zone for Evacuation

N

SHAH-I-KOT VALLEY

0 Miles   .25   5

0 Kilometers   5

to Gardez (15 miles)

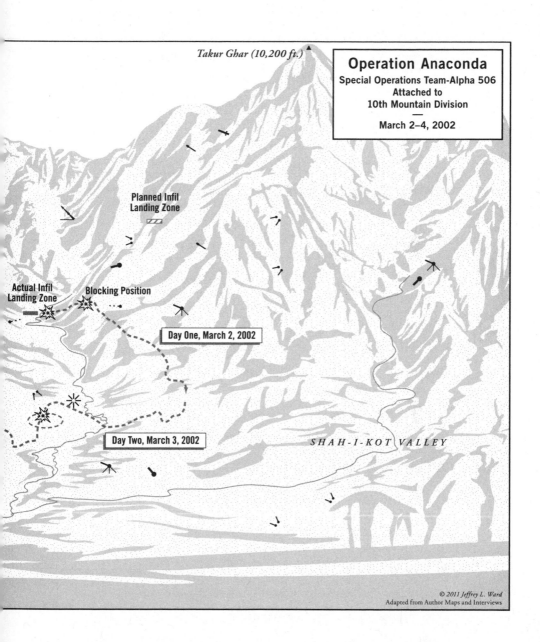

Takur Ghar (10,200 ft.)

Operation Anaconda
Special Operations Team-Alpha 506
Attached to
10th Mountain Division
—
March 2–4, 2002

Planned Infil
Landing Zone

Actual Infil
Landing Zone

Blocking Position

Day One, March 2, 2002

Day Two, March 3, 2002

SHAH-I-KOT VALLEY

© 2011 Jeffrey L. Ward
Adapted from Author Maps and Interviews

Taliban that day as well. "They were brave to a fault," Captain Crombie says of the enemy he faced. "A lot of it is cultural and some of it is obviously training. We respected them, but it was also apparent that they were not very accurate with their weapons and there wasn't a lot of collective training. They did some things, though, like field craft, camouflage, and some more command-type skills, like understanding terrain and positioning weapons systems in terrain that protects the weapon and allows it to fire undetected and have a huge field of fire."

The good news for the Americans was, as Patriquin later explained, "Slim [al-Qaeda and the Taliban] is a bad shot." The al-Qaeda and Taliban frontline fighters were enthusiastic at putting out high volumes of fire, but their accuracy was generally poor. Their shooting technique was mainly of the "spray and pray" style.

The ambush split the Americans into two groups, and Patriquin got pinned down with an element led by a 10th Mountain Division sergeant. The fire was getting so intense they could not move forward and had to hunker behind whatever cover they could find.

Patriquin was lying facedown in a creek bed ditch. "I'll never forget this," recalls Mauldin. "We're pinned down with sniper fire and mortar fire on both sides, and I am not shitting you, he's laying there on his belly and he digs a little hole in the dirt to light a cigarette and blow the smoke into it so as not to give away our position. He takes a hit from the cigarette and a sip from a little flask of whiskey."

"If I'm going to go out like this," said Patriquin, "I'm going to have a cigarette and a drink before I go. Rory, would you like some?"

"No, thanks, dude," replied Mauldin.

Patriquin quickly realized that with Crombie and Passero pinned down elsewhere, as a lieutenant he was not just the team leader of a three-man SOT-A team, he was also the senior officer in a group of twenty-one infantry troops fighting for their lives.

It was a startling, eerie feeling. In the midst of combat, he was suddenly the leader. Patriquin's mind flashed back to the year 2000, to a lecture given to him and all incoming students at Officer Candidate School at Fort Benning by the commander, Colonel David Osborne. "The mantle of leadership is so heavy it's like the yoke around an ox's head," Osborne said. "Everybody is looking to you to make decisions, and all your actions are under a microscope."

"Now I understand what he meant," thought Patriquin.

To Mauldin it seemed like all the enlisted men were looking at the officer with a beard, Patriquin, to get them out of there. "You're the guy in charge, tell us where to go," said one soldier. "We want to follow you."

"Hey, I think I can shoot this guy on the ridgeline," one young soldier with a sniper rifle said, then asked Patriquin, "Can I shoot him?"

"Of course you can," Patriquin said and chuckled, "by all means, please!"

"I directed sniper fire onto the eastern ridgeline and the sniper killed at least two enemy snipers," Patriquin recalled. From their position in a ten-foot ravine, Patriquin, Mauldin, and the others launched suppressive indirect fire up into the cliffs, including small M203 grenades launched from tracks on the bottom of their M4 rifles. They established radio contact with the rest of the formation, and soon the soldiers began linking up into one formation.

Eventually they noticed that whenever American aircraft flew overhead, the enemy fire stopped. Using this insight, the men managed to relay-run through the fifteen-hundred-meter kill zone in one piece. They killed at least ten enemy fighters along the way.

"Heroics is not just killing the enemy," Lieutenant Passero remembers of Patriquin, "but putting your men in the right place and time while you're getting shot at." Captain Crombie had not worked with Patriquin before, but was impressed by how the SOT-A team leader was "instantly likable and user-friendly, and spoke his mind in a tactful way." Patriquin was "unflappable, mature, had a lot of common sense and was always calm and level-headed," Crombie reports, adding, "He knew how to move under fire, how to fire, and how to direct his team through the whole experience. He was a good guy to have by your side."

"There wasn't an hour that went by that day that the three of us weren't under at least fairly accurate mortar fire," recalls Mauldin. "Patriquin stayed very calm and he made it seem easy. He got us out of there."

That night, a team of soldiers tried to return to the spot where many of them had dropped their heavy rucksacks during the fire-fight. But through their night-vision goggles they saw an al-Qaeda fighter guarding the sacks, so they marked the area with infrared strobes and radioed for attack aircraft to eliminate him.

Instead, a UH-60 medical evacuation helicopter heading to pick up a casualty from a different unit mistook the strobes to be markers for their operation. The aircraft swooped in close, drawing highly dangerous unwanted attention to Patriquin's group.

"Go back, go back!" Patriquin shouted as he tried to wave the chopper off, but the crew couldn't hear him above their rotor noise until they landed. He ran to the helicopter and demanded, "What the hell is going on? What do you want?"

"We're a medevac—where's the casualty?" replied a crew member.

"We don't have any yet, but if you don't get out of here, we're going to have some!" Patriquin announced, waving them away.

The second day of battle was ending, and most of the soldiers were parched and famished, with the officers and team leaders having gone forty-eight hours with next to no food in their bellies.

Patriquin sat down with several soldiers beside a dry creek bed and they shared the last bits of food Patriquin could find in his pockets—a pouch of MRE peanut butter, a package of shelf-stable bread, and five packs of Hickory Farms Summer Sausage his mother-in-law had shipped him in a care package. Someone scrounged up a few mouthfuls of cheese tortellini from an MRE, the military's ubiquitous "meal ready to eat."

That night, they huddled together in their bivvy sacks, wrapped in ponchos and makeshift emergency blankets improvised from their poncho liners, and tried again to ride out the freezing cold. One infantryman drifted toward hypothermia, so the soldiers put him in the middle of the squad and everyone pulled in tighter to heat him up.

On the third day they all finally made it safely to the 101st Airborne landing zone, where Patriquin and his Special Forces team were evacuated by helicopter, along with troops from other SOT-A teams who had endured their own ordeals elsewhere in the valley. "We ran fast to the landing zone," remembers Rory Mauldin, "jumped in the back of the helicopter, the crew chief threw blankets on us, and we went into a dead sleep."

Instead of being extracted, the forty 10th Mountain Division troops were reequipped and ordered to remain in the valley for the next thirteen days, search for enemy fighters, and blow up and seal enemy caves. Seven of the soldiers were awarded Bronze Stars. Several of them suffered PTSD, posttraumatic stress disorder.

When he reached Bagram Air Base after being flown out of the valley, Travis Patriquin called his family on a satellite phone to tell them he was okay.

On the phone, Patriquin had what he called a post-combat "adrenaline dump" reaction. He broke down, cried, shook, and felt angry. He saw his colleagues go through similar emotions when they called home to their loved ones.

"What I thought was interesting," Patriquin quipped, "is we did it on the phone with our wives, girlfriends, and mothers, though not on the same phone call."

He wondered what soldiers did before satellite phone technology was available. "Did they just hold that in, or did they let it out with their buddies? The breath control stuff does help, but if you don't stay in your 'front brain' it's hard to tell yourself to take a deep breath. That's what I always have to do; I have to remind myself (and breathing helps to set the mood) that I am a front brained human, who CAN get control of the situation. If you spend too much time back in the 'Rat brain' you can get stuck there. And that ain't pretty." He told his wife of one overpowering emotion he felt: "As long as I live, I never want to be cold again."

Patriquin had proven himself in battle. He brought his men unscathed through a gauntlet of enemy fire. He had survived and distinguished himself in three days of combat and extreme physical punishment. And somehow, his bum knee held up.

For his actions in the battle, Patriquin earned the fourth-highest combat award in the U.S. military, the Bronze Star medal for meritorious achievement. The citation, issued by Special Forces Command, read: "First Lieutenant Patriquin was instrumental in identifying and collecting on several crucial targets. [He] took command of 21 members of the combined element, supervising the placement of key weapons and defensive positions. His calmness under fire was a constant source of inspiration to his teammates and the infantrymen around him."

The Battle of Shah-i-Kot Valley fizzled out to an ambiguous

conclusion. The Americans won the battle in the sense that the enemy was killed or fled, and U.S. and Afghan forces occupied the battle space when the fighting stopped. In total, eight American military personnel were killed and over fifty wounded. Somewhere between one hundred and three hundred enemy were killed, including fighters from Arab countries, Chechnya, and Uzbekistan. If there were any senior al-Qaeda leaders in the valley, they escaped capture and slipped away to freedom, just as they did at Tora Bora.

The U.S. military declared it a victory, and U.S. commanding general Tommy Franks concluded that "the last al-Qaeda sanctuary in Afghanistan had been destroyed" and would never be rebuilt.

But nine years later, the war ground on with no end in sight, and the Taliban were dominating over 70 percent of the country and striking inside the capital city of Kabul.

The army brass had called this battle Operation Anaconda to evoke a snake squeezing and devouring its prey.

When it was over, Travis Patriquin had another name for it:

Operation: Where the Hell Is the Main Effort?

CHAPTER 2

THE EDGE OF THE ARABIAN DESERT

The lights of Wadi Rum switched off at ten p.m., and the clear desert sky revealed a star canopy of stunning brilliance.

It was one of the greatest moments of Sergeant Travis Patriquin's life.

To another U.S. Army Special Forces soldier camped out next to him in the open air, it looked like he was in heaven.

For three years Patriquin had been thinking about Arabia, studying its history, language, and peoples. He'd absorbed Arabic lessons from Syrian, Egyptian, and Lebanese instructors at the Defense Language Institute, where for fifteen months he'd studied Modern Standard Arabic for five hours a day.

He'd memorized passages of Arabic poetry, and studied the Koran in Arabic, marveling at its grandeur and striking paradoxes. He relished the self-transfigurational prose of T. E. Lawrence's combat epic *Seven Pillars of Wisdom: A Triumph*, and he pondered the notion of how far a man could immerse himself in a foreign culture, and how it would change him.

The year before, in 1998, Patriquin had traveled to an Arab

country for the first time, to Kuwait, on a ninety-day Special Forces training mission, where he was first able to exercise his language skills with regular Arab citizens. The high point of the trip was when Patriquin and his colleague Ken Baker, a fellow Arabic linguist, stopped at a Kuwaiti truck stop in the middle of nowhere and began an animated discussion in Arabic.

Overhearing their curiously accented speech, the Kuwaiti proprietor asked, "I can't tell—are you Tunisian, or Lebanese?"

"We're Americans," replied Patriquin.

"America?" said the Kuwaiti. "But that's not an Arab country!"

Introducing himself, a delighted Patriquin said he was from outside Chicago.

"Chicago? That's not an Arab country, either!"

"Travis was really proud of that one," recalled Baker.

Now, in the summer of 1999, Patriquin and Baker found themselves in Jordan, on the northwestern edge of the great Arabian Desert, which sprawls into Iraq and the Saudi Arabian peninsula. They and five colleagues were on a thirty-day 5th Special Forces Group mission to refresh their Arabic language skills and immerse themselves in the culture. The 5th Group was based at Fort Campbell, Kentucky, and their designated slice of the world was the Middle East.

Patriquin and Baker were camped out on rented two-dollar mattresses, surrounded by a remote natural wilderness so striking that even the stoic local Bedouins were awed by its beauty.

Wadi Rum was a desolate ocean of sand pierced by titanic mountains that soared to over five thousand feet, creating a labyrinthine superhighway that ran for 120 kilometers through southern Jordan. It was perhaps the most beautiful natural scenery in all of Arabia.

"Whenever I describe Travis to someone, it sounds like a movie," recalls Baker. "But the thing is, some movies are true." And now they were inside some of the greatest cinematic scenery on Earth, the place where David Lean filmed parts of the 1962 classic *Lawrence of Arabia*.

Patriquin was thrilled by the fact that in this exact spot in 1917 and 1918, his hero T. E. Lawrence set up a guerrilla camp with his Arab irregulars and planned strikes on Ottoman military trains and on the strategic port of Aqaba. This was one of Lawrence's favorite places on the planet, and he rhapsodized about it at length in *Seven Pillars of Wisdom*, describing it as "this irresistible place: this processional way greater than the imagination" that was "vast and echoing and God-like."

Patriquin was spellbound by Wadi Rum's history, its beauty and its magnificent sky. If he wished to ponder his life so far and where it might lead, it would be a perfect place.

Travis Patriquin was a man for whom patriotism came naturally, and he was intensely proud of the United States and its military. Beyond his devotion to his wife and his first child, a newborn daughter, the U.S. Army was his whole life, his entire reason for being. "I came into the military," Patriquin explained to a friend, "and I found a home." He loved the globe-trotting adventure and the unpredictability of army life, and the nobility of its mission.

Travis Lyle Sallee Patriquin, the oldest of four children, was born in a suburb of St. Louis, Missouri, on August 15, 1974, the week after Richard Nixon fled the White House and over a year after the last U.S. combat troops left Vietnam.

His ancestors were French, Swiss, and English, and his seventh great-grandfather was John Hart, a New Jersey farmer who was one of the original fifty-six signers of the Declaration of Independence. Late in his life, while doing genealogical research, Patriquin learned he had Native American blood, which thrilled him, as he had a lifelong fascination with Indian history and ritual dances.

His father, Gary Patriquin, wanted to name him after Trampas, a character played by Doug McClure in the 1960s TV series *The Virginian*. He always liked that name. But Gary had a few beers to celebrate the night his son was born, couldn't remember exactly how the name was spelled, and it wound up "Travis."

When he was in third grade, Patriquin announced he was quitting school since, he claimed, he'd already read all the classics of world literature and there was nothing left for him to learn. He stayed in school, and spent much of his life reading books by the box load, like the *Lord of the Rings* trilogy, Plato's *Republic*, *Bulfinch's Mythology*, *Conan the Barbarian*, the *Foxfire* books of Appalachian folklore, classics of English literature, war histories, poetry, George MacDonald Fraser's *Flashman* series, Joseph Campbell's *The Hero with a Thousand Faces*, and countless other works.

His family moved to Chicago when Patriquin was nine, but disagreements over family discipline led him to move back to the St. Louis area to live with his aunt's family, and in 1992 he graduated from Francis Howell North High School in St. Charles, Missouri. He joined the army the same day he graduated, at age eighteen. He was married once, right out of high school, a union that ended in 1996 in his first year at the Defense Language Institute in Monterey.

Patriquin wanted to be a soldier as far back as he could remember. In grade school he spent recess periods with his buddies discussing GI Joe characters, and drawing pictures of tanks, jets and battles. His decision to join the military was, he explained, directly inspired by adventures he enjoyed in books like *Starship Troopers*, Robert Heinlein's science fiction epic about space-borne infantry paratroopers dropped onto planet surfaces by space pods (a favorite line: "I always get the shakes before a drop"), and from TV shows from the 1980s, which Patriquin considered the Golden Age of American Television.

"Those shows were full of Vietnam badasses trying to make their way in the world," Patriquin later explained. "Every episode of *Magnum, P.I.* had someone having a flashback, *Riptide* boys were Air Force Search and Rescue guys, *Simon and Simon* had the Marine Force Recon Brother, Edward James Olmos of *Miami Vice* was some sort of badass ninja from the Cambodia ops. Ahh. Total bullshit, of course, but enough fuel for the imagination to get my happy ass hooked on the military forever!"

In bonding with his fellow soldiers, Patriquin often jokingly portrayed himself as a low-culture-loving "knuckle-dragger." He once wrote, "I've always said the best thing about the infantry is that we convince people we're stupid, so they'll do the work." But his tastes embraced epic poetry, like two of his favorite works of literature, Homer's *Iliad* and *Odyssey*, from which he recited passages from memory.

For a volunteer soldier like Patriquin, one scene in the *Iliad* had special poignancy, when Achilles tells of the two futures he must choose between: "I carry two sorts of destiny toward the day of my death. Either, if I stay here and fight beside the city of the Trojans, my return home is gone, but my glory shall be everlasting; but if I return home to the beloved land of my fathers, the excellence of my glory is gone, but there will be a long life left for me, and my end in death will not come to me quickly."

In 1993, after army basic training at Fort Benning, Georgia, Patriquin was assigned to a military intelligence detachment of the airborne 7th Special Forces Group at Fort Bragg, North Carolina, where he'd find any excuse to strap on a parachute and jump out of an airplane, which he did many dozens of times before losing count.

Patriquin spent much of his early military career as a radio specialist on SOT-A teams, a job he volunteered for soon after enlisting. A SOT-A usually consists of four men and an arsenal of portable radio gear. The teams are attached to a Special Forces battalion as specialized support soldiers and technicians, and their job is to provide intelligence gathering, reconnaissance, threat identification, and force protection to Special Forces troops in the field. Many SOT-A soldiers, like Patriquin, were trained in foreign languages, like Spanish, Arabic, Russian, Persian, and Korean, as well as Morse code.

With his wide, lopsided grin, obvious talent, and powerful charisma, Patriquin impressed one of his early Special Forces commanding officers, then captain Butch Bowman, as a standout from the beginning: "When I met him, Travis was a Private First Class radio operator, eighteen or nineteen years old. He was a hard charger and a quick learner. He came in as a young gung-ho radio man and showed an amazing aptitude for anything he did. As the communications guy he routinely carried ninety-plus pounds in his ruck and could keep up with any of the SIGINT [signals intelligence] soldiers or Green Berets he deployed with. I will always remember standing around his makeshift antenna farms at Fort Chaffee, Arkansas, knowing that one of this young soldier's jury-rigged antennas would keep us in communications with our teams in the field. We would sit and smoke cheap Honduran cigars, drink very bad coffee out of canteen cups, and solve the world's problems. It became evident to me very quickly that this was a very special young man. He had a superior intellect, he was a real thinker, he was physically tough, and just a pleasure to be around. Travis was a super-stud SOT-A guy, a warrior-poet, and one of the finest people I've ever met."

Patriquin's personnel records echoed Bowman's assessment, and through the years superiors rewarded the young soldier with written accolades like: "tremendous leadership potential," "we must promote him to captain," "outstanding," "well above his peers," "a motivated self-starter who can accomplish any mission," and "I wish I had 10 soldiers like him." Technically, Patriquin was a Special Forces support soldier, not a full-fledged SF soldier, as a bureaucratic fluke prevented him from entering the notoriously intensive Special Forces Qualification Course, or Q Course, graduation from which would have entitled him to wear the fabled Green Beret. Instead, Patriquin was proud to wear the red beret of a paratrooper.

From 1993 to 1996, Patriquin was deployed to Latin America as a SOT-A team member on counternarcotics missions. Army officials realized Patriquin was something of a language prodigy and sent him to Spanish classes, and he acted as a radio operator and communications intercept specialist and linguist specializing in Spanish and native South American dialects. His missions took him to Venezuela, Colombia, Panama, Ecuador, Peru, and Bolivia, and he spent long hours in remote jungle eavesdropping posts with headphones on, hunched over a radio.

On one mission he was posted at a giant secret U.S. radar complex carved out of the Amazon rain forest near Leticia, Colombia, where he monitored the radios for threats to the base, helped track unidentified suspected drug-carrying aircraft, and passed intelligence to the American and Colombian military commands. One day he heard Spanish-language voices discussing an attack on government VIPs they planned for the next day. Patriquin flashed an alert that made it far up the chain of command to what a military document called "national-level decision makers." The dignitaries canceled their visit, the attack was thwarted, and Patriquin and his team were rewarded by being chosen to represent the U.S. Army in the competition for the National Security Agency Director's Medal.

Patriquin scored so well on the Defense Language Aptitude Battery, the U.S. military's foreign language aptitude test, that in 1996 his superiors assigned him to intensive training in a highly complex Category 4 foreign language, of which there were only four: Japanese, Chinese, Korean—and Arabic.

He was packed off to the Defense Language Institute, where in sixty-three weeks of study he became an Arabic linguist, and one of the relatively few skilled American-born Arabic speakers in the U.S. military. In his off hours he relaxed at the Mucky Duck Tavern with his buddies, one of whom remembered, "We'd play darts, chug beers, hit on Air Force girls, get rejected by those extremely picky Air Force girls, and listen to Travis's alcohol-fueled stories about fighting the 'War on Drugs' in South and Central America."

"I thought he was a bullshit artist," one classmate remembers thinking upon hearing Patriquin's yarns, like the one about his taking on a boa constrictor in hand-to-hand jungle combat. "Then I found out the stories were true," he adds.

Another classmate, Alton Lippe, remembers the vivid impression Patriquin made: "He was very good at making you feel important. I think that's why a lot of people liked Travis. Travis could make you feel that whatever your positive attributes, they were very impressive to him. He was really good at assessing people, finding what your buttons were, and pushing them. He was just brilliant, but almost like creepy-brilliant sometimes. He'd say something and you'd think *woooo, that's out there*, and you waited for *X Files* music to start playing in the background. Sometimes I figured he wasn't really from this planet. I don't mean that in a bad way. But every once in a while I'd think there was just so much more to him that he wasn't revealing. I had a hunch, I didn't know for sure, but I got this little strange feeling that he was just awash in a much deeper ocean of things."

In the barracks one day, Patriquin and Lippe were practicing martial arts, doing kicking and punching drills. Patriquin stopped, walked over to a framed map of the world on the wall and said, "You know what? Every time I look at the map, I wonder which one of these shitholes I'm going to die in."

In one of his classes, as his first marriage was ending, Patriquin was assigned to help tutor a striking woman named Amy Alston, an Air Force Senior Airman, fellow classmate, and Arabic linguist in training. They got married in 1998, eventually having a daughter and two boys. After graduating from language school Patriquin was assigned to the 5th Special Forces Group at Fort Campbell, where he started putting his Arabic language training to work.

During his month in Jordan in the summer of 1999, Patriquin's group attended intensive Arabic language studies at Yarmouk University at the northern city of Irbid, close to the former Israeli-Syrian war zone of the Golan Heights. They wore civilian clothes, and were under orders not to advertise the fact that they were American soldiers, but not to lie about it if asked, either. They acted like college students. On weekends and evenings they roamed the country, soaking up the atmosphere and resolving to live as close to the locals as they could, riding the crowded little commuter buses with the Jordanians, absorbing their colloquialisms, and enjoying their food.

The army had chosen Arabia as a destiny for Patriquin by virtue of the language they assigned him, but now that he was actually living in the heart of Arab and Bedouin culture, he was captivated by it.

Patriquin danced in a disco in the capital of Amman, floated in the Dead Sea, and snorkeled in the Red Sea off the port of Aqaba. He explored the remains of the Roman city at Jerash, inspected the grand battlements of the Islamic anti-Crusader castle at Ajlun, and was flabbergasted by the splendor of the ruins of the lost city of Petra. He was invited to a Jordanian home for a three-course family meal, and was beckoned to feast and dance in a raucous Jordanian wedding party he happened to pass by.

At Mount Nebo, he stood on the peak where Moses was said to have been shown the Promised Land and was later buried, and where on a clear day the view Patriquin saw encompassed much of the history of the Middle East in one long sweep of the eye: the hills of the West Bank, Jericho, the Dead Sea, the distant rooftops of Bethlehem and Jerusalem, and the area surrounding the reed-flanked spot on the River Jordan where, it was thought, John the Baptist baptized Jesus Christ.

Through it all, Patriquin tried out his Arabic skills with as many Jordanians as he could, and he absorbed the rituals and rhythms of Arab street life. "Anywhere we went," recalls Patriquin's buddy Ken Baker, "he immediately fit in—he loved everything about the culture."

Patriquin was fearless in his approach to speaking Arabic. He knew that he might never achieve native-level fluency and was guaranteed to make mistakes. But he knew these mistakes could be softened by eagerness, so he plunged into conversations with such fearlessness and expressive body language that Arab audiences were routinely charmed by his efforts, and understanding of his messages. His wife, Amy, explains that on a scale of 1 to 5, with 5 being full Arabic fluency, Patriquin was technically about a 3, but his positive energy could jump him over 4 so that he sometimes functioned closer to a 5, at least in relatively brief everyday street conversation.

One day, Patriquin visited a teahouse near campus with a book of Arabic poetry.

He knew how proud Arabs could be of their literature, and how excited they could be when outsiders expressed interest in it. He struck up a conversation with a man at the next table, then began reading from his book. His new acquaintance was thrilled to hear Patriquin's voice wrapping around the passages in their original Arabic, and beckoned for other men to enjoy the reading.

"Come here, come here, there's an American who can read Arabic poetry!"

"He reads it beautifully!"

Before long, an excited crowd of hookah-smoking poetry lovers formed around Patriquin's table, enthralled by the performance. When he finished, they rewarded him with a burst of applause and a round of tea.

Patriquin was a lifelong Roman Catholic who'd served as an altar boy and church volunteer and remained a devout churchgoer throughout his life. But he was also accepting of, and fascinated by, all other faiths and forms of worship. He was intrigued with the reputed mystical powers of "the Jesus Prayer," a simple meditative incantation rooted in both the Gospel of Luke and in Eastern Orthodox tradition. It's simplest form involved breathing deeply in, and then out, while praying words like those of Luke 18:13: "God, have mercy on me, a sinner."

For a time later in his life, Patriquin became so impressed by the fellowship of one Methodist Church congregation that he attended services there twice a week. But in his wife Amy's words, "He believed in the magic of the Catholic church. He would wear on his dog tags the St. Michael medallions blessed by the priests. He very much enjoyed being Catholic, and probably would have loved to convert anyone who was willing. He also couldn't accept the idea that his religion was right and everyone else was wrong."

In Jordan, Patriquin discovered a widely devout, tolerant Islamic nation at peace with Israel, a nation that came close, he believed, to an ideal example of how the authentic Islamic faith could inspire and guide a society, while simultaneously respecting and protecting the rights of non-Muslims. Christians, for example, comprised only about 3 percent of Jordan's population but had complete freedom of worship and served in prominent positions throughout the government and society. Christian churches were guaranteed their own laws independent of Islamic influence. Like any other society, it wasn't perfect, but Jordan was close to a model for this part of the world, he thought. In Jordan, Patriquin saw that it was indeed possible for everyone to "just get along" in the explosive cauldron of the Middle East.

But there was one way of seeing Islam that especially enraged Patriquin.

Patriquin was, in the words of his roommate in Jordan, Ken Baker, "really pissed off" with the argument made by some non-Muslims that Islam was by definition a religion of intolerance or terrorism. He was well aware of the acts of terror committed by some who called themselves Muslim fundamentalists and claimed Islamic sanction for hostage taking and the slaughter of civilians. And to a degree deeper than many Americans, Patriquin was familiar with the "sword verses" of the Koran that seemed to endorse aggression against nonbelievers. In fact, he insisted on studying the Koran in its original archaic Arabic, to avoid being misled by the myriad sloppy, inaccurate, and misleading translations and interpretations made of the holy book over the centuries.

Patriquin's conclusion from his careful study of Islam was simple. He believed there were good and bad people in all religions, and that the overall thrust of authentic Islam was tolerance and respect for all people, including Christians and Jews, who where "People of the Book" and fellow children of Abraham.

Patriquin knew that sections of the Islamic, Christian, and Hebrew scriptures were ambiguous, or contradictory, or objectionable, or relevant only to ancient times, and could be twisted out of context to justify evil today. But Patriquin also knew that for every such passage, there were many others in the Koran that exhorted Muslims to charity, forgiveness, tolerance, compassion, respect for captives, and a resort to war only as a last resort in self-defense—such passages as "There shall be no coercion in matters of faith," and "Those who believe, those who follow Jewish scripture, the Christians, the Sabians, any who believe in God and the Last Day, and do good, all shall have their reward with their Lord and they will not come to fear or grief."

And Patriquin would have also known that the Old Testament and Torah books, such as Exodus, Leviticus, and Deuteronomy, that were revered by both the Christian and Jewish faiths contained "sword verses" of their own, like "Kill any friends or family that worship a god that is different than your own"; "I will make mine arrows drunk with blood, and my sword shall devour flesh; and that with the blood of the slain and of the captives, from the beginning of revenges upon the enemy"; "And whoever blasphemes the name of the Lord shall surely be put to death."

Patriquin disagreed with how certain Islamic traditions were expressed by some people. He disapproved of the inferior status granted to women in some Muslim societies, a tradition that sometimes fueled the tragedy of denying women education, or the horror of "honor killing," which happened even in Jordan. He disapproved of the hypocrisy of some adherents in places like Saudi Arabia and Kuwait, who made ostentatious displays of being devout and then spent much of their private lives in pursuit of wealth and hedonistic pleasure.

He had no illusions about the danger posed by those who would pervert Islam into acts of terrorism or aggressive war, just as centuries earlier Christianity was twisted into the Inquisition and the Crusades, epochs of Christian and Muslim violence and counterviolence that spanned over five hundred years. A few years after his Jordan experience, Patriquin made an offhand quip to a buddy about the tenacious Islamic fighters he faced in the mountains of Afghanistan. "They're fanatics over there. There's only one way to deal with fanatics. It's a crazy thought, and hopefully there's another way to do it, but maybe we should nuke Medina, their second holiest city, and tell them to straighten their ass up, because if they don't, Mecca's next!" His friend responded, "Whoa, Travis, that's kinda far out there!" Patriquin replied, "Well, as of right now, that's kind of the way I feel about it."

But on the whole, Patriquin believed that the authentic visions of true Islam, Christianity, and Judaism were three branches of the same tree. Thinking of the centuries of conflict between followers of Islam and followers of Christianity and Judaism, Patriquin considered a provocative idea: "What if it's all just a misunderstanding?" What if all the "sword passages" were canceled out by other scripture passages in all three faiths?

What if, Patriquin asked Ken Baker, quoting from an old Islamic parable, the fundamental differences between Islam, Christianity, and Judaism were no bigger than a line in the sand drawn by a stick?

Before he left Jordan, after weeks of searching, Patriquin finally found one of the few remaining craftsmen who could make him a customized, authentic Bedouin-style sword. He asked the artisan to forge a sword and scabbard that captured his attitude to Arabia, a vision crystallized in his days at Wadi Rum, the Dead Sea, Mount Nebo, and the sun-drenched plazas of Amman.

The sword scabbard featured traditional Arabic designs and inscriptions.

And alongside them, displayed in positions of equal prominence as Patriquin instructed, were a crucifix of Jesus Christ, rosary beads, and the Lord's Prayer—written in Arabic.

CHAPTER 3

THE CITY OF DEATH

In May 2006, Captain Travis Patriquin found himself in the epicenter of the Iraqi insurgency, a city that one visiting journalist called "the most fucked-up place on Earth."

Ramadi was the capital of Iraq's al Anbar province, a city of 400,000 that was also the de facto capital of the al-Qaeda caliphate in Iraq, and a place that was by some measurements more violent than Baghdad, a city six times its size.

The city had no working government. The brutal insurgent federation known as "al-Qaeda in Iraq" ruled nine of Ramadi's fifteen districts, and kept coalition troops pinned down in bases, bunkers, and convoys under showers of mortar, rifle, and rocket fire.

Upon arriving in Ramadi, Patriquin's brigade commander, Colonel Sean MacFarland, felt like a drowning man about to be consumed in an ocean of violence. He was sure that scores of his troops were going to die.

"I'm going to lose maybe a hundred soldiers in the next few months," he thought. He did not want to leave Iraq in defeat or stalemate. "If I'm going to lose a hundred soldiers, it had better be for something. I want something to show for it."

MacFarland and Patriquin knew that over the next few months, American soldiers were probably going to die in many ways.

They would be mortared, rocketed, and grenaded. They would be shot by snipers hiding in mosques and apartment blocks. They would be incinerated in truck-bomb gasoline detonations, chemical explosions, and blown up by God knows how many kinds of explosive devices, hidden in vests, roadsides, fruit stands, cars, booby-trapped houses, and even thrown at them point-blank.

They would be attacked by small arms, rocket launchers, and rocket-propelled grenades. They might be kidnapped, tortured, and beheaded. Many soldiers would be wounded for life, some blinded, or needing fake limbs, or requiring intensive psychiatric care for posttraumatic stress that would never end.

Seventy miles west of Baghdad, on the banks of the Euphrates River, the city of Ramadi and the surrounding farmlands and desert of al Anbar province were the heart of darkness for the Americans. Reporters scampering through the city in 2006 compared it to the ruins of Stalingrad, Dresden, and Hiroshima. "Ramadi was known for IEDs the way certain French cities are known for wine," wrote one correspondent.

The roads were laced with every manner of IEDs, from bombs disguised as garbage on curbsides to complex subsurface IED belts, rendering much of the city a no-go zone for U.S. and Iraqi army troops. One captured insurgent explained to an interrogator, "You Americans own the street for one hour a day when you come and patrol through, but we own it for the other twenty-three." The insurgents used ingenious networks of spotters, kite signals, and carrier pigeons to track and ambush American troops. Al-Qaeda fighters regularly sliced the heads off accused collaborators, and playful neighborhood kids were said to comb the hair and shove cigarettes in the lips of the severed heads on public display.

The city had no mayor, and little phone service, police, functioning schools, electricity, or running water. At least half of the population had fled. The titular governor of the province, Maamoun Sami Rashid al-Awani, was the target of thirty-one assassination attempts so far, and his deputy governor and press spokesman had both been recently shot to death.

Patriquin was soon attending meetings with Governor Maamoun, a former engineer and member of the Iraqi Islamic Party, which was until recently a fairly obscure and weak political group. One American soldier, marveling at Maamoun's massive girth, dubbed him Jabba the Hut. Patriquin could admire Governor Maamoun's guts—his predecessor, Governor Raja Nawaf Farhan al-Mahalawi, had been abducted and killed. But Patriquin had a very low opinion of Maamoun's actual authority, which in 2006 was microscopic. Guarded by a U.S. Marine Corps rifle company, he influenced events inside the four walls of his office, and little else.

In June 2004, marine General James Mattis visited Ramadi and issued an order to a marine battalion that was absorbing the worst casualties of the war: "Ramadi must hold or the rest of the province goes to Hell." But that year, when U.S. forces retook the city of Fallujah, many insurgents moved to Ramadi, just thirty miles to the west, and took over most of the city. After two years of frantic sweeps by seventy-ton M1 Abrams tanks, raids, air strikes, and counterattacks, another marine officer was preparing a report that concluded that Ramadi and Anbar province were lost and the coalition essentially beaten there.

Patriquin's colleague Major Thomas "Andy" Shoffner recalls that "Ramadi itself had basically been declared al-Qaeda–owned, and they wanted to make it the capital of their new caliphate. They had poured everything into Ramadi. If you wanted to make a name for yourself as an insurgent you would infiltrate into the country and go to Ramadi. It was like the Super Bowl of insurgents. The best snipers, the best explosives experts come to Ramadi to make a name for themselves. When we got there in May 2006, you could not walk anywhere in the city without taking massive casualties. The city was for all intents and purposes lost. Al-Qaeda was using Ramadi as kind of their headquarters. It was the first stop from neighboring countries to train foreign fighters, to train local Iraqis to go into Baghdad and elsewhere as trained insurgents."

"The sheer scale of violence in Ramadi is astounding," noted Todd Pittman of the Associated Press, who visited in early 2006. "It's out of control," announced army Sergeant First Class Britt Ruble, from behind a sandbag in an observation post. "We don't have control of this, we just don't have enough boots on the ground." The Iraqi colonel Ali Hassan agreed, "We just go out, lose people and come back. The insurgents are moving freely every-where." If you toss your hat in the air, quipped the locals, it will come down with twelve bullet holes in it.

Patriquin discussed the importance of Ramadi in a conversa-tion he held late in the year with a young sheik. The Iraqi explained to Patriquin, "As goes Ramadi, so goes the province, then so goes Iraq. Al Anbar is the largest province in Iraq, and a spiritual center for the Bedouin heart that resides in most tribal Sunnis. Even for the Iraqi middle class, deep inside them exists the love of the des-ert and Bedouin culture. For some it's like a passing fancy similar to your interest in the Wild West, but for others, it's a deep-rooted spiritual connection. Most Iraqis have relations and roots in the tribal areas, and feel a connection to them. Even Mohammed the prophet, who was by rights a middle-class city dweller, spent time in his youth on his uncle's camel and sheep train, where he learned the Bedouin ways."

The existential bleakness of Ramadi was starkly described in a U.S. Army report: "Pro-coalition and neutral tribal leaders were kidnapped, tortured and killed. Local citizens lived in fear. Public services were nonexistent and public schools, religious centers and medical facilities were all under AIF [anti-Iraqi forces, or insurgents] control. The Ramadi General Hospital had become an AIF headquarters. The al Anbar University had become a recruiting ground for impressionable minds that processed IEDs and generated AIF propaganda."

The city of Ramadi represented one of the first cases in history where forces identifying themselves as "al-Qaeda" had managed to seize and hold so much of a large population center. For the local people in Ramadi and elsewhere in Anbar province where al-Qaeda held sway, many of them disempowered Sunnis who thoroughly hated the American presence to begin with, the reality of living inside an al-Qaeda "mini-caliphate" on a day-to-day basis was becoming much worse than anything the occupation could inflict. Lieutenant Colonel Anthony Deane, a battalion commander in Patriquin's brigade, reported, "In response to the Iraqi army checkpoint established at al Anbar University, al-Qaeda had issued a decree that they would kill the children of Anbar if they attended school. Al-Qaeda was also attempting to implement strict sharia law throughout Ramadi, including a ban on smoking, which caused an uproar with the local population."

According to Sheik Sabah al-Sattam Effan Fahran al-Shurji al-Aziz of the Abu Mahal tribe in western Anbar province, "It was a disaster when al-Qaeda entered our country, killing and executing Iraqis. Whatever the Tatars did against humanity, al-Qaeda did it worse, worse than anyone that you can think of." He added, "They were foreigners who entered from Yemen, Saudi Arabia, Syria, and they called themselves emirs. They wanted to have their word and their opinion over us. In our personal experiences with them, they dealt violently and toughly with all Iraqi citizens."

"Ramadi became a ghost town," remembered the Sunni cleric Dr. Thamer Ibrahim Tahir al-Assafi, "universities, schools, factories, and institutions were all shut down." One female community leader in Ramadi later told a team of U.S. Marine Corps historians of the reign of terror the city endured: "The ugliest torture was committed by al-Qaeda. If discipline didn't work, the people were abducted and slaughtered. The head was put in a container and thrown away, or the neck cut and the head placed on the back. They killed doctors and said that it was because they treated Americans. The doctors fled the country. They killed mullahs and said that it was because they liked Americans. Soon there were no men left to kill, so they started killing women and children. They killed women and said that it was because their husbands were policemen. They killed children and said it was because their fathers were policemen. I cannot describe the horror we lived in. Those were very bitter days. Those days we lived in hell. We looked like ghosts out of a cemetery."

Patriquin once asked a resident of Anbar, a young sub-sheik, how al-Qaeda managed to gain a stranglehold on the area. The Iraqi told him: "When the Americans came, they didn't fire a shot. We heard they were coming, and we went to welcome them down Route Michigan at the Government Center. The Americans called us all heroes, because at that time, Anbar was a peaceful place, and we were beginning to rebuild the security forces. But soon the uprisings in the South began. Many people were emboldened and took up arms against the Americans for perceived and real wrongs, like the injuring of innocent people in escalation of force incidents. Also foreign interests entered al Anbar, especially the areas between Fallujah and Ramadi, and found tribes that would work with them and began to infiltrate them and corrupt the minds of young people and disaffected people."

The sheik explained to Patriquin that al-Qaeda employed a methodical, step-by-step strategy of murder and intimidation to seize control of the area: "They enter a village and call a meeting of the imam, sheik and other important members, and present them with the al-Qaeda philosophy. If the sheik or imam refuses to go along with them, they are killed, and a weaker man is installed in his position. If the next in line refuses, he is killed, and so on, until al-Qaeda leadership is firmly in charge. Then al-Qaeda pays the poor and weak-minded people good money to lay IEDs and fight the coalition forces. Once the weaker tribal areas were co-opted in this manner, al-Qaeda started to go after the larger tribal sheiks."

The man given the herculean task of turning around the city of Ramadi was Colonel Sean MacFarland, Patriquin's commander. A career army armor and cavalry officer, MacFarland was a West Point graduate from upstate New York, as well as the son and grandson of army colonels. He was a decorated veteran of combat in the First Gulf War, and peacekeeping tours in Kosovo, Macedonia, and Bosnia. He was soft-spoken, laconic, and highly respected by his troops. He had no swagger, but was clearly in charge, and Travis Patriquin greatly admired him.

MacFarland is a man "you would dream to have as a commander in combat," says Lieutenant Colonel Tony Deane, one of his battalion commanders. "He is level-headed, unflappable, very, very intelligent and very disarming when you talk to him. He's a man for all seasons. He shared the danger with his men, and he was out there with them. My guess is that every casualty took a piece of his soul. He was the ideal guy for the situation, very smart and very willing to empower those who could run with the ball. He was not afraid of pushing the envelope and clearly recognized that we had nowhere to go but up in Ramadi, and the intractable situation called for innovation."

Patriquin and MacFarland also knew that fighting insurgents in Iraq was like squeezing a balloon. Push them out of one spot and they'll pop up someplace else. The Americans and their Iraqi allies faced a brutal, stubborn enemy in Anbar province, an invisible, highly mobile legion that easily numbered in the thousands of fighters and active sympathizers.

"There were various flavors of enemy in Ramadi," explained MacFarland. "At the very top of the pyramid was al-Qaeda in Iraq, dominated by foreigners for the most part from Syria and elsewhere. Then below them, you have the homegrown version of al-Qaeda called the JTJ [Jama'at al-Tawhid wal-Jihad]. They were the locals who had drunk al-Qaeda's Kool-Aid and believed in what al-Qaeda's goal was, which was to create a caliphate with its capital in Iraq, in Ramadi to be specific. Then below them on the insurgent food chain, you had former Ba'athists. Ramadi was home to a large number of Sunni former government and military officials, many with professional combat training. This was the group that was privileged under Saddam Hussein, the people who felt most dispossessed by his departure. Then below them, you had just criminals. And there was a fair amount of organized crime going on at that time."

Al-Qaeda had a large pool of fighters at the bottom of the pyramid: military-aged males, many of them resentful of the Americans, with no jobs, zero prospects, and no way to put food on the table to feed their families. For these men, a $200 offer to plant a bomb to kill U.S. troops was a no-brainer. They were cannon fodder, and provided thousands of volunteers who could be called on both by al-Qaeda and by nationalist insurgent groups. Patriquin wrote a paper at the time that pointed out that the true "center of gravity" for the insurgency lay with this local population, and not with foreign terrorist leaders. He wrote: "Some coalition figures still refuse to acknowledge the obvious, and assert instead that the insurgency is in the main a terrorist conspiracy fueled by foreigners working for Osama bin Laden. The major problem with this assertion is that very few of the insurgents captured or killed have been foreigners. Outsiders are certainly playing a role, especially as suicide bombers, but hardly in the numbers one would expect if they were to be regarded as the driving force of the insurgency."

Colonel MacFarland's boss was Major General Rick Zilmer, the commander of the I Marine Expeditionary Force (Forward) (often shorthanded to First MEF, or simply MEF), which was headquartered at Camp Fallujah and oversaw all of Anbar province, including the Ready First Combat Team's (RFCT) new battle area of operations, called AO Topeka. Zilmer and his boss, Lieutenant General Pete Chiarelli, the commander of Multinational Corps–Iraq in Baghdad, outlined a plan that called for the RFCT to slowly retake Ramadi by "clearing, holding, and building" one neighborhood at a time.

"We were considered kind of an economy of force effort," Mac-Farland explains, "to go out there and try to keep a lid on things, do what you can but we don't expect much out of you." He described the thrust of the orders he received as: "Try to fix Ramadi, but don't destroy it—don't do a Fallujah," referring to the destructive 2004 coalition reconquest of that city, which generated bad international press and much local resentment.

MacFarland's Ready First Combat Team was built around his First Brigade, First Armored Division (1/1 AD), made up of five battalion-sized maneuver elements. He had at his disposal about fifty-seven hundred army troops and engineers (largely from the 1/1 AD, but including a battalion of the 101st Airborne); thirteen hundred marine troops and air controllers; twenty air force personnel to help coordinate air strikes; and three hundred navy personnel, including medics, sailors for patrols along the Euphrates River, Seabee construction engineers, and two platoons of Navy SEAL Special Operations troops for countersniping missions, Iraqi security force training, and hunting and killing "high-value targets," or insurgent commanders. These regular forces had a variety of tools at their disposal: tanks, giant self-propelled artillery pieces, Bradleys, boats, attack helicopters, and jets they could call in from the air force, marines, and other army units.

MacFarland could also call on Special Operations forces and unmanned aerial vehicles from JSOC, the Joint Special Operations Command, and operatives and high-tech eavesdropping tools from the CIA, the Defense Intelligence Agency (DIA), the National Security Agency, and various civilian intelligence contractors, all of which were widely deployed across Iraq in secret command posts connected to the main U.S. bases. At Camp Ramadi, many of the CIA, DIA, and Special Operations people were housed in a nearby facility called Shark Base. American technicians had recently developed sensors and techniques that enabled them to penetrate insurgent computer networks and intercept both wireless and even satellite phone calls placed by insurgents.

As a former "special operator" support soldier, Travis Patriquin soon became a frequent guest at Shark Base, sharing beers and burgers and swapping war stories and intelligence with people he called his "secret friends": Navy SEALs, military intelligence officers, and civilian contractors working for the CIA who were trying to track and capture the most wanted insurgents and terrorists.

Patriquin's brigade could also call on twenty-three hundred

troops from two Iraqi army brigades and a handful of Iraqi police to try to keep the peace, but the troops were mostly far from combat-ready, and the few police were usually too afraid to set foot outside their stations. All told, it was an "economy of force" operation. To properly seize, hold, and patrol the Ramadi battle area, MacFarland really needed about twenty-five thousand troops. He had barely a third that many.

But MacFarland quickly realized he had a powerful asset in his tribal and civil affairs officer, Captain Travis Patriquin.

Patriquin had come to Iraq through a series of career twists and turns.

Even before his experience in Operation Anaconda and during his fairly brief stint as a rifle platoon leader in the 82nd Airborne the year before, Patriquin had entertained hopes of rejoining a Special Forces unit and eventually becoming an SF team leader, but he came to realize that chance was probably passing for him, by virtue of his age and the lousy condition of his knee.

After his service in Afghanistan, Patriquin had focused on family life, and he took a leave of TDY, or temporary duty assignment, completing a bachelor's degree at Campbell University near his base at Fort Bragg, North Carolina. It was nearly a year and a half of study, civilian life, and much-needed family time.

By then it looked like two of Patriquin's career dreams would not come true. He was not one to look back or wallow in disappointment, but it looked like he was destined to get neither a Ranger tab nor an SF team leader slot. So he took a look at the regular army and figured there was still time to try to be a company commander, hopefully in Iraq, obviously where most of the action was in his profession right now.

Patriquin seemed to have what it took to potentially be a great commander of troops and an inspirational leader. Russell Wagner, an officer he served with in the 82nd Airborne Division, described Patriquin's contagious enthusiasm and his "absolutely positive outlook on everything."

Wagner recalled of Patriquin, "He was most often smiling, telling stories, or helping somebody out. He had a great rapport with junior soldiers, probably from having risen through the ranks. His war-fighting, can-do attitude was infectious. He used to walk around the office constantly talking about being 'warriors' and 'fighting for freedom,' and unlike a lot of officers, he truly meant it. His soldiers responded to him with admiration and respect because they knew that he truly believed what he said, he always gave them straight answers, and he always looked out for their well-being. He was probably one of the best leaders I've ever met. His soldiers loved him, the leadership loved him, he was technically and tactically very, very smart. His knack was being able to take a complex subject and break it down to very basic language that soldiers could understand."

Patriquin confided to his colleagues that if someone stays in Special Forces their whole career, then "none of that good stuff you learn gets spread around." Plus, he thought, there was a chance of earning more recognition in the regular army than the notoriously tight-lipped Special Forces. He noted in an e-mail to his colleagues, "Every once in a while, when I'm reading about Anaconda, I'll run across a reference to SOT-A or SF guys attached to 10th MTN and 101st, or Men with Beards who were good shots and filled leadership gaps. I just smile and nod, and remember that it's no fun being secret unless you can tell everyone."

"I used to think that if you weren't in SOF you weren't shit, but I've come around on that thinking," Patriquin later wrote in an online posting. "I plan on working my way back [to Special Forces], but I'm thankful to have this tour to see 'big army' for the first time in a thirteen-year career."

In 2005 Patriquin was assigned to the brigade staff of the Ready First Combat Team at its headquarters in Friedberg, Germany, to plan for deployment to Iraq. His job was first as assistant brigade operations and planning officer, or AS3, which was strictly a staff job. The trouble was Patriquin hated staff jobs. He was, in fact, a lousy staff officer, and being one drove him crazy. He hated writing reports, pushing paper and sitting in meetings, listening to other officers yammer on as they slogged through their two hundredth sleep-inducing, statistics-clogged PowerPoint presentation slide.

Patriquin's dream was to command his own infantry company in the field, leading troops in action. That was where the glory was for a career soldier. The job Patriquin yearned for was to command the brigade reconnaissance company, a prestigious slot that, in the cold war battlefield orientation of the army, reported directly to the brigade commander and served as his forward eyes and ears on the battlefield as a highly mobile scout force, though in occupation-era Iraq, recon troops were usually assigned a fixed battle space. Patriquin was "chomping at the bit for it," in the words of one colleague. It was just a matter of timing and waiting his turn, and he hoped the slot would open up.

As the brigade prepared to deploy to Iraq in late 2005, Patriquin was assigned to be the brigade S5 (later called S9), or Civil-Military Operations (CMO) officer, in charge of coordinating civil affairs projects, community outreach, cultural affairs, and tribal engagement.

In retrospect, it was the perfect job for Patriquin, given his language skills and personality, to be advising the brigade on tribal outreach and key local leader engagement. It still included a fair amount of office work, which Patriquin hated. His colleague Captain Aaron Dixon recalls, "Once he knew he was going to be stuck as our cultural advisor and even more, discovered that he was gifted in that role, he abandoned his disappointment [company command] and set himself to being the best S5 he could be. He even made the decision to follow that aptitude for the rest of his career and told me that he was going to make the transition to Civil Affairs permanent following our deployment."

The midcareer switch from Special Forces to the regular army wasn't an easy transition for Patriquin. "I hate the fucking big army," Patriquin once griped. "Motherfuckers won't listen." One of his complaints: "When I got here, no one in my section full of captains was qualified on their damn rifles. Now, everyone I go to the range with is at least a sharpshooter. Maybe it's the ex-NCO in me, but that makes me happy. Man, you wouldn't believe how they run a frippin' zero [shooting] range over here. But instead of bitchin' about it, I just try to change things one day at a time."

As a highly skilled marksman and gun buff, Patriquin took it upon himself to organize extra marksmanship training for the soldiers in his brigade, and a "squad designated marksman" training program. A colleague remembers, "The intent of the training was to bring in a team of shooting experts from the infantry center to work with soldiers to get them up to speed on how to engage at the middle distances. A normal soldier without enhancement is trained to shoot and kill out to three hundred meters, a sniper can shoot and kill at seven hundred–plus meters, and the squad designated marksmen were to fill that three-hundred- to seven-hundred-meter gap with better weapons and optics. It was right up Travis's alley, and he dove into it full bore. After the training he kept up with the soldiers who had been trained, and followed up on their sustainment training, were they getting used by their units for their roles, what equipment they needed, etc. He didn't have to follow up, he just did."

In January and February of 2006, troops of the Ready First Combat Team flew to their new assignment—the relatively secure northwestern Iraqi city of Tal Afar—with Travis Patriquin as the brigade's civil-military affairs and tribal affairs officer.

Tal Afar was a city of roughly 250,000. It was ethnically largely Sunni Turkoman, and had been plagued by ferocious off-and-on insurgent attacks until the arrival in 2005 of the Third Armored Cavalry Regiment. Commanded by the innovative Colonel H. R. McMaster, the unit leveraged a high troop-to-civilian ratio, aggressive combat operations, and equally ambitious community outreach to "clear, hold and build" the city into a relative oasis of stability, so much so that their successors in the RFCT found much of their workdays focused not on combat but on Patriquin's specialty, civil and tribal affairs, training the Iraqi police, and trying to develop a city government and essential services. McMaster's experience was being widely hailed as apparently the Americans' first sustained counterinsurgency success in Iraq.

In Tal Afar, Patriquin plunged into the local culture as much as was possible for an American soldier, getting to know the city's Iraqi officials, local sheiks, and police over chai tea, cigars, and cigarettes. He struck up conversations with Iraqi shop owners, army contract interpreters, and regular Iraqis on the street, honing his dialect skills and startling almost every Iraqi he met with his very-good-for-an-American Arabic, and jovial, deferential personality.

In addition, he cultivated a habit that was becoming a kind of magnificent obsession for him: learning everything he possibly could about Iraqi culture, customs, religion, folklore, and tribal structures. He learned it online, through books, and through constant conversation with Iraqis, with whom he would quote a parable from the Koran to illustrate a point. For his fellow officers, Patriquin held classes three times a week in Arabic language and culture, dubbed the "Travis Patriquin School of Arabic Studies," with classes like "How to Talk to an Iraqi" and "How to Get Them on Our Side."

By their own admission, American officers sometimes showed up armed to the teeth for meetings with Iraqis, dominating conversations with an aggressive communications style, and reading off meeting agendas on paper with a "let's get things done" can-do attitude, going bang-bang through the list of items. They didn't realize it, but they came off as rude to the Iraqis they were trying to work with. From the moment they set foot in Iraq, a number of Americans suffered from a lack of cultural awareness that crippled any hopes they might have had of a successful occupation and timely withdrawal. Brigadier Nigel Aylwin-Foster, a British general who served with the Americans in a training mission in 2004, put it this way: "It seemed to be an enigma, the U.S. military as an entity. They're polite, courteous, generous, humble, in a sense. But you see some of the things going on, if I could sum it up, I never saw such a good bunch of people inadvertently piss off so many people."

Travis Patriquin, on the other hand, knew that deference, humility, and cultural respect were force multipliers in dealing with Iraqis. In fact, without them, the Americans had much less chance of getting anything done. It took endless hours of literally "man-kissing" and holding hands, talking about family, and socializing over tea, cigarettes, and goat-meat buffets before Iraqis felt comfortable talking business with an American. As in much of life anywhere in the world, personal relationships were essential to success.

Patriquin's insights on Arabic culture were based on his personal experiences in Jordan and Kuwait, on his friendships with Arab nationals who taught his language classes at the Defense

Language Institute, on his constant conversations with Iraqi interpreters, and from his ravenous reading of books by Arab authors
and by Westerners like Karen Armstrong and Bernard Lewis. It
was an approach very much in line with the recommendations
made by Patriquin's hero T. E. Lawrence, who in 1917 offered
these tips in the *Arab Bulletin* to his fellow British officers: "The
beginning and ending of the secret of handling Arabs is unre-
mitting study of them. Keep always on your guard; never say an
unnecessary thing: watch yourself and your companions all the
time: hear all that passes, search out what is going on beneath the
surface, read their characters, discover their tastes and their weak-
nesses and keep everything you find out to yourself. Bury yourself
in Arab circles, have no interests and no ideas except the work in
hand, so that your brain is saturated with one thing only, and you
realize your part deeply enough to avoid the little slips that would
counteract the painful work of weeks. Your success will be propor-
tioned to the amount of mental effort you devote to it."

In Iraq, Patriquin gave his fellow American officers tips about
how to interact with the locals: "The only way to win in Iraq is to
drink thousands of cups of tea and smoke hundreds of cigarettes.
When you meet an Iraqi, you need to chat back and forth first. You
need to build trust on a personal level. Sheiks want to hear about
your hometown, they want to hear about New York and Chicago.
Go around and introduce yourself, tell them where you went to
school, where you grew up. Show them pictures of your family.
Don't rush things. Don't go into a meeting and expect to cover ten
topics."

Patriquin knew that one of the biggest and most painfully obvious problems the Americans had was they didn't speak the language. Only a relative handful of U.S. personnel in Iraq spoke any
Arabic beyond a few pleasantries. An Iraqi once asked Patriquin,

"Why aren't there more Americans who speak Arabic and understand Arabs the way you do?"

"Arabic is considered a very difficult language for an American to learn," he replied, "and we often avoid languages that are too difficult, preferring to study Spanish or German or French in our secondary schools. This is a regret of many soldiers, and many of them are trying to learn Arabic on their own."

Patriquin explained, "The more we engage the local Iraqis on a one-to-one basis, the better off we'll all be. One of the reasons Americans are sometimes nervous around Iraqis is because of the deep cultural differences. For example, though German is a different language, culturally the Germans and Americans are about 70 percent the same, while Iraqis and Americans don't enjoy that same degree of cultural familiarity, which creates misunderstandings and fear."

Lieutenant Colonel Pete Lee was the executive officer, or XO, for Patriquin's brigade, and the designated "hard-ass/bad cop," whose job was to knock heads together and try to run the organizational aspects of the unit. He remembers of Patriquin, "I personally thought the absolute world of the guy, even though in my view I failed because I couldn't get him to produce a goddamn staff product [report] to save my ass. I used to try to get Travis to focus on the staff aspect of what he was doing. But rather than sit in meetings, Travis would usually find an excuse to go off the FOB [Forward Operating Base] to meet with a sheik."

Lee tried to give Patriquin career advice in a kidding way, saying, "Travis, look at you, come on! You chain-smoke, dude! Look at you! You can't run around the frickin' block without getting winded and having to bend over! Infantry is not going to be your forte." He recalls, "Travis had all the knowledge and expertise to be a very, very good infantry company commander, but the problem was he did not personify the lean, well-shaven, clean-cut, high-and-tight look of a typical hard-nosed infantry officer. I didn't think he would be given a fair chance, in part because of the way he looked. He had been injured, he'd put on a few pounds, he had long hair and a mustache, he pretty much chain-smoked, and was a little bit overweight." Another one of the brigade officers, Lieutenant Colonel Tony Deane, saw Patriquin in a similar light: "Patriquin was a guy straight out of Hollywood, kind of like William Holden in *Stalag 17*. A reluctant hero. He needed a haircut, and he was not the most physically fit guy."

"Travis's gift was with people," explained Pete Lee. "The reason he did so well with the local sheiks was because of his personality. He spoke the language, understood the customs, his look and demeanor fit in perfectly in Iraq. He had such a huge connection with the sheiks. He gained access for battalion commanders and the brigade commander that they would never have earned on their own."

Patriquin's colleague Captain Aaron Dixon recalled, "He spent all of his waking hours researching the history of the land and the nuances of the local culture. If he couldn't find it online, he spent time with our Terps [interpreters]. If he couldn't get it from them, he researched during normal conversation over chai [tea] and cigarettes. Showing interest in another man's culture, remembering it and respecting it is one of the highest forms of respect you can show the people of your host nation. Travis understood the importance of the tribes and families and would inquire after family members or see the trickle-down effects from one tribe to another before they were even mentioned. Iraqi tribal leaders respect that kind of involvement, and respect builds trust. But he also had the ability to take that knowledge and break it down into simple and practical dialog for our military leaders to incorporate into the campaign."

Another colleague, Captain Will Bardenwerper, remembers that when Iraqi merchants working at the American base at Tal Afar saw Patriquin coming, they "fell all over him, dropped what they were doing, offered him free packs of cigarettes and DVDs, and treated him like royalty." Soon, through informal conversations over chai tea and smokes, Patriquin was developing such good intelligence on the local insurgency, says Bardenwerper, "I thought he was getting better intelligence than the brigade intel staff."

In Ramadi, Colonel Sean MacFarland was increasingly amused and impressed by Captain Patriquin. He recalls, "Travis was just an amazing, amazing guy, introverted and soft-spoken, but also a jovial, witty Renaissance guy. He stepped into a moment in history that is really important at the strategic level. Without a lot of direction from me, Travis went out and built relationships with Iraqis. I gave him a lot of latitude. I'd always rather have a guy I have to reel back in a little than a guy I have to kick in the butt. And I never had to kick Travis in the butt."

Based on their experience in Tal Afar and on plain common sense, Patriquin and MacFarland believed that the tribes were a key to turning the war around. They simply could not prevail in the battle for Ramadi and Anbar province without the help of at least some of the powerful local tribal bosses. Patriquin knew that Iraq, like Afghanistan, had been a strongly tribal society for centuries.

For many Iraqis the tribes were a social organization that was of parallel importance to the government. As in many Middle Eastern societies, tribal sheiks were local power brokers and neighborhood bosses who had influence over their own extended clan and family networks. They were expected to adjudicate disputes, provide security, look after the welfare of tribal members, and intercede with authorities on their behalf. In Iraq, a sheik's position was based not only on lineage and family ties but on a rough grassroots democracy that asserted when a sheik failed to deliver for his constituents, and he could quickly find himself without popular support and the patronage power, or wasta, that flowed from it. Like politicians in many countries, sheiks had to build consensus behind their decisions, and sell the decisions to the people.

To the American military, Iraq's tribes presented a murky, Byzantine complexity that could baffle attempts to map or categorize them. One tribe could have many sheiks. Men could step forward and identify themselves as sheiks and turn out to be con men. Intermarriages between tribes were common. One part of a tribe could be planting IEDs against American troops by night, and another part could be volunteering to join the Iraqi police the next morning. Sheiks could be legitimate businessmen and smugglers simultaneously. Tribal identity seemed to weaken among city dwellers and highly educated Iraqis, but the tribe still seemed to hold a mystical place in their hearts.

Saddam Hussein saw the tribes as a nuisance and a competitive threat to his secular one-party dictatorship, but he knew that tribalism was ingrained in the Iraqi soul and would be devilishly hard to eradicate. After the disasters of the Iran-Iraq War and the Persian Gulf War, Saddam decided in his typical brute Machiavellian style to cultivate tribal support, by showering preferred tribal leaders with favors—and reshuffling the national deck of over seven thousand sheiks to keep them all off balance, adding new sheiks and disempowering others.

The idea of engaging tribes in Iraq was nothing new for the Americans.

American marines and soldiers by the thousands had been reaching out to Iraqi tribal leaders since the war began, trying to involve them in local government, intelligence gathering, security, and reconstruction projects.

The CIA had been carefully courting Iraqi tribal leaders since before the invasion, establishing relationships with both exiles and with tribal leaders inside the country. Currently the agency was nurturing relationships with sheiks across Iraq, including Anbar province.

As long ago as the earliest days of the almost universally loathed reign of Coalition Provisional Authority (CPA) viceroy Paul Bremer, American officials paid their respects to Iraq's tribes, holding meetings, posing for pictures, handing out certificates, making grand pronouncements, and trying to bring tribal leaders into the politics of the new Iraq.

Patriquin, like others in the military and many in the world at large, held Paul Bremer and his CPA in contempt for many reasons, including what they saw as repeated attempts by the CPA to push the tribes aside and deny them influence in the early days of the occupation, in favor of shoring up the fledgling Iraqi central government. Bremer's CPA had gained a reputation for interfering with tribal outreach efforts attempted by both the military and the CIA.

Paul Bremer, who became a historical punching bag for much of what went wrong in Iraq in 2003 and 2004, claims the opposite was true: "I met with tribal leaders all the time. I met with them in the south; I met with them in Ramadi, Mosul, and Tikrit. I launched an outreach program to draw Sunni tribes into the political process. I gave permission and funds to the new Ministries of Oil and Electricity to pay tribes to protect oil and electrical power lines because they were being attacked by insurgents and criminals. We weren't trying to obliterate the tribal structure in Iraq, nor were we trying to ignore it. And if somebody on my staff was stupid enough to say the tribes are a vestige of the past, well, there's no accounting for stupidity."

But as a 2009 Rand Corporation analysis titled "Occupying Iraq" reported, "These efforts had only limited impact." The reason was simple, and it explained much of the torment the Americans and Iraqis would endure through the war and occupation. For the minority Sunnis, the invasion was a political apocalypse, the sudden, humiliating, and bloody end to their fourteen-hundred-year rule. "The Sunnis, still chafing over their loss of position, privilege, and influence," concluded the Rand study, "resisted being drawn into the political process, and the insurgency raged on." One Sunni man remarked, "We were on top of the system. . . . Now we are the losers. We lost our positions, our status, the security of our families, stability. Curse the Americans."

A few days after they took up their new post at Camp Ramadi, Colonel MacFarland turned to Patriquin with an urgent request.

"Travis, you've got to help me out. I really don't know who all the tribes, sub-tribes and clans, sheiks and sub-sheiks are.

"Find out everything you can about the tribes."

CHAPTER 4

THE EARTH WAS ON FIRE

P atriquin thought about the war he was in, and he marveled at how spectacularly fucked up it was.

"We came into this country with no plan to fix it," he thought, "no plan to occupy it, and no plan to put it on a road to democracy. We are fighting this war in entirely the wrong way. We are on our ass."

Patriquin was a connoisseur of history and an amateur archae-ology buff, and he was garrisoned in a land that was the very womb of human civilization: Iraq's ancestor kingdoms had given birth to agriculture, writing, accounting, mathematics, navigation, law, astronomy, commerce, and war itself. The first war for which there is detailed evidence climaxed in 2525 BC when infantry of two Sumerian city-states clashed on the plain of Lagash in present-day southern Iraq, a battle that ended with lions and vultures feasting on the corpses of defeated combatants.

It was early summer, and temperatures would soon climb to a pulverizing 120 degrees at Camp Ramadi, a sprawling dust- and mud-choked American base that sat astride the fabled Euphrates, one of the four rivers that, according to Genesis, flowed from the Garden of Eden.

To the west the country was largely desert, wild and desolate. But near here began the fertile alluvial plains that spread down to the gulf, dotted with green fields, palm trees, and pockets of languid river landscapes described generations ago by the British explorer Austen Henry Layard, who jotted in a notebook as his barge drifted down the Tigris River: "We are now amidst the date groves. If it be autumn, clusters of golden fruit hang beneath the fanlike leaves; if spring, the odor of orange blossoms fills the air. The cooing of the doves that flutter amongst the branches, begets a pleasing melancholy, and a feeling of listlessness and repose."

Within a day or two ride of Patriquin's billet at Camp Ramadi were the sites of Ur, mankind's first major city and the birthplace of Abraham, father to Judaism, Islam, and Christianity; Baghdad, the medieval capital of the golden age of Islamic culture; and Babylon, the ancient supercity where Alexander the Great died at age thirty-two in the midst of his campaign to subdue Mesopotamia. Over the centuries, the invading Persians, Mongols, Turks, and British would follow, and now the Americans were trying to hold Iraq.

On balance, they seemed to be failing terribly. Patriquin strongly believed in the American mission in Iraq, which he saw as defeating the insurgency and giving Iraqis a better life. In an e-mail to his younger sister Karrie back in the States, he wrote, "I've buried quite a few friends, and I'll bury more before it's over, but I am confident that we are doing the right thing and that these people need our help. Iraq could be the Arab Turkey, it used to be and can be again, and through it, it can be an example to all the other Arab nations."

But Patriquin simply could not believe how badly America's

leaders had run this war. It was screwed up from the start. According to his wife, Amy, he thought U.S. forces should have gone into Iraq much faster and harder with a much higher number of troops, especially Special Operations troops.

Three years after the American invasion, Iraq was a carnival of human slaughter.

Full-scale civil war was erupting, as insurgents, criminals, terrorists, freelance sadist gangs, and renegade government death squads roamed and slaughtered across much of the country at will. Baghdad's central morgue took in a staggering 1,855 bodies in the single month of July 2006, with eyeballs drilled out, limbs gouged off, and a multiplicity of other hideous mutilations and tortures.

Ultimately, Patriquin felt, there were only three American officials responsible for the colossal mess in Iraq: Vice President Dick Cheney, Defense Secretary Donald Rumsfeld, and President George W. Bush.

Patriquin was largely nonpolitical, in keeping with the nature of his job. He wasn't especially pro-Bush or anti-Bush, and he often identified more with Republicans than Democrats. In fact, he feared that a new leadership team in Washington might even mess things up worse. But Patriquin had by now privately concluded that George Bush, as the commander in chief, was so far disconnected from the reality on the ground in Iraq that he was almost irrelevant to its outcome, or worse. "As long as Bush is running this war, we're never going to get anything accomplished," Patriquin confided to his brother Danny. "We're not going to do anything right over here."

Think back to what Bush, Cheney, and Secretary of Defense Rumsfeld were saying in 2003, Patriquin mused in an online discussion with fellow soldiers. "It's shocking that we've all collectively forgotten what they said back then."

Back then, President Bush was saying things like: "Major combat operations in Iraq have ended," "Bring 'em on!" "We've got the force necessary to deal with the security situation." Vice President Cheney: "We know Saddam Hussein's trying to produce nuclear weapons and we know he has a long-standing relationship with terrorist groups, including al-Qaeda." "We will be greeted as liberators." Rumsfeld: "It could last six days, six weeks. I doubt six months." "We know where the WMDs are."

There had been coalition victories in Iraq, to be sure, like the initial invasion, the "Thunder Runs" into Baghdad, the shattering of most of the Republican Guard, the capture of many towns and villages in a hundred forgotten battles and skirmishes, the pacification of certain sections of the country, notably Kurdistan, and the capture of Saddam Hussein, his sons, and many of his gang of corrupt, thuggish Iraqi leaders.

There had been national democratic elections as well, and some lurching, back-and-forth political progress toward creating some embryonic outlines of an actual functioning Iraqi government. These victories came from the ingenuity and boldness of countless coalition troops and commanders and the blood sacrifice of hundreds of thousands of coalition soldiers and their Iraqi allies. But there was a long, nightmarish procession of public relations disasters, failures, mistakes and tragedies, too, like Abu Ghraib, Haditha, and Fallujah; the weapons-of-mass-destruction mega-fiasco; and total casualty counts of military and civilians in the many tens of thousands, and growing.

The horrible truth was that now, in 2006, the Iraqi insurgency seemed to be out of control, and riding seemingly ever-escalating waves of chaos as open civil war appeared to be under way. The Iraqis had an expression for the violence they were enduring: "the Earth was on fire."

For three years the United States had tried and failed to stabilize Iraq. The blame for this, thought Patriquin, lay not with American soldiers or their commanders, although mistakes had been made even by the best of them.

Take the case of the previous commander of Patriquin's brigade, Colonel Pete Mansoor, who led the Ready First Combat Team in 2003–2005, a man whose sense of humor and intelligence greatly impressed Patriquin. Mansoor, recalled Patriquin, was a "genius" who had subdued the Mahdi Army militia of the militant Shiite cleric Moqtada al-Sadr in Karbala in 2004 and restored the city to coalition control, earning the unit a Presidential Unit Citation for collective valor in combat. But even Mansoor wasn't a counterinsurgency master, Patriquin believed; in fact, he thought that heavy-handed tactics by some of Mansoor's battalion commanders during his first Iraq tour probably fanned the fires of the insurgency in Baghdad immediately after the 2003 invasion.

However badly botched the war had been until now, thought Patriquin, the job now was to win it. And Patriquin was in the thick of it, at the very tip of the spear, which was exactly where he wanted to be.

Soon after their brigade entered Ramadi in May of 2006, Patriquin was hitching rides on patrols, trying to chat with Iraqis in the street and absorb information, gossip, and clues to the power dynamics of the city and surrounding province.

He started building a tribal map of the highly complex local tribal structures and relationships so he, MacFarland, and the brigade intelligence staff and battalion commanders could start to figure out which people and neighborhoods were most dominated by insurgents, and which might eventually be receptive to being "flipped" to the side of the coalition.

During his first days in Ramadi, Patriquin canvassed as many knowledgeable key people as he could find. Armed with a pen, a notebook, and cartons of Marlboros and Gauloises, he sat down with young Iraqi police recruits, soldiers of the outgoing American brigade, Arabic-speaking contract interpreters, and CIA and military intelligence officers with experience in Ramadi and Anbar province going back in some cases for three years.

Patriquin was a student of the history of counterinsurgency, a field of study that had been widely neglected in the post-Vietnam regular American army, and he would have agreed with the blunt logic expressed in 1963 by Lieutenant Colonel John Paul Vann, the famed U.S. advisor to the South Vietnamese army: "Guerrilla warfare requires the utmost discrimination in killing. Every time we killed an innocent person we lost ground in our battle to win the people." Patriquin's roots were in Special Forces, a military branch where the fundamentals of counterinsurgency never fell out of favor, and where institutionally, tactics like living among the population, protecting them, learning the local languages, and projecting cultural sensitivity were all second nature.

Patriquin actually thought this war might be won, or at least brought down to much lower levels of violence. And although he was only a thirty-one-year-old junior army officer, he was forming a clear vision of how to do it.

Patriquin's strategy boiled down to a series of concepts he was forcefully expressing to his colleagues, his bosses, to army and marine brass, and to anyone who would listen: to prevail in this war, the Americans must project extreme cultural understanding, sensitivity, and modesty to Iraqis; they must protect Iraqi civilians at all costs; and they must treat the Iraqis as if they were blood brothers.

Tactically, his strategy included two difficult, controversial steps: work with the traditional power brokers of Iraq, the local tribal sheiks, who were periodically embraced by various U.S. military and intelligence officers but largely sidelined by U.S. civilian policy-makers; and welcome "reconcilable" former insurgents over to the American and Iraqi government side, an explosive concept that had been flirted with and attempted by U.S. military and civilian officials but never implemented in force.

In other words, the Americans had to do much the opposite of what they were doing until then. Patriquin believed that all the firepower in the world would not save the American mission in Iraq unless these ideas were put into action, and fast.

In the spring and early summer of 2006, Patriquin poured out his thoughts, frustrations, and geopolitical observations into a series of online postings and e-mails to his family and friends: "Every counterinsurgency manual back to Caesar says the population is the target in an insurgency. Win the population over. And heavy-handed reaction isolates you from the populace. Sound familiar? Well, it is. Too many times in this war I've seen a good idea spread around a division, brigade, or battalion staff, and it gets cut off by well-meaning but incorrect squad and team leaders who say, 'Screw 'em. We're here to fight, not hold hands and man-kiss.'

"I think the crux of everything is that we just didn't train good enough, hard enough, or well enough on how to fight a counterinsurgency, mainly because no one wanted to admit we were fighting an insurgency. . . . But for our leaders, schooled for years in 'maneuver warfare and crushing the enemy's tank formations on the battlefield,' an insurgency wasn't in the cards. If they didn't admit it was a problem, they wouldn't have a problem, right?

"Sitting in a room with my fellow captains listening to what they had to say about the first year of the war, I was absolutely shocked to the core at some of the things I heard. Infantry lieutenants and captains have no business running whole city infrastructure (power plants, sewage, food distro), but after 'de-Ba'athification' that's exactly what they ended up doing. Of course they were going to make mistakes and further alienate the populace. Who wouldn't?

"But more importantly, who in the name of Jebus thought it was a good idea to fire everyone who was running the country at the same time, on the same day, with no plan to replace them? Paul Bremer? Rumsfeld? Cheney? I don't really know where the decision came from, but in my opinion, that one decision led more to the insurgency than anything any one unit did.

"Let's take a million-plus people and make them unemployed, and also, let's make sure that the jobs they were doing were in positions to make endearing ourselves to the locals harder (electric, food, water, services). Yeah, that'll work! Then let's put some 22-year-old infantrymen in charge of those positions. Great! Iraqi army and police? Disband them! That fits with our 6-week occupation plan, right?

"This is the life I've chosen. I have only myself to blame for sitting in the sand speaking Dirka [Arabic] right now!

"And if Arabic is a hobby," Patriquin wisecracked, "and you're not in the weeds with the few of us that speak the language, that aren't afraid of 'real' Iraqis—then kiss my ass twice."

As he took up his new command, Patriquin's boss, Colonel Mac-Farland, decided his troops had to go on the offensive in Ramadi, and quickly. "I believed if I was aggressive and offensive and put the enemy back on its heels," he explains, "I probably wouldn't lose that many more guys than I would have if I'd just stayed on the defense."

Some top U.S. military planners felt the presence of American troops on the streets of Iraq was an irritant to the population, pouring fuel on the flames of the insurgency. A number of units largely pulled back to their bases and ventured outside the wire only in limited vehicle patrols. Since the Iraqi police and army were rarely able to fill the void, this withdrawal effectively ceded large chunks of territory to the insurgents and deprived coalition forces of local intelligence and local relationships.

It was a special problem in Ramadi, according to Colonel Mac-Farland and Major Niel Smith, who later jointly wrote, "Past coalition operations in Ramadi had originated from large FOBs on the outskirts of town, with most forces conducting 'drive-by counter-insurgency' (or combat)—they exited the FOB, drove to an objective or patrolled, were attacked, exchanged fire, and returned to base. Because the physical geography and road network in Ramadi enabled the enemy to observe and predict coalition movements, nearly every movement into the center of the city was attacked multiple times by improvised explosive devices, RPGs, or small arms, often with deadly results."

At this point in the war, however, some army and marine units were experimenting with the more classic counterinsurgency approaches of living close to the population in smaller fortified outposts, patrolling on foot, and protecting the population, all done in close partnership with Iraqi security forces whenever possible. Hopefully, once security was established, reconstruction could begin. This approach, made famous by Colonel McMaster's Third Armored Cavalry Regiment in Tal Afar, was christened "seize-hold-build," and made a lot of sense to Colonel MacFarland and his marine bosses in Fallujah.

A key piece of the concept was the COP, or combat outpost, a small garrison of about eighty soldiers dropped into enemy territory. "Our methodology was to drop combat outposts deep in the heart of AIF [anti-Iraqi Forces]-dense areas, live there as a platoon or company, and control the area while living in the city," explained Patriquin's colleague Captain Aaron Dixon. "Additionally, these combat outposts (COPs) would provide a civil-engagement hub for the locals to bring issues directly to one of our officers. Platoon leaders would have this same charge to engage the locals every time they patrolled out from these COPs. As we captured or drove out AIF, gained the trust of the locals, and improved security, ISF would take over the COP and we would move on to the next hot spot. MacFarland called this the 'inkblot' method."

The hope was that with new outposts established through the city and rural areas, coalition forces could wrest control of large areas away from the insurgents. The danger was that al-Qaeda in Iraq seemed capable of mounting complex mass attacks of twenty or more fighters, and they might theoretically be able to wipe out and overrun a small combat outpost, which would signal a huge psychological victory for the insurgents.

Patriquin and MacFarland agreed that everything hinged on protecting Iraqi civilians and building new alliances with local tribal leaders at the same time they waged war on insurgents. It was the only way to swing the population away from the grip of al-Qaeda and deny the insurgents a safe haven. The sheiks were the key, MacFarland and Patriquin reasoned. If they could be persuaded to push local Sunni men into the Iraqi police, and in big numbers, they would have a much better chance of pulling off some kind of positive result.

MacFarland recalls of Patriquin, "Coming from Special Forces, he had an appreciation for working unconventionally with indigenous forces, which was exactly what we were trying to do. Travis was adamant about engaging the tribes. He was the motivator and cheerleader inside the brigade to connect to the tribes. The most important thing in a counterinsurgency is to separate the people from the insurgents. I'm a bit of a student of history and I know that one of the most effective things we did in Vietnam or any counterinsurgency was to create indigenous forces with legitimacy among the people we were trying to protect, and Travis intuitively grasped this from the start."

The trouble was that about the only sheiks still remaining in the area were minor figures like the highly charismatic but until now obscure young Sheik Sattar, whose compound happened to be perched right across the road from Camp Ramadi's main entrance.

Some U.S. Marine Corps staff officers at MEF headquarters at Camp Fallujah wanted nothing to do with Sattar, a suspected smuggler and highway bandit. Instead they preferred that Mac-Farland work through established channels with the exiled sheiks in Amman and with the stillborn Iraqi government in Baghdad, through the powerless provincial governor Maamoun. Various marine generals and CIA officers had been shuttling to Amman, Jordan, ever since 2004, assiduously courting "top-tier" sheiks from Anbar who had fled the mushrooming violence following the U.S. invasion. But these contacts hadn't produced much of any consequence.

Surveying the landscape in late spring 2006, MacFarland decided that "the exiled sheiks have nothing to offer. The contacts with them are going nowhere. Maybe there's a power struggle going on between the sheiks in Jordan and the sheiks in Anbar."

"Let's pick a horse and back it," MacFarland thought. "Let's back the sheiks in Anbar. They're all we've got to work with. If the exiles come back, they probably won't have any authority and legitimacy among the people. We can't influence them, either."

Right away, three things were painfully obvious to Patriquin and his colleagues: in addition to attacking al-Qaeda forces in the city head-on with a great deal of carefully placed firepower, they had to rebuild the shattered local Iraqi police force, and they had to reach out to the area's Sunni tribes.

But Patriquin thought it wasn't too late to turn everything around. In the weeks surrounding his arrival in Ramadi, he wrote briefings for his fellow officers that offered a candid assessment of the predicament faced by his brigade. "As in any other counterinsurgency fight, the population is the center of gravity in the battle for the soul of Ramadi," he wrote. "To win a populace in the Iraqi insurgency, you don't have to 'win' them over to your side. This is a common misperception, and seems like an insurmountable task. So insurmountable, in fact, that many coalition units make a halfhearted attempt, if they make an attempt at all, in doing so. To win the populace in Ramadi, our goal is simple: We simply have to convince them not to side with the insurgency, especially the extremist insurgency represented by al-Qaeda."

Patriquin continued, "Coalition Forces are losing the information operations battle. To put it bluntly, we're on our ass when it comes to IO. Untrained, unskilled operators who don't speak the language or understand the culture and its subtle nuances cannot hope to fight native propagandists who speak the language, and know what tugs the 'heart' of the Arab people. Not only are we losing the IO [information operations] battle with the Iraqi people, we're losing it on the Arab street, and more importantly, our own street. How do we reverse this trend? In addition to aggressive media engagement, we must mirror the enemy's propaganda.

"We're supporting the insurgency by our absence on these fronts. Our inaction is action in a negative direction. If we don't learn from the successful actions of our enemy, then we're doomed from the start, because he learns our successes quickly and moves to exploit them."

He added, "We must use religion to our advantage in this fight. Our failure to do so has led us down a path where again, we are losing. Iraqis do not want an Islamic caliphate in Iraq, or anywhere in the world. They were once one of the most secular Arab nations on the planet. But our inaction in the face of *takfirist* and other extremist philosophy has made us fools in the eyes of the Iraqi people.

"We must capitalize on the mistakes of those who went before us. That paid for their mistakes in blood. In order to effectively isolate the insurgents in Ramadi, we must aggressively take him on in all systems of operation, from information operations to civil affairs as well as kinetically."

If the Americans did everything differently, Patriquin thought, they still had a chance. If they used religion, propaganda, money, and common sense, linked with military force, euphemistically re- ferred to as "kinetic effects" by the American military, they might turn things around.

It was not too late, he hoped, to turn the tide of battle.

At the beginning of his deployment to Iraq, Patriquin took part in a brigade officer training exercise where he conducted a simu- lated media interview.

"Captain, do you like the Iraqi people?" asked the interviewer.

"I love the Iraqi people," Patriquin responded. "I think they are a very proud people with a great, great past and culture. And the ones that are standing next to us and fighting next to us are some of the best men around."

He continued, "I see a people that are anxious to get on with their lives, and that want to rebuild. I see people that are fed up with the insurgency. And we want to help all those people in any way we can."

His interlocutor asked, "What's it going to take to stop the fighting?"

Patriquin said, "It's going to take time and understanding."

"Do we have enough time, or understanding?"

Patriquin paused carefully for a moment.

Then he said quietly, "*Inshallah*. God willing."

CHAPTER 5

A TIME TO STRIKE

"Y ou guys are way too cocky," said one marine officer serving under the outgoing U.S. Army–led Second Brigade Combat Team, Twenty-eighth Infantry Division (2/28 BCT), Pennsylvania Army National Guard, commanded by Colonel John Gronski, which held the Ramadi battle space from May 2005 until May 2006.

"The brigade before you is surprised," the marine officer said to one of the new interpreters in Patriquin's brigade. "You guys think they're a piece of crap and you're going to do wonderful things. You're going to get a lot of people killed. You guys are going to get yourselves killed. You don't know what you're doing. We've tried this tribal engagement idea before. It doesn't work."

In late May and June 2006, Patriquin and his brigade's deputy commander, Lieutenant Colonel Jim Lechner, were crisscrossing the city of Ramadi in convoys on dangerous roads in broad day-light, including the notorious Route Michigan, which was a mag-net for IED and RPG attacks.

The two officers were paying courtesy calls on the handful of Iraqi government and security officials who dared show up for work, and introducing themselves to any sheiks they could find who looked like they might hold promise. "When we got to Ramadi there was no contact with the locals," recalled Lechner. "Travis and I had to start from scratch. We did that initially by trying to talk to the governor of Anbar and the police. Our battalions were going around slowly familiarizing themselves with who the leaders were in their area.

"Travis and I learned in Tal Afar that sheiks don't want to talk business directly, they don't want to soil their hands talking about money and fees and business arrangements," Lechner recalls. "The sheik wants to do the pleasantries and be a good host. Sattar was like that. Every sheik has a deputy in a suit, who is a brother, a cousin, or close confidant. The guy in the suit will handle the business discussions. In Ramadi, in a reversal of our normal command roles, Travis was the one who dealt more with sheiks even though he was a junior officer. I was the one who had to do the negative scutwork with the deputies. It was a 'good cop, bad cop' approach. When we needed a big, positive heavy hitter, we brought in Colonel MacFarland."

Lechner explains, "Our higher headquarters had been trying to deal with the Anbar sheiks that were living outside of the country. In Bedouin culture you have hereditary lines of sheiks going back hundreds of years. But a lot of these sheiks had left Ramadi and were living in Amman and Damascus in a form of self-exile. Our higher headquarters were generally on the right track. They might have thought Sattar was a bandit trying to make a bid for power. They were trying to support the elected government in Anbar and they were trying to court these exiled sheiks. The problem was they had been doing that for about a year with absolutely no success."

Soon, Patriquin was giving out cell phones and prized Thuraya satellite phones to sheiks like Sattar who might be influential, programmed with his own number so they could reach him whenever they needed to.

The brigade's convoys were getting hit with IEDs in these first few weeks, but no one was getting killed. The Ready First Combat Team (RFCT) entered Ramadi with a confidence and optimism that flowed from their four months of success in Tal Afar following the city's famous turnaround by McMaster's unit.

But Patriquin's brigade was initially striking some American military and intelligence officers with more experience in Ramadi as arrogant and reckless. In the case of one officer in a unit already serving in Ramadi who had been carefully cultivating a relationship with a pivotal tribal sheik, Patriquin's enthusiasm to meet the same sheik caused deep resentment. "Patriquin didn't set out to fuck up the relationship, but that's what was happening. He was overeager, and therefore clumsy and counterproductive. I had him declared persona non grata from our area."

Some officers in Patriquin's incoming brigade, including Patriquin himself, thought the 2/28 was not aggressive enough, was exhausted and somehow fumbling the handoff, or "rotation in place" and "transfer of authority," which occurred from late May through June 11, 2006.

Patriquin was critical of the 2/28 in one online posting he wrote in the summer of 2006, in passages that seemed to reflect a sentiment sometimes held by other regular army troops rotating into new assignments in Iraq: the idea that the previous unit screwed things up. "Having been somewhere where the unit before me did things 'right' (Tal Afar) and 'wrong' (Ramadi)," Patriquin wrote, "I can tell you one thing—good unit handovers are a big key to winning this war on our terms. When units just leave you the keys to the base and you can tell they really didn't care, and are just happy to be alive at the end of the year, well, you know you're in for a shit storm. When a unit looks longingly at its terrain, has tears in its eyes at TOA [transfer of authority], and embraces local leaders like they're brothers, and has people weeping in the streets, well, then you know it will be a pretty good year."

Eighty-two American soldiers of the 2/28 BCT were killed in action from July 2005 to June 2006 while trying to bring peace to Ramadi. And in a sense, they accomplished some small miracles, given the meager resources they had and the ferocity of the enemy they faced. "My perception was the RFCT had little respect for the job we did," declares John Gronski with bitterness at how his brigade is sometimes portrayed, but with what he calls "pride in how we actually performed." He explains, "For anyone to say that we were FOB-bound and didn't set up combat outposts doesn't know what they're talking about. We had a cordon of combat outposts set up around that city. All we needed was more combat power to be able to seal it off. We put combat outposts in Malaab near the soccer stadium. In Jazeera, an area heavily controlled by insurgents, we fought our way in and put outposts in that area. We also set up combat outposts in the Lake Habbaniya area. Also, the marine battalions based at Camp Hurricane Point had built three outposts inside the city."

Additionally, soldiers of the 2/28 launched civil affairs projects to try to improve sewer, water, energy, medical, and school facilities. They reached out to tribal sheiks, Sunni clerics, and other community leaders in Ramadi, hammering away repeatedly at a single message: "The sooner you encourage young men to join Iraqi police, the sooner Americans will leave your city." Patriquin's predecessor in the job of coordinating tribal affairs, Lieutenant Colonel Mike McLaughlin, was a smiling, charismatic, dynamic officer who was gaining wide respect among tribal leaders for his enthusiasm and dedication to connecting with sheiks and improving the lot of the civilian population. The sheiks nicknamed him "the Gold Colonel" and "the Star Colonel," and he was increasingly personifying the hopes that some sheiks were starting to place in the Americans as possible partners rather than enemies.

Patriquin's brigade arrived in Ramadi at the same time a transformation was happening there just below the surface, a change that had been brewing for at least a year. The most important history of this chapter of the Iraq War has yet to be written, and it will probably be created when the war is over, by the Iraqis who rose up against al-Qaeda themselves. But based on the available evidence, including what Iraqis have told U.S. military officers and historians, it appears clear that in late 2005 and early 2006, a shift in the mind-set of many sheiks and citizens in Ramadi was occurring. They decided they were fed up with al-Qaeda, probably because the group had become both very bad for business and excessively brutal in its tactics against Iraqis.

One of the most cogent analyses of the probable reasons for the shift is offered by former U.S. Marine intelligence officer Ed Sullivan, who reasons that the sheiks permitted al-Qaeda to operate with relative impunity because it was to their direct political and financial benefit. "They had no trust or real representation in the national government, and viewed that government as Iranian stooges. AQI [al-Qaeda in Iraq] therefore served as a legitimate bulwark against feared Shia aggression," he reasons. "A larger reason, though, was that the sheiks were making huge money off of the chaos. Chaos was good for business. They were able to rob and pilfer convoys or individual drivers, they were able to profit in huge ways from construction contracts [with coalition forces] that were themselves grossly inflated in terms of price, and they had complete immunity from legal prosecution of anything they chose to do."

But by 2006, Sullivan argues, al-Qaeda grew so powerful that it posed "an existential threat to the sheiks and their way of life" by opposing "all of the vices through which the sheiks profited." Sullivan explains, "When the sheiks initially protested against AQI excesses, the brutality of AQI's response seemed to be the final straw for the sheiks. It became clear what the choices really were for Anbar. They could side with AQI, and drive themselves to extinction and lose all the wealth they had created in a short time, or they could ally themselves with the U.S. and the Iraqi government and in the process they would legitimize the monetary gains they had made while simultaneously allowing them to form the backbone of the security services that would be in the future charged with enforcing the law. Choosing us ensured them of a stake in a future Iraq, under a legal, legitimate framework, in which they would have a controlling stake in law enforcement operations and governance, thereby ensuring their future prosperity."

Fractures within insurgent factions, and between insurgents and the population, were already appearing during the 2/28's time in Ramadi. In mid-2005, some Iraqis in the city began sporadic, scattered actions to try to overthrow the rule of al-Qaeda over much of their city.

The actions were evidently triggered not only by al-Qaeda's brutality and by its disruption of most economic activity in the city, legal and otherwise, but also by al-Qaeda's attempts to incorporate all insurgents in the area under the single command of al-Qaeda, including a powerful faction called the 1920 Revolution Brigades. It was a group consisting largely of former Ba'athists and Iraqi military officers who had killed hundreds of Americans but was considered, in the relative scheme of things, more nationalistic and less existentially bloodthirsty than al-Qaeda in Iraq. Until now they had been happy to opportunistically cooperate with al-Qaeda, but had no intention of being forced under their command.

In August 2005, dozens of Sunni Dulaimi tribesmen took up automatic weapons and grenade launchers in a gun battle to defend small Shiite enclaves in the city against their threatened expulsion by forces loyal to Abu Musab al-Zarqawi, a Jordanian by birth and the leader of al-Qaeda forces in Iraq. "We have had enough of his nonsense," declared Sheik Ahmad Khanjar. "We don't accept that a non-Iraqi should try to enforce his control over Iraqis, regardless of their sect, whether Sunnis, Shiites, Arabs, or Kurds."

There had been scattered, localized, and often unpublicized conflicts between Sunni tribal figures and insurgents before else-where in Iraq, as well as disputes between radical foreign-led terror groups like al-Qaeda and relatively more moderate Iraqi national-ist insurgent groups like the 1920 Revolution Brigades. The splits and skirmishes broke out in places like Hit, Haditha, Rawah, Kubaysah, Amariyah, Khalidiyah, and as early as 2003 in Bagh-dad, where a group called the Eagles Cell provided intelligence about insurgent activities to coalition forces. In some of these dis-putes, U.S. Army, Marines, Special Forces, and intelligence people got involved, but many others were strictly Iraqi affairs.

The first really big break came in late 2005, in the far western Anbar city of Al Qaim, when an intertribal dispute caused Sheik Sabah al-Sattam Effan Fahran al-Shurji al-Aziz of the Abu Mahal tribe to turn against al-Qaeda and its allied local tribes. He formed an anti-insurgent militia force of several hundred fighters he dubbed the Hamza Brigade, later called the Desert Protectors, and, after some false starts, confusion, and missteps, joined sides with U.S. Marines commanded by Colonel Dale Alford in Operation Steel Curtain, a joint mission to clear the city of insurgents. This spark represented both the first major case of an open Sunni revolt against al-Qaeda and the first sustained battlefield cooperation between Sunni tribal forces and coalition troops. Some consider it the earliest spark of what would later be called "the Awakening." But, in fact, the Al Qaim events, while they did provide a case history of how al-Qaeda could be taken on and beaten, had no immediate direct effect on events elsewhere in the province—it did not catch on as a movement beyond the city of Al Qaim.

In November 2005, American commanders in Ramadi held an open public conference attended by scores of Iraqis, including sheiks and religious leaders, to discuss restoring security. This was soon followed by a group of sheiks and nationalist insurgents banding together as a self-appointed "Anbar People's Council (APC)" to resist al-Qaeda and channel Sunnis into voting in the national elections scheduled for December.

On December 15, 2005, something astonishing happened. As many as 40 percent of the voters of Ramadi turned up to vote in largely peaceful democratic elections, up from only 2 percent who voted the previous January. In Anbar province and across Iraq, it looked like the Sunnis were reappearing on the political stage.

"My God," thought Colonel Gronski, "we finally made some headway here with the sheiks and imams."

But the devil was in the numbers, and Gronski never had enough troops to tame the enemy in Ramadi. He was stretched far too thin and couldn't possibly fully cover and hold his battle space, given the fiendish talents and power of the blossoming insurgency. "We were only a brigade combat team operating in an area large enough for a division," he explains. He remembers listening in disbelief as Secretary of Defense Donald Rumsfeld bantered in late 2005 about withdrawing thirty thousand troops from Iraq.

"Please," thought Gronski, "send some troops over here, I can use them."

According to Major Alfred "Ben" Connable, a marine intelligence officer at MEF in 2005 and 2006, this was a potential "tipping point" for Anbar province, but it was "flubbed" because "we never really established security, we simply didn't have enough troops." The Americans "promised a great many things," he said, "and of course we couldn't deliver them."

On January 3, 2006, an amazed Colonel Gronski was sure he was witnessing a transformation before his eyes when he saw a crowd of hundreds of Iraqi men patiently standing in line on the second day of an Iraqi police recruiting drive being held by his brigade at the site of a former glass factory, near his headquarters at Camp Ramadi.

The "Gold Colonel," Lieutenant Colonel Mike McLaughlin, had worked extremely hard with key sheiks to make the recruiting drive a success. "Up to that point, when recruiting events occurred, we were lucky to have five to ten men show up," remembers Gronski. "On January 3, we had hundreds come to join. We were beside ourselves with joy. We knew we had won the confidence of the sheiks, because that type of cooperation with coalition forces would never occur without sheik encouragement. On January 4, hundreds more signed up for the police. The 2/28 BCT leaders were euphoric. We felt we reached a tipping point with the support from sheiks and tribal leaders."

On the third day, which was supposed to be the last day of the drive, the crowd swelled to over five hundred. The Americans were ecstatic. "I made the decision to conduct the recruiting drive at the glass factory for four straight days. In hindsight I made a mistake. When conducting counterinsurgent operations a commander should never allow a unit to do the same thing for four days in a row.

The insurgents will observe and find a vulnerability if you create a pattern of activity."

This gave the al-Qaeda commanders just enough lead time to recruit and equip a suicide bomber with a vest packed with explosives and antipersonnel shrapnel like nails and ball bearings.

Almost a thousand Iraqis showed up on day four to join the police force.

When the bomb exploded at around eleven a.m., Gronski was giving an impromptu pep talk to a crowd of eager young Iraqi police applicants near the entrance to the glass factory, telling them, "We are so proud of you. You are going to take back your city. . . ."

In a nanosecond, disaster struck.

Lieutenant Colonel Mike McLaughlin fell, mortally wounded, and as he lay dying he comforted his rescuers, saying, "I'm okay, go check on my boys." U.S. Marine dog handler Sergeant Adam Cann was also killed in the explosion, as were about sixty police applicants, and over a hundred of them were wounded. Police recruitment collapsed, a setback to square one for the Iraqi police in the province.

The insurgents quickly followed up with a wave of carefully targeted killings in January and February that doomed Gronski's tribal outreach efforts. "We simply didn't have enough security to keep these sheiks alive," recalls Gronski. "The murder and intimidation campaign drove a wedge between my brigade and the people. It severed our leader engagement. The initiative was lost." Tribal affairs remained stalled until Patriquin's brigade arrived in late May 2006.

On paper, Patriquin's incoming unit had at least four advantages over its predecessor. First, because it was based on an armor brigade, Colonel Sean MacFarland's Ready First Combat Team had more heavy firepower at its disposal than the 2/28 BCT, which was based on a light-infantry model. Second, thanks to a "mini-surge" of manpower, it was assigned several hundred more troops over Colonel Gronski's force, on top of which its area of operations was reduced by about 20 percent. It was still an "economy of force" operation, but all told the RFCT enjoyed a roughly 30 percent surge in troops and combat power per square mile over the 2/28 BCT when it arrived in Ramadi.

Patriquin knew his unit had another advantage that played directly to the growing persecution complex of Anbar's Sunnis and their fears of being dominated or attacked by the Shiite-dominated central government in Baghdad. In a briefing to his brigade staff, Patriquin argued that the idea be exploited for maximum psychological effect: "The Sunnis of al Anbar and the ERV [Euphrates River Valley] are extremely distrustful of the Shia. If we broadcast that message in front of and during our arrival, two things will occur. One: We will establish the RFCT as a force to be reckoned with, having destroyed a respectably sized army of Iraqi insurgents only a few short years ago. Two: We will play automatically to the side of the hatred of the Shia shared throughout the Sunni Arab population of Iraq. This hatred of the Shia, especially Moqtada al-Sadr, is so great that the population will instantly give more credit to the RFCT for having defeated them in battle. This is a touchy subject, but as long as second- and third-order effects are studied, it is an entirely realistic course of action that could pay huge dividends for the RFCT in our crucial first days on the ground."

Patriquin also thought there was a huge opportunity for the Americans to exploit the growing splits within the insurgency. He argued in a briefing paper, "While Iraqi insurgents decidedly do not want us here in Iraq, they and their families do not desire a Taliban-style 'caliphate' either. A general amnesty and laying down of arms, as well as a cessation of all anti-CF activities, could support the RFCT's destruction of AQIZ [al-Qaeda in Iraq–Zarqawi] in Ramadi. At the very least, we need to actively target the local insurgents with a heavy IO [information operations] campaign, urging them to choose Iraq over chaos."

Patriquin continued, "Successful engagement would pave the way to having powerful individuals who could secure their neighborhoods against incursion by AQIZ, and allow us to concentrate on more heavily infested areas of Ramadi." He concluded, "Playing to the Iraqis' inherent distrust of armed foreigners, while downplaying our long-term strategic goals in Iraq, is a strategy that will work to separate the population from their support of AQIZ in Ramadi. By combining kinetic [combat] operations designed to capture or kill insurgents with nonkinetic operations designed to drive a wedge between the insurgency and their popular support, we can hit the enemy in Ramadi in a way he hasn't been hit before, limiting his Center of Gravity support while limiting his freedom of movement."

On June 7, 2006, two laser-guided five-hundred-pound bombs dropped from a U.S. Air Force F-16 jet struck a remote safe house north of Baqubah, killing the chieftain of al-Qaeda in Iraq, Abu Musab al-Zarqawi. The event triggered a decision by American military planners to jump-start combat operations in Ramadi, in the hope of catching a newly leaderless al-Qaeda at a vulnerable moment. One U.S. military report noted, "it was time to strike, and strike hard." Human intelligence sources indicated that local insurgents expected a huge coalition attack, and, according to the report, local people "were afraid that the city would be smothered in combat like previous CF operations in Fallujah."

On June 17, Colonel MacFarland gave the go-ahead for U.S. and Iraqi forces to pounce into Ramadi's streets and begin rapidly building a series of thirteen combat outposts to try to complete the cordoning off of the city begun by the 2/28 Brigade Task Force before them. The purpose of the outposts was to secure permanent footholds in the city and establish "inkblots" of security that could expand out and eventually connect with each other.

It was an impressive feat of logistical planning, engineering, and synchronized maneuvering, as an RFCT paper described: "To rapidly emplace barriers, wire and life support, hundreds of tons of materials and equipment were massed, palletized and moved with internal lift assets within six hours of the initial seizure of key terrain. Ninety-six hours later, the last of the life support was completely operational. The result was consistently clear. In just four days, the RFCT drastically disjointed AIF freedom of maneuver every time a new COP was established."

On July 24, al-Qaeda launched a fierce counterblitz of platoon-sized attacks across the entire city of Ramadi, staging what Colonel MacFarland called a "massively synchronized" strike at over fifteen targets in the space of just thirty-two minutes. The attacks were repulsed with at least twenty-eight insurgents killed. One of the two American fatalities that day was army Captain Jason West, the brigade adjutant.

The death of Captain West hit the brigade hard, especially his good friend and bunk mate Captain Patriquin. That night, the job fell to Patriquin to gather up and pack West's personal effects to be shipped to his wife. It was one of the hardest things he ever had to do in his entire life.

But at this moment in the summer of 2006, all that was needed to spark a revolt against al-Qaeda in Ramadi was for an Iraqi leader to step forward, some Americans to help him, and an incident to galvanize the support of the people.

The incident would occur in late August.

The leader who would step forward was Sheik Sattar abu Risha.

The Americans who first helped him were men like Tony

Deane, Pat Fagan, Jim Lechner, Teddy Gates, Sean MacFarland, and a small group of their colleagues in the U.S. Army, Marine Corps, and intelligence agencies.

And for Sheik Sattar, the American help would increasingly be symbolized by the face of one man sitting next to him—Travis Patriquin.

CHAPTER 6

BEFORE THE DAWN

☆

"Fuck the Iraqis."

A young U.S. Army private muttered the oath inside Patriquin's Humvee.

The private was acting as a military police guard on Patriquin's personal security detail, and he felt comfortable enough with the avuncular captain to "shoot the shit" with him with unvarnished bluntness.

The private was fed up with what he saw as treachery and double-dealing by Iraqis he'd dealt with. "I hate them all. Everybody hates Iraqis. They're shady and two-faced. Let's just get rid of 'em all."

Patriquin understood where the sentiment came from. He thought some Iraqis were schemers and scammers, skilled in telling Americans what they wanted to hear, making promises and not delivering. But Patriquin knew why Iraqis sometimes acted as they did. They were victims of decades of Saddam's medieval-style dictatorship, and of an economy shattered by three wars and crippling international sanctions.

"The Iraqis haven't been taught like we were," Patriquin told the enlisted man. "They just need help like anybody else to be self-sustaining. Like any other culture, there's good people and there's bad people. Not all people here are bad people. The majority of them are good people. But they get threatened and they have to make decisions to save themselves and their families. They don't have the privilege of calling the police if something bad happens to them. There are no police."

There were no police. That was the horrible truth.

In many parts of Iraq, despite billions of dollars' worth of American arms and training, the local police were ineffective, corrupt, and badly led. In Ramadi, the police force was practically nonexistent. Without local police, the city had no hope of experiencing any semblance of civil society. It was a prehistoric shell of occupation, combat, and chaos, a living nightmare for Iraqi civilians.

Compounding the Americans' predicament in Ramadi, Patriquin believed, was a culture of corruption and criminality that flourished in the city, in the midst of many thousands of skilled potential local insurgents with military training. In a paper to the staff of his brigade, Patriquin explained: "Corruption, graft, and greed have always been a staple of the Ramadi lifestyle. Apparently, since the initial founding of Ramadi, the city has been, and continues to be, a haven for the unseemly and illegal. Purportedly the best forgers in the Iraq AO [area of operations] come from the Sofia area of eastern Ramadi. To this day, your best bet in Iraq for needed forged documents is to go to Sofia [also spelled "Sufiyah"] and have their 'experts' make what you need. From money to fake passports, Sofia has always been the place to go to procure world-class forgeries. Their talents are still sought out for facilitation of foreign fighter movement and fake documentation of all kinds.

Weapons and the men who know how to use them are available at the buyer's leisure in Ramadi."

But in June 2006, a deal was struck that would shape the course of the war in Anbar province, a deal that held promise to bring back some semblance of law and order.

The arrangement was first made between Lieutenant Colonel Anthony Deane, battalion commander of Task Force 1-35 Armor, and the two leaders of the relatively minor rural Abu Risha tribe, Sheik Sattar and his older brother, Ahmed, who lived in Deane's "battle space." The two brothers were still battalion-level contacts for the Americans, one level down from being brigade contacts, which would have made them primarily Travis Patriquin's responsibility.

It was a deal about police, and it was inspired by what Deane calls a "blinding flash of the obvious" that all three men had at about the same time. The deal was struck soon after Travis Patriquin first met Sheik Sattar, and while Patriquin was not involved in the initial negotiations, the dividends the arrangement yielded would soon dominate his work for the rest of his life and sharply increase the odds his brigade had to succeed in its mission to stabilize Ramadi.

It was clear to Deane, Sattar, and Ahmed, as it was to Patriquin and the other American officers in the city, that the crucial first step in providing stability in Ramadi was to get local men into the police force, and lots of them.

The Iraqi police were the key to turning everything around.

But police recruitment in Ramadi was crippled by three problems. The recruiting locations were hard to secure and under severe threat of attack by al-Qaeda. The recruits signed up, then went home until their training began a week or two later, leaving them vulnerable to intimidation attacks and murder. And once their training at the police facilities in Jordan or Baghdad was complete, they were likely to be assigned to one of the three functioning police stations in the city, at locations that were usually far from their own homes and neighborhoods, causing them to fear for their families.

The Iraqi police held huge potential as leverage to sharply boost the manpower the coalition could field to patrol the streets, gather intelligence, and pursue insurgents. The numbers of the American forces were fixed. The numbers of Iraqi army troops were fixed, and even declining, due to high rates of desertion. But in June 2006 the Iraqi government Ministry of Interior had authorized 3,386 slots for police in the area, of which only 420 were filled. And of those, less than 150 ever showed up to work, and they rarely went out on patrol. If large numbers of the open slots could be filled, the police could theoretically tip the balance of the order of battle for the city in favor of the coalition and Iraqi government.

Lieutenant Colonel Tony Deane urged Ahmed, Sattar, and other sheiks to recruit their tribesmen to the police force, in exchange for new police stations in their areas. "We can give your men jobs, money, and the ability to protect their homes. We'll take half of the police recruits you send us and we'll create a police substation in your tribal area to protect your families and your routes back to work. And we'll take the other half and put them in places where we need them, like central Ramadi."

Sheik Ahmed proposed a simple trade. "If you want to recruit police," he told Deane, "then do it here at our compound and build us a police station in our area." Similarly, his brother, Sheik Sattar, told U.S. Marine Corps police liaison officer Major Teddy Gates, "I want to fight al-Qaeda with you, as long as you'll support me and give me the weapons and give me a police station."

Lieutenant Colonel Deane figured at this point that Sattar and

Ahmed were "midlevel management" in the war-fragmented tribal hierarchy of the city. Deane recalls that the dapper, nightlife-loving Sattar "was widely considered Ahmed's dumb-ass little brother, more prodigal son than knucklehead." But in the early summer of 2006, with most of the remaining tribal leaders in Ramadi too terrorized by al-Qaeda to move openly against them, Deane saw the brothers as "the only guys we could work with and about the only people who appeared to be on the team. We could use them to make contacts throughout the tribal network to get more police recruits. They seemed to be respected by other sheiks and could bring in recruits."

Deane worked with his own tribal affairs officer, Captain Pat Fagan; with the brigade's deputy commanding officer, Lieutenant Colonel Jim Lechner; with marine police implementation officer Teddy Gates; with battalion commander Lieutenant Colonel Dan Walrath, whose battle space included the Jazeera area on the north side of the Euphrates River; and eventually with Captain Patriquin to come up with a new plan to funnel recruits into the police. They started with a recruiting drive at Sattar and Ahmed's compound, which was easily guarded by U.S. troops from Camp Ramadi across the highway. The "flash of the obvious" idea was that they would ship new police recruits to Jordan or Baghdad for training on the same day they screened them, rather than waiting a week or two, to reduce the risk of al-Qaeda intimidation.

There was one big bureaucratic hurdle. Certain staff officers at MEF, the marine division headquarters in Fallujah that oversaw Patriquin's brigade, were adamantly opposed to building new police stations in tribal areas, fearing it would lead to generating de facto tribal militias. They would hit the roof if this happened. The Ministry of Interior in Baghdad probably wouldn't be too happy if they found out, either, for similar reasons.

So in a creative bookkeeping maneuver, one officer in Patriquin's brigade "fudged" the creation of several new police stations by calling them "temporary substations" attached, on paper, to two functioning stations downtown, without making it clear where they would be built. What the marines and the Ministry of Interior didn't know was that the planned so-called substations were being built nowhere near the open stations downtown, but in more rural tribal areas. The maneuver would later cause a huge mess and interoffice combat between RFCT and MEF officers, but for now it worked, enabling Ready First Combat Team officers to strike deals by trading recruits for the promise of new police stations. One of the new "substations" was promised for Sattar and Ahmed's neighborhood.

"The situation was a winner any way you looked at it," reported Lieutenant Colonel Deane. "The tribes soon saw that instead of being the hunted, they could become the hunters, with well-trained, paid, and equipped security forces backed up by locally positioned coalition forces. For the sheiks, this was a great proposal. The Sunnis wanted to secure their families and villages and hold jobs that were prestigious in their communities, such as military officers or police officers. Previously, coalition forces had offered them jobs as garbage collectors or street cleaners. They wanted al-Qaeda out of Anbar, but were unable to fight them alone. The sheiks had constantly asked for authorization to arm militias to fight al-Qaeda, a proposal that was unacceptable to the coalition. In the bargain, the government of Iraq would assume the burden of paying their tribesmen to provide their security. By putting the young men into the Iraqi police, we linked the tribes with the central government, and began investing Sunnis into the political process, which paid dividends later."

Patriquin's brigade commander, Colonel Sean MacFarland,

had no major problems with the idea of reaching out and doing business with Sattar, despite the sheik's unsavory reputation. He had read the intelligence reports on the sheik, but he knew that in the postapocalyptic, *Sopranos*-esque landscape of Anbar province, these were the only kinds of people he had to work with. "You don't get to be a sheik by being a nice guy," MacFarland later explained. "These guys are ruthless characters. That doesn't mean they can't be reliable partners." He added, "A lot of people say, well, he was not a choirboy before we found him and began working with him. I went to Catholic schools, and a nun used to tell me that every saint had a past and every sinner has a future."

The first "test-drive" of a new tribally backed police recruiting event happened at Sattar and Ahmed's house on the Fourth of July 2006. Nearly a hundred men showed up to join the force. "We were mortared," Deane recalls, "but the Iraqis were undeterred." It wasn't the hundreds hoped for, but it was a good start, and triple the number of recruits yielded by the outgoing brigade the month before.

Patriquin and Lechner urged Sattar to reach out to other sheiks to join the recruiting campaign. According to a brigade after-action report, "The RFCT continued to meet with key tribal leaders and encourage the reestablishment of a council that represented the people. The RFCT believed that if the cooperative tribes could unify and begin supporting an effective government in the city of Ramadi, it would pave the way for the provincial government to follow."

On the streets and back roads of Ramadi, the word from the sheiks began spreading among military-aged Iraqi men, including some who were recently insurgents, or insurgent sympathizers, or even freelancers who accepted money from al-Qaeda to plant IEDs against American forces—it was time to switch sides and join the Iraqi police.

The next recruiting drive, in late July, was a bonanza. Two hundred men showed up at Camp Blue Diamond, the marine base on the north side of the Euphrates. The turnout was so large that the Americans had to close the doors at noon, and it took until eleven p.m. to process all the recruits through biometric scanning, medical screening, and a battery of paperwork.

Patriquin and his colleagues were delighted. Patriquin mingled with the Iraqi police recruits, asking them in Arabic, "What tribe are you from? Who sent you here? Why are you here?"

Patriquin knew how painful it was for American troops to welcome former insurgents into the Iraqi police. "This wasn't easy emotionally for us who had lost friends," recalls Captain Mike Murphy, who helped run the event, "but Travis realized before most of us that if we didn't do this, all we were doing was repeating the same vicious cycle."

Patriquin asked Murphy how many recruits were from a particular tribe. "About ten," Murphy replied.

"That's bullshit!" said an angry Patriquin. "They promised three dozen—that's what we should have."

"What's the deal?" asked Patriquin when he got through to the appropriate tribal leader on the Thuraya phone. "I thought we had an agreement—pony up!"

By the end of the long day, a jubilant Lieutenant Colonel Jim Lechner realized things might be poised for a turnaround in the city. The police stations, he thought, would be the catalyst to give the sheiks security and give coalition forces more combat power to prosecute operations.

"This is fantastic," Lechner told his colleagues as they got ready to leave Camp Blue Diamond. "This is exactly what we need to have happen." Travis Patriquin couldn't have agreed more.

At the next recruiting events in early August, a record-setting

395 Iraqis showed up to join the police in Ramadi, thanks to the sheiks and the constant prodding of Patriquin and his U.S. military colleagues.

To sweeten the pot, cash rewards were paid out to recruits at the recruiting drives as signing bonuses. The piles of cash were discreetly supplied by the Central Intelligence Agency. This CIA money acted as a very effective lubricant in generating the new flood of police recruits, and was greatly appreciated by officers of the RFCT, who had much shallower pockets to dip into. As in many scenes in the Iraq War, the CIA was working in the shadows, cultivating relationships with key players, and, when necessary, acting as an ATM with vast reserves of cash.

The sudden influx of Iraqi police produced immediate psychological benefits, according to a brigade report: "We deliberately placed our first IP stations manned with newly recruited Sunni tribesmen where they could protect the tribes that were supplying us with additional recruits. This tactic gave the IPs added incentive to stand and fight and effectively ended al-Qaeda's murder and intimidation campaign against the men serving in the ISF. In a significant change of circumstance, the newly minted IPs quickly became the hunters, arresting a number of insurgents and uncovering tremendous weapons caches. By the end of July 2006, AQIZ was definitely feeling the pinch."

Travis Patriquin and Sheik Sattar were impressed with each other from their very first meeting, and with the successful recruiting police drives of July and early August, a close partnership began to grow between them.

One man who watched the friendship build was brigade interpreter Majd Alghabra, a Syrian-born American citizen who sat in on many of Patriquin's meetings with Sattar and other Iraqis and became Patriquin's primary interpreter. Alghabra recalls that in the first few weeks, the two men circled each other somewhat warily. Both had cause for hesitation, according to Alghabra. Patriquin couldn't be sure if Sattar could be trusted to deliver on his promises, and he couldn't be sure of Sattar's motives.

Sattar, in turn, couldn't be sure if Patriquin and his colleagues could deliver on their promises, either. He had seen several American units rotate in and out of Ramadi harboring initial high hopes, which were always dashed. Sattar seemed to be testing Patriquin in these early weeks by calling up and asking for minor favors. Patriquin always came through, both by delivering on his promises and by not overpromising.

"This is one of the reasons Sattar and the other sheiks came to love Patriquin so much," recalls Alghabra. "In Arabic and Bedouin culture, they take men by their words. You're not a man if you say something and you don't do it. Whatever Patriquin promised them, he would do. And they would see that. They had seen many U.S. officers before his unit came to Ramadi make promises, then come back and apologize that they couldn't do it. Their commanders wouldn't authorize it. But with Captain Patriquin it was so different. He would do whatever he promised them, no matter what. I saw him arguing with his commanders when they'd tell him something can't be done. He'd tell them he gave his word—it had to be done."

Through his actions and his striking personality, Patriquin was demonstrating something else to Sattar and the other sheiks and citizens of Ramadi, according to interpreter Sa'ad Mohammed: "He was in love with Iraq. He was addicted to the culture. He was obsessed by it. He loved the food, the people. He loved everything about Iraq."

"No one I ever heard of connected to the Iraqis like Captain Patriquin," marvels another Baghdad-born brigade interpreter,

Atheer Agoubi. He explained, "Iraqis can like you, but they *loved* him, for a lot of reasons. He had a magical, trustful personality and a trustful face. His presence was noticed immediately. Iraqis love to talk to men with a mustache, and he had a mustache, a suntan, dark skin and a big, muscular body, which made him look like an Arab. Besides that, his heart was really connecting to these people. For the average American soldier a lot of Iraqis are very hard to even say hello to. But when Iraqis sat down to eat with Captain Patriquin they could tell he enjoyed eating with his hands just as they did, and he didn't fake it. They felt he was telling them, 'I love you guys and I'll do whatever I can to show you that I'm genuine.' He gave Iraqis the most honorable and honest picture of the American people and the American military in particular. I think he changed a lot of hearts when he worked with the tribes. Because they thought he was really the true American heart."

Patriquin's Iraqi colleague concludes, "My God, there is no one in the world who could have formed a closer connection with the Iraqi people than Travis did. They adored him."

"For meetings with the sheiks, there was lots of casual talk," recalls Alghabra. "We would take off our shoes and boots, sit down on the floor and drink tea forever. Travis sat on the floor with them and ate food with his hands. For Arabs, you really have to like us to do that. His body language and attitude made people love him. He made them feel like he's one of them. The key was his personality. He looked more Eastern European or Mediterranean. He had a very positive attitude that made Sheik Sattar and the other sheiks like him. His deep understanding of the Arabic culture helped him a lot. He did not sit with Sattar as an officer, or an occupier, or an enemy, but as a friend."

With each successful police recruiting drive, Sattar was proving himself to the new American brigade that he was a man who could also deliver on his promises. Patriquin and Lechner noticed how much influence Sattar was suddenly commanding with other sheiks in the area. Something was happening behind the scenes among Sattar and the sheiks; the Americans weren't sure what it was, but with the ranks of the Iraqi police rapidly swelling, it looked like something wonderful.

Sattar was soon proving very adept at telling American military officers things they enjoyed hearing, and laying it on thick with declarations, such as, "Thank you, Bush, father of free Iraq." "Abraham Lincoln was the father of America, and George Bush is the father of Iraq." "I will liberate Iraq from those criminals [al-Qaeda]. One day Americans will be in Anbar and they will walk the street with their head high, very soon, God willing." At least one U.S. Marine officer scoffed at such comments, seeing them as typical of some Iraqis' talent for silver-tongued ingratiation of flattery-starved Americans.

The personal connection between Patriquin and Sattar grew at their next few meetings in July and August. Captain Mike Murphy, who watched the friendship take off, remembers that "Sattar absolutely adored Travis." At the meetings, Sattar regaled Patriquin with stories of how he and other sheiks arranged for the peaceful entry of U.S. combat troops to Anbar province. "When the Americans came to Iraq we did not fire one bullet," Sattar said. "I went to welcome them with flowers! We had white flags everywhere. This is a sign that we are very peaceful people. When the Americans came in, we did not fight them, but then the Americans did not help us. Now we want to help ourselves, and we are ready to help ourselves—if you are willing to help us.

"The people of Ramadi are sick and tired of al-Qaeda," Sattar declared, reiterating ideas he expressed at his initial meeting with

Patriquin. "They are looking for someone like the Gold Colonel to help us," he added, referring to the late Lieutenant Colonel Mike McLaughlin.

Patriquin replied, "We're here to help you. We need to build a police force. What do we need to do? How can we make the city secure without guns? We don't want to lose more soldiers and we don't want to hurt civilians."

"Ramadi will never get fixed by coalition forces," Sattar reiterated. "Ramadi will get fixed by Ramadi people. If we don't recruit our own people, our own army, there's no way we're going to win. The people have no jobs—they depend on al-Qaeda to support themselves. If we can support these people and get them on our side, we can kill al-Qaeda sooner. The best way to start is to start with the sheiks."

"We're going to do it just like your Gold Colonel," Patriquin assured Sattar. "Let's get all the sheiks together. We'll find out what all the sheiks want, what we want, and we'll work together for the people of Ramadi. Don't worry, I'll try to finish Colonel McLaughlin's mission, on the track he took."

Before long, according to interpreter Majd Alghabra, the two men "were like brothers." Sattar lit a cigarette for Patriquin every fifteen minutes, which Alghabra told Patriquin was a great honor. Sattar was very relaxed with Patriquin, and conversations turned to each other's families and life experiences. Patriquin told Sattar everything about himself, of his exploits in South America and Afghanistan. "How's your brother doing?" Patriquin inquired of Sattar's brother, Ahmed, who was away on business that summer. "What kind of contracts did he get in Baghdad?"

Eventually, the conversations drifted into intelligence matters. Sattar told Patriquin about suspected insurgent locations and forwarded tips about possible IED sites. In exchange, Sattar asked for small favors like extra fuel deliveries.

One day, Sattar introduced Patriquin to a moderate Sunni religious leader in Ramadi. The cleric and Sattar were discussing how they could team up to expel the radical imams who had taken over the mosques in the city.

"What are you going to do?" the cleric asked Patriquin. "What are your ideas? You came here in 2003 without a plan. Do you have a plan now?"

Patriquin was impressed by the dynamic clergyman, a former commando in the Iran-Iraq War, and saw him as a perfect example of a voice of authentic, mainstream Islam. He told the cleric, "Yes, we have a plan, we are working together with Sheik Sattar to make this happen, to free you from al-Qaeda in the province, and to free Iraq from the terrorists."

The friendly conversation turned to religion, and Patriquin said, "I respect Islam as a religion. I respect Muslims and I have worked with many Muslims through my life and career. I have no problem with Islam at all. Al-Qaeda is causing great confusion among the people by calling us Crusaders and infidels fighting a religious war. We're not here to fight for a religion, we're not here to fight Islam. We're here to fight people who use Islam as a justification to do bad things."

The Islamic scholar replied approvingly, "There are many incidents in the history of Islam when Christians helped Muslims, and Muslims helped Christians."

The two discussed the eminent position of Jesus Christ in Islamic theology, the ascension of Jesus into heaven, and other points of scripture.

Patriquin left the meeting convinced that the cleric held one of the keys to victory in Ramadi. If he could wrest control of the mosques from al-Qaeda, he could issue religious fatwas, or decrees, that could help bring peace to the city.

As Iraqi police recruiting took off, other sheiks started stepping in to support Sattar, and the sheik kept delivering on his promises to the Americans. Patriquin began making pep talks about tribal outreach to Colonel MacFarland, to his fellow officers in the brigade, to officers at Marine Expeditionary Force headquarters at Fallujah, and to anyone else who would listen. Patriquin became a one-man cheerleading squad and motivational force for Sattar inside the U.S. military.

By most accounts, Travis Patriquin was the first American officer to grasp the full potential of the moment that was opening up, and he was the driving day-to-day force inside the American military to make tribal outreach through Sattar succeed, working along with Jim Lechner, Tony Deane, Pat Fagan, and a handful of other officers.

"There's something inside of me telling me that Sattar is not playing with us," Patriquin told his interpreter Majd Alghabra. "I trust him."

At about the same time, Sattar may have been thinking the same thing about Patriquin and his brigade.

CHAPTER 7

A BAPTISM IN BLOOD

The Awakening of Iraq was anointed with the blood of terrorists, spilled by death squads in the night.

One day Patriquin spotted a dead male body dumped on the side of the road with a sign strung around its head. It read: "This is what happens when you work against the people of Anbar." It was signed "Thawar al Anbar," or "Revolutionaries of al Anbar."

More bodies appeared. Americans in Ramadi had been quietly discussing names of insurgent "high-value targets" with a few local Iraqi contacts, including Sheik Sattar, and now some of these "most wanted" were showing up dead on the streets.

The mysterious perpetrators, dubbed TAA by the Americans, seemed to be using al-Qaeda's terror tactics against al-Qaeda itself. The TAA killings had been going on for months, and were orchestrated by a small secret network of local leaders who were, apparently, seething with frustration over al-Qaeda's abuses and increasing disruption of society, the complete lack of law and order in the province, and the Coalition prohibition against launching tribal militias. So they took things into their own hands with direct vigilante action, and they were killing terrorist suspects by the dozens.

The early stages of the campaign briefly became public in March 2006 when a *Washington Post* article quoted a sheik of the Abu Fahd tribe as saying that what he called American "military officers" were present at early meetings of the TAA group, and they helped by providing "all kinds of financial support." The article reported that "a U.S. military spokesman in Baghdad denied that American forces were funding the militia." The sheik went on to say, "We have killed a number of the Arabs [non-Iraqi al-Qaeda figures], including Saudis, Egyptians, Syrians, Kuwaitis, Syrians, and Jordanians. We were also able to foil an attack by [al-Qaeda in Iraq chieftain Abu Musab al-]Zarqawi's men who were trying to attack an oil pipeline outside Ramadi. We killed four Iraqis trying to plant the bomb under the pipeline."

One key TAA figure later confidentially explained to an American contact how the group started. "We just came up with it," the Iraqi explained. "The Americans weren't doing anything against al-Qaeda. The Iraqi army wouldn't. We had almost no Iraqi police, and few weapons to fight against the terrorists. So we just thought the only way we could scare them was to identify who they are, and warn them we're after them. Local people knew who's who. We knew who al-Qaeda was." With the help of sympathetic moderate Sunni clerics, TAA volunteers posted lists of terrorist suspects in the mosques, he explained, with notices announcing, "We know who you are. You are working with the terrorists against the people."

Caught between the counterterror strikes of the TAA on one side and the wide spectrum of lethal combat operations being prosecuted by various units of Patriquin's brigade on the other, al-Qaeda fighters in Ramadi appeared to be shifting abruptly from battlefield élan to nervousness, even fear. An intercepted al-Qaeda situation report from the period referred to the TAA as "this vicious organization."

The greatest strength the TAA had in terrorizing al-Qaeda was its own amorphous, shifting, and impenetrable secrecy. It operated as a group of masked gangs in the dark of night, and few knew exactly who they were or who was behind them.

Patriquin wrote up a report of a conversation he held with an Iraqi with inside knowledge of the workings of the TAA death squads: "TAA is a group of friends or relations who have been wronged by al-Qaeda in the past, and want revenge against al-Qaeda. They will find other people or groups who have been wronged by al-Qaeda. These groups will band together and fight al-Qaeda as if they were terrorists, using the black masks, AK-47s, OPEL cars, night movements, etc. They are literally terrorizing the terrorists by using their own tactics against them, and any time that this goes on, it's called TAA. TAA is a problem self-created by al-Qaeda. In tribal law, when parties are wronged, they usually rely on intervention by sheiks to solve problems between the two parties. Since al-Qaeda has killed many of the sheiks in the tribal areas they control (Obayd, Fahad, Khalifa) or intimidated the sheiks of their areas into fleeing to Jordan or Baghdad, there is no other tribal justice recourse for the young men of the tribes besides vengeance, and there is 14,000 years of history backing up their desire to 'settle the score.'"

Patriquin concluded, "My own opinion is that TAA attacks will increase in areas that are contested and then decrease and taper off once an area becomes more secure (i.e., IP patrols). When the area is still under questionable security, that's when TAA moves into the area and begins murder and intimidation campaigns on al-Qaeda. This understandably de-synchs the al-Qaeda forces and allows IP recruitment, training, and staging to gain momentum.

Coupled with CF [coalition forces] involvement, TAA vigilante action is a valuable tool for gaining momentum in stagnant areas. It also gives the perception of Iraqi people fighting back against al-Qaeda independent of CF, which helps set the stage in the contested areas for eventual support of Iraqi police."

During afternoon prayers one Friday in September, a squad of TAA fighters burst into the Abdel Rahman Mosque in South Central Ramadi, an insurgent-infested area the Americans had trouble getting into. The Iraqi vigilantes dragged ten al-Qaeda suspects into the street, executed them with gunfire, and then raced off.

"That was good stuff for us," recalled one American officer in Patriquin's brigade. In this period, he says, "TAA was blamed for up to twenty vigilante killings of al-Qaeda, which was fine by me." Reportedly, one group of American intelligence operatives followed up on the TAA attacks by putting word out on the street aimed at al-Qaeda fighters: "There's a secret organization that knows where you are, and is coming to kill you."

There is no evidence available of this or any more direct coordination between TAA and any U.S. military or intelligence groups, but if there was such contact, it happened at a level so secret that Patriquin wasn't aware of the specifics. That wouldn't be unusual, since despite Patriquin's personal ties with many of the American "special operators" and intelligence people working in the area, there were still many secrets they held to very tightly in their highly compartmentalized world of shadows.

In the late summer of 2006, Patriquin was intrigued by the anti–al-Qaeda death squads of the TAA and was trying to follow them, as he suspected they probably connected directly into some of the relationships he and the brigade were now developing. At least one of Patriquin's colleagues thought Sheik Sattar was a boss of the TAA.

"We don't know who these people are," Patriquin told MacFarland.

"Let's not ask too many questions," replied the colonel.

"It's good for us to stay unconnected," he added.

On August 21, 2006, two things happened that Travis Patriquin immediately thought could create a tipping point in Ramadi.

Days earlier, al-Qaeda leaflets appeared in neighborhoods of the Abu Ali Jassim tribe demanding that tribesmen stop joining the Iraqi police and turn in any weapons they had.

The tribe refused the al-Qaeda order, and a sheik of the Abu Ali Jassim tribe named Khaled A'rak Ehtami Al-A'layawi'a went to speak with members of the Abu Aetha tribe about opposing al-Qaeda.

On August 21, al-Qaeda fighters abducted the sheik, killed him, and held his body hostage. In a gross violation of tribal and Islamic custom requiring a swift burial, the al-Qaeda fighters dumped the sheik's body in a remote field, where it remained for several days. The calculated outrage struck many tribal leaders as a final straw in the group's reign of terror.

On the same day the sheik was killed, al-Qaeda firebombed the new Iraqi police station in the Jazeera district with an enormous suicide vehicle-borne improvised explosive device, or "SVBIED." The bomb was delivered by a dump truck packed with fuel enhancers and accelerants, and it created a fireball so big that it reached over blast walls to hit the station.

In a stirring scene that reminded Colonel Sean MacFarland of the flag-raising at Iwo Jima in 1945—and signified for him "a true turning point in the war"—the Iraqi police at the station refused to abandon their post, declined offers of evacuation from coalition forces, ran up a tattered Iraqi flag, and resumed patrols on the same day. "They stood their ground," recalls MacFarland, "and proved they wouldn't be intimidated."

The attack on the Jazeera station, according to Major Teddy Gates, the U.S. Marine Corps liaison officer to the Iraqi police, "was the point at which we really knew the police were here to stay." He explains, "We were able to replace vehicles, weapons, ammunition, body armor, and uniforms the same day. Station after station was hit, and each time we rallied behind the Iraqis and rebuilt, rearmed, and reequipped. As we stood by them and they stood firm in the face of the attacks, even the local populace began to support the IPs and provided them with invaluable information. It was not the main turning point, but it was clear evidence that we were winning."

Patriquin thought the enemy had made a huge mistake by killing the sheik and desecrating his body, and he saw a big opportunity opening up.

"I'm going to kill them! I can go and shoot them! I will kill them all!"

A bemused Patriquin looked on as Sheik Sattar raged at the murder and desecration of Sheik Khaled A'rak before a group of sheiks gathered at Sattar's compound. He shook his head and smiled faintly at Sattar's gung-ho attitude, and asked if he could address the group.

"Look, this is who they are," Patriquin told the sheiks. "They say they are your brothers. They say that they are Muslims like you, and they want what's best for you. But here they are showing who they really are. They killed the sheik and they hid his body. These people are not Muslims. They do not feel obliged to follow Islamic law, only when it suits them.

"We're beating the streets trying to find the sheik's body as well," he continued. "But we're here not only to help you to transition to a government and an authority that works for Iraq, we're here so that once that's in place, we can leave. We're not here forever. What you need to do is band together as tribal leaders and stand in opposition. And the way to do that is to have your men join the Iraqi police and the Iraqi army.

"We're sorry you lost a good sheik and a good tribal leader. We're here to help you stop the killing. We're here to protect you and work together with you. We will help you, you will help us, and we can do it."

Sattar seemed affected both by Patriquin's words and his earnestness in trying to communicate how steadfastly the Americans would stand with the sheiks. The sheiks in the audience seemed impressed, too.

Sattar deadpanned to Patriquin, "Now, you deserve a cigarette."

Suddenly, in this moment, Sheik Sattar was emerging as the galvanizing force to bring a nucleus of furious sheiks together to strike back hard, and openly, at al-Qaeda in Iraq.

And Travis Patriquin was emerging as the key personality binding the sheiks to the Americans at the brigade level.

"If we don't stand up together," Sattar told the group, "al-Qaeda is going to pick us apart one by one, like they did last time."

A few days later, in the last week of August, Majors Dave Raugh and Chuck Bergman of Lieutenant Colonel Tony Deane's battalion paid courtesy calls on Sheik Sattar to discuss items like police recruitment.

They stumbled into a historic moment in the making.

In his meeting room, Sattar was huddling up with about fifteen sheiks and planning a revolution. He explained to the Americans that he had a vision of building an alliance of tribes to formally, openly stand and fight against al-Qaeda.

"I think I can get these tribes united," he explained. Sattar produced a draft declaration that spelled out a series of points the sheiks were fine-tuning. He continued, "We want to declare our independence from the *salafists* [fundamentalists], and regain control of our country for our families. I want to present this personally to President Bush."

The idea of the diminutive, obscure, back-country Sheik Sattar sitting down with George Bush amused Major Raugh, who thought to himself, "Well, I don't think that is going to happen."

Bergman and Raugh alerted Deane, who on September 2 met with about twenty sheiks at Sattar's compound. "They were declaring an Anbar Emergency Council to bring peace to al Anbar," Deane wrote later. "They claimed that the Iraqi Constitution authorized formation of an Emergency Council and brought out lawyers with copies of the Iraqi Constitution to prove their point. The sheiks stated their desire to work with coalition forces to rid al Anbar of al-Qaeda and to restore peace in the region. They wanted to work openly with the coalition forces and the government. What we had been trying to do with the sheiks for months was now on the table."

The sheiks also wanted Governor Maamoun thrown out of office. They hated him for his alleged incompetence and corruption, and they even accused him and his Iraqi Islamic Party of being insurgent sympathizers and collaborators. In fact, Maamoun was already on al-Qaeda's local top-ten list of Iraqis to be killed.

Deane told the sheiks he applauded their commitment, but he had to take this all to his chain-of-command superiors. He realized it might soon be time to kick Sattar one level up the food chain and "promote" him from a battalion-level contact to a brigade-level contact.

Deane alerted brigade commander MacFarland and his staff. As he did, Deane realized how much his impression of Sattar had changed in the three short months he'd known the Iraqi. Sattar had originally impressed Deane as a striking, powerful, and hot-headed character, as well as a "knuckleheaded dumb-ass."

But by now, he realized four things about the Iraqi.

The guy had charisma. The guy had balls. He was a natural leader.

He just might be the man to pull off a revolt against al-Qaeda.

CHAPTER 8

THE AWAKENING OF IRAQ

Just after eleven a.m. on September 9, Captain Travis Patriquin and Colonel Sean MacFarland walked in as honored guests to a historic tribal council already under way at Sattar's compound.

They were joined by other American officers and three brigade interpreters, including Sterling Jensen, a twenty-nine-year-old, Arizona-born Mormon with a highly eclectic, globalized background.

He'd spent a year in Mexico as a teenager, did a two-year religious mission in Italy when he was nineteen, and attended a Brigham Young University study-abroad program in Jerusalem. He lived in East Jerusalem near Palestinian districts, and developed a great fondness for Arab people and culture. In 2003 he went to Damascus, Syria, as part of a State Department–funded Arabic language program, then won a Boren Fellowship for a year of intensive Arabic study at the University of Damascus. He went to Iraq as a contract interpreter to make money for graduate school, and was assigned to Patriquin's brigade as interpreter and cultural advisor in April 2006.

Jensen and Patriquin were kindred spirits in their affection for Middle Eastern history and culture, and were forming a close partnership in the war zone of Ramadi, just as Patriquin was doing with the interpreter Majd Alghabra. And for the three history buffs, there was much to savor about the scene they were witnessing.

To Colonel MacFarland, it felt like they were stepping into what he calls "a *Lawrence of Arabia* moment." Sattar led the brigade commander to a seat beside him at the head of the assembly.

The place was packed with over forty sheiks in flowing robes, plus their deputies and bodyguards. The sheiks represented eleven of the area's twenty-one tribes. Patriquin had given MacFarland a briefing before the meeting on who was who among the probable attendees.

Patriquin, in line with his relatively junior rank, stayed in the background of the room, discreetly taking photographs for later discussion and analysis with his colleagues. He and Jensen wanted to get everyone's name and picture, so they could build a "people map" of the emerging anti–al-Qaeda alliance.

Tribal strongman and powerful Sattar ally Sheik Hamid al-Hayes of the Abu Thiab tribe was there. A distinguished-looking Iraqi in a Western-style business suit was there, too, circling the room and shaking hands. He was Faisal Gaoud, a former governor of the province who had been a notable figure in supporting the 2005 revolt against al-Qaeda in the far western Anbar city of Al Qaim, and also had personal ties to exiled Anbar sheiks in Jordan. Gaoud was emerging as a key mainstream ally of the erstwhile upstart Sattar, and his presence was a statement by Sattar that this alliance was not aimed against the institutions of the Iraqi government. To MacFarland, the former governor appeared to be "senile, or a bit of a nut case."

With Colonel MacFarland sitting beside him, Sattar announced that the men in the room were starting a new campaign to rid the province of al-Qaeda, a campaign called Sahwa al Anbar (the Americans were soon shorthanding it as SAA), and establishing an al Anbar Emergency Council (also called the Anbar Salvation Council, among other names) to literally take over the provincial government until elections could be held. The word *sahwa* was soon popularly translated into English as "awakening," but Patriquin and Jensen felt a more precise translation in this context was "a sudden, gasping realization to the real danger."

Sattar explained, "There's an Iraqi law that says if the Provincial Council isn't meeting in the capital three consecutive months then you can dissolve them and create an emergency government, which is what we'll do. Then we'll start a political party.

"We've got our friends the Americans here," said Sattar, warming to his sudden and fairly improbable new role as provincial power broker and potential statesman. "This is the American commander at Camp Ramadi. Colonel MacFarland, we've seen that you are supporting the police, which is good. We have a common enemy. We want to fight al-Qaeda. We are here to announce that we are having this tribal conference, and we are against al-Qaeda.

"The Americans are our friends," Sattar assured the sheiks. "We have seen that they are trying to help us."

Echoing Travis Patriquin's belief that there were many relatively moderate and reconcilable people in nationalist insurgent groups like the 1920 Revolution Brigades, Sattar held out an olive branch to them, saying, "We invite all the honorable resistance fighters to the table, and to put down their weapons."

One sheik spoke up to express a widely held theory among Anbar's Sunnis that linked Iran, or "Persia," to supporting both radical Shiites in Iraq and Syria's facilitation of radical Sunni foreigners coming into western Iraq and then Ramadi.

"If someone wants to take over the Middle East you must win

Iraq," the sheik declared. "To win Iraq, you must first win Anbar. The Persians are killing the Sunnis, and they are behind the attacks in Anbar. The U.S. forces are the only ones who can really defend the Sunnis from the Persians."

Sattar stood up and summarized the points of the public declaration the group was working on: "Coalition forces are friendly forces, not occupying forces. Anyone who attacks them is attacking us. Al-Qaeda are thugs and criminals. We want no tribal militias. The only people to carry weapons are those authorized by the Ministry of Interior and Ministry of Defense. Anyone who is not a government of Iraq authorized security officer we'll consider an enemy." In addition, their new Emergency Council would replace the governor and the largely inactive Provincial Council.

For many of the sheiks in the room, this was the first time they had a chance to meet Colonel MacFarland and size up the commander.

On the spot, when asked if the United States would support the eleven-point proclamation, MacFarland said, "Yes, I can certainly agree to that on behalf of the coalition, except the point about ejecting Governor Maamoun and the Provincial Council. I can't agree to that. We have to work on that. You can call for provincial elections. You guys need to make sure no accidents happen to Governor Maamoun while we work on a constitutional way to move him out."

"We will support the government in Baghdad," said Sattar. "And if Baghdad doesn't support us, we'll do it anyway!

"We have ten thousand men ready to fight," he claimed, directly addressing MacFarland and the Americans. "But what is the role of the Iraqi police? When Mickey Mouse business and corruption is going on in the government, the Iraqi police won't want to work. Here is a window of opportunity. Use that opportunity to use us.

There are former officers who now want to come back and work and go through the process. But it sounds like the U.S. is hesitant.

"America is a great country," he added, "but we have a saying that the Americans want to stay in their barracks. We will fight the terrorists."

"We will not stay in our barracks," countered Colonel Mac-Farland. "We will help you fight. Our problem is not a lack of forces but a lack of information. That keeps us from defeating the terrorists. The terrorists are fish in the sea and we don't know where to drop our line or what bait to use.

"We will support you, we will be with you in the fight," said MacFarland. "We are here to help you. We are not here to kill you, and we are not here to occupy you or take your land. We have a mission. We are going to accomplish it and then we're going to go back home. Then we'll leave it to you so you can take care of your own country by yourselves."

"What are you going to do if al-Qaeda continues killing us, killing our tribal members?" asked one sheik who lived in an area surrounded by al-Qaeda fighters, no doubt remembering the wholesale slaughter of sheiks who supported the Anbar People's Council earlier that year. "Are you going to protect us if anything happens? What are you going to do?"

"You will be protected," MacFarland replied. "We will do our best. We are with you and we stand with you. It's all our battle, it's not only ours and not only yours. But I am very concerned about your lives. I want you to be very careful."

"Don't worry," said Sattar. "We are brave, we are tribal members and we can do it. We are not afraid of anything. We know what to do when it comes to fighting. We've fought a lot in our history."

MacFarland knew that the emergency expulsion of the governor, no matter how ineffective he was, was an incendiary idea, and it would be a nonstarter with his bosses at Marine Expeditionary Force headquarters, as well as with the Iraqi central government authorities in Baghdad. He needed to cut this discussion off immediately.

"Change is good," MacFarland said. "You need change in government, or it will become stagnant and lose touch with the people. Hopefully this meeting will be a catalyst for change, and elections in Anbar. But I am caught between sympathy for you and responsibilities to my leaders. We must work with the Iraqi government. If you want to replace the governor, then do it democratically—have an election—vote! Encourage your people to vote. But as far as you telling us to disregard [Governor] Maamoun, it's just not going to happen. We will help you and work with you, but the governor is an elected official and he represents the government in this province.

"This could be really historic," concluded MacFarland. "You're very wise to say you're going to work with the central government. This council is wonderful, but you've got to make it legitimate, by working with the governor."

One American in the room thought from the way he looked and presented himself, MacFarland came across like a novice in the cutthroat world of Iraqi tribal politics. MacFarland did have an all-American Jimmy Stewart or Gary Cooper–style earnest demeanor, but at this moment there was no doubt that MacFarland was the man with the most power in the room. His words carried the brute force of a thousand weapons he held in his pocket—troops, guns, tanks, artillery, jets, helicopters, heavy weapons, and influence over millions of dollars of U.S. construction contracts, reconstruction aid, and CIA money. Everyone in the room knew that Mac-Farland represented what the author Bing West later dubbed "the strongest tribe."

MacFarland later said that the experience felt like a mixture of *Lawrence of Arabia* and Independence Hall in Philadelphia in 1776: "It felt like they were declaring their independence from al-Qaeda."

After the meeting with Sattar and the sheiks, MacFarland checked with Patriquin and Jensen for their impressions of what just happened. "What do you think?" he asked them.

The two young men were almost euphoric.

"I think this is awesome!" said Jensen. "This is great!" He thought they needed many more of these meetings, and they had to get the Iraqi army and Iraqi police into the room, as well as more tribes, but this was a fantastic start. "The tribes are going to have their own interests, but for them to say all these things out loud is incredible."

"That was the real deal," said Patriquin. "That was genuine, I could tell they really meant it. This is a great movement—this is a popular movement against al-Qaeda. And we've got to support it."

"I think so, too," agreed MacFarland. "I think it's awesome."

The next day, Sattar secretly pulled off a major coup for the Awakening and for the Americans. He managed to switch off a major portion of the insurgency.

Privately, Sattar had asked Colonel MacFarland an explosive question: "I'm talking to Latif and the 1920 Brigades, would you like to meet him?"

Sattar explained he had entered into negotiations with Mohammad Mahmoud Latif, the area commander of the most powerful nationalist insurgent organization in Anbar province, the 1920 Revolution Brigades, a Sunni group that had killed scores of American troops but was increasingly fed up with al-Qaeda. Local insurgents from another radical group, Hamas of Iraq, were involved in the talks, too.

MacFarland was intrigued with the discussions, but he adamantly rejected the idea of coming face-to-face with Latif.

"That guy is an absolute insurgent," he replied to Sattar, "and if you're going to introduce me to him I will be happy to take him into custody. You can talk to him. If he's willing to stop attacking U.S. forces, that would be great, and I can work through you to him. But directly, it's not going to work."

MacFarland explains, "Our rule was if you wanted to partner with us you can't directly have been involved in attacks on U.S. forces, or we couldn't find evidence of it. There were guys coming in who had blood on their hands, but nothing we could prove, so we didn't pursue it if they wanted to be a new ally of ours. But a guy like Latif was a known enemy. I was catching a lot of heat from my higher headquarters about going kind of rogue in dealing with these insurgents, or creating an extra-governmental militia, so I just couldn't bring in a guy like Latif without setting off all kinds of alarm bells. I couldn't deal with him directly. I needed some separation between me and Latif."

He instructed Sattar, "Listen, you work with him, and keep him at least one degree of separation away from me. I'm not going to pursue this guy if he's going to lay down his arms. You can be our interlocutor."

Patriquin later learned that on September 10, 2006, Sattar traveled to an unknown location and held a summit conference with Latif and other insurgent leaders. Patriquin wrote in his report, "Sattar held a meeting of as many Hamas of Iraq and 1920 members as he could gather. Many attended, including their leadership, and they agreed at this meeting to lay down their arms against American forces and join SAA, realizing after the failed People's Committee uprising earlier in the year that cooperation with U.S. forces was the only way to get rid of al-Qaeda in the area and that U.S. forces weren't really the enemy. The contact informed me that a large percentage of our Iraqi police recruits over the last few months were people who'd been actively against us in one of these organizations."

Suddenly, with this cease-fire agreement, Sattar was truly poised to be the kingmaker of Anbar province.

"We're going to do this," Sattar told Patriquin on the night of September 13. "Tomorrow I'm going to announce the Emergency Council, read the declaration, and we'll call for provincial elections."

"Remember, we are with you," a delighted Patriquin told Sattar. "We support you one hundred percent."

On the morning of September 14, 2006, Sheik Sattar and his tribal allies made the first open, public declaration of the Awakening.

Sattar was filming the event for distribution to Arab satellite networks, and he alerted Baghdad press bureaus that on this day he was launching an open revolt against al-Qaeda in Iraq, with the goal of expelling them from Anbar province, and eventually all of Iraq. No national reporters showed up. Travel was too dangerous around Anbar province, besides which, the announcement was so unusual, few could be expected to take it seriously. The world in Baghdad and beyond knew little or nothing about the simmering revolt in Anbar.

Sheiks and their deputies filed into Sattar's horseshoe-shaped outdoor *diwan* meeting tent. No American officers were present at the meeting, as they wanted it to look like a purely Iraqi affair. The Americans did help provide perimeter security for the event, and a U.S. Apache helicopter droned overhead, its crew surveying the landscape for trouble.

After guest readings of inspirational Arabic poetry and Koranic verse, Sattar strode to the lectern, wearing sunglasses, formal

Arabic dress, and flanked by his nine-year-old son, Sattam, and a machine-gun-wielding bodyguard. The young Sattam, who had become a pickup soccer buddy of Travis Patriquin's, stood next to Sattar as his father faced the crowd.

For this meeting, Sattar had managed to gather forty-one sheiks representing twelve of Anbar's roughly forty tribes. The sheiks came largely from smaller and more rural tribes like Sattar's, and like Sattar many of them had had tribesmen and relatives killed by insurgents.

The sheiks had at least three things in common: They were fed up with the savagery and disruption of al-Qaeda to their lives and businesses, they detested the Anbar provincial government of Maamoun Sami Rashid, and they all knew that by showing their faces here today they were signing their own death warrants.

Some Americans thought that Sattar was more of a figurehead leader of SAA and that the real brains of the movement were his brother, Ahmed, Sheik Hamid al-Hayes, and Tariq Yusif Mohammad al-Thiyabi, an advisor to Sattar. But Sattar was the public face of the revolt, and as such he was putting his life very much on the line.

"My dear brothers, the sheiks," Sattar began. "It takes real men with real will to join this meeting today.

"When the Americans first came to our country, the bad people said it was Christianity against Islam. But the truth of it is we didn't see the Americans destroy any mosques and build churches over them. They didn't even build any new churches. Now it is clear that the Americans really are here to help us."

His next words, which Sattar had been repeating over the last weeks and were perhaps inspired in part by conversations he'd had with Travis Patriquin, Tony Deane, and Sean MacFarland, were no less than electrifying, and signaled the public announcement of a potentially seismic shift in Sunni Iraqi sentiment.

"We have to accept the fact that the United States is in our country," Sattar proclaimed. "It's a fact. They're not going to stay here. So why don't we try to learn from this experience? Why don't we learn from Japan and Germany? The United States was at war with both of these countries. And look at them now. They are superpowers. They are super in technology, in manufacturing, in education. They are among the top countries in the world in everything. It's a good lesson for us. There was another country that was at war with the United States, Vietnam, but they were hard-line communists. The Americans lost to them and look at them now. They're not huge powers like Germany and Japan. You want to be poor? Move to Vietnam!

"I ask all of you, do we agree that we need new leadership in our province, a leadership who lives what we are living?"

"Yes, yes, yes, Abdul Sattar, we agree, you are the man!" yelled a voice in the audience, in the familiar call-and-response style of Iraqi politics, where speeches can be interrupted by exuberant cheers, sometimes planted, from men jumping to their feet.

Sattar continued with a slap to the powerful Anbar sheiks who had fled to Jordan and Syria. "The real mujahedeen are the people who stay and fight, not the leaders who leave the country to do their meetings and negotiations.

"Let us fight as one hand. We ask for an election that represents the people of al Anbar."

"You are the man, Abdul Sattar," a man chanted, "you are the man who will bring us together as one hand!"

Sattar held up a copy of the Koran, placed his hand upon it for a few moments, and seemed to choke up. He may have been reacting to rumors he was lining his pockets with enormous sums of cash from American contracts.

"I swear on this holy book," announced Sattar, "what I'm saying here is from my heart, and that I'm trying to do what's right for our province."

For a moment, Sattar appeared to be weeping.

A chalkboard was produced and an impromptu election held, where each sheik declared his support for Sahwa al Anbar, for Sattar as its chief, and for the eleven-point proclamation.

The document called for reconciliation and political engagement "on a large scale" with the central government in Baghdad. There was to be no cooperation or negotiation with al-Qaeda. American forces were to be considered friendly and not attacked. Tribal sons were to join the Iraqi police and Iraqi army, not militias. The judicial system would be reopened, agriculture and industry immediately rebuilt, and unemployment would be addressed. It also called for "open dialogue" with two pivotal groups: "ex-Ba'athist members who have not committed any crime against Iraqis, and did not support terrorism, and to help them get jobs," and "coalition forces to schedule withdrawal from Anbar, after the complete formation of the Iraqi police and Iraqi army."

Sattar kept the demand to oust the governor in the proclamation, but in the coming weeks this point would wither in the face of strong objections by the Americans.

The meeting went off without a hitch.

One by one, forty-one sheiks voted in favor of the proclamation.

And at that moment in history, Anbar province, and Iraq, began to awaken into the daylight.

The next day, Lieutenant Colonel Tony Deane and his battalion's tribal affairs officer, Captain Pat Fagan, paid a visit to Sattar to discuss the launch of the sheik's new movement. Over the coming weeks, Travis Patriquin, as the brigade tribal officer, would become Sattar's main contact, but for now the Americans officially also kept Sattar on as a lower-level battalion contact, as they didn't exactly know where his Awakening was going, and they didn't want to prematurely elevate him at the expense of other sheiks.

But excerpts from the U.S. Army report of Sattar's September 15 encounter with the American officers captured Sattar in action as he grasped at the levers of power in the province with the confidence of a seasoned CEO: "The Emergency Council would like to use [U.S. Marine Corps base] Camp Blue Diamond as the new Provincial Government Center. Sattar explained that only three tribes have not been invited due to their ties to terrorists. Sattar explained the video of the Council's Proclamation was sent to Al Zawra, Al Arabiya, Al Sharqiyah, and Al Jazeera networks and should be aired very soon. Zaif Jassem, a known terrorist, has fled the Jazeera area due to the area's tribes trying to turn him in. Sattar is demanding every tribe that participates in the Emergency Council provide a list of their men to join the IPs and a list of known terrorists in their area. . . . Sattar explained that the Emergency Council is awaiting a response from the prime minister, the parliament, and the U.S. ambassador to continue their work on standing up a provincial government."

Four months earlier, Sheik Sattar was an obscure alleged gangster and country bumpkin.

Suddenly he was poised to change Iraqi history.

Event Timeline for the Awakening of Iraq, 2003–2007

2003–2006: CIA, Army and Marines cultivate Sunni tribal sheiks in multiple outreach efforts.

2004–early 2006: al-Qaeda (AQ) conquers much of Anbar Province, launches parallel government and headquarters of planned caliphate.

2005: Abu Mahal tribe and Desert Protectors overthrow al-Qaeda in city of Qaim, joined by Col. Dale Alford's Marines. Sheiks in Ramadi begin scattered attempts to resist AQ, crushed by AQ in early 2006.

April–May 2006: Captain Travis Patriquin's brigade arrives at Camp Ramadi, jumps to offensive push into city.

Summer 2006: Iraqi Police recruitment jump-started by Sattar, MacFarland, Deane, Lechner, Patriquin and colleagues. CIA provides start-up funds.

August 21, 2006: AQ kills Abu Ali Jassim sheik, wouldn't return body, inciting tribe to rise against AQ; major catalyst to Awakening.

Sept. 2006: Sheik Sattar and tribal allies publicly announce Anbar Awakening and 11 point platform. Sattar reaches agreement with 1920's Revolution Brigades to stop attacking coalition forces. Anti-AQ death squad pulls 10 AQ suspects out of mosque and executes them in broad daylight.

Oct. 2006: AQ fortifies in Sufiyah and other areas of Ramadi, launches attacks on key tribes.
   -Sheik Sattar named senior advisor to counter-terrorism operations in Anbar by Iraqi Ministry of Defense.
   -Patriquin circulates PowerPoint presentation.

Oct. 17, 2006: Sheik Sattar meets with Governor Maamoun.

Oct. 25, 2006: Insurgents behead three teenagers in Sufiyah, one insurgent is executed in public as revenge.

Oct. 29, 2006: Awakening members meet with Prime Minister Maliki in Baghdad; Maliki legitimizes the group. Iraqi Police recruiting takes off across Ramadi through summer and fall.

Fall 2006: CIA station chief and State Department officer in Ramadi alert superiors that "game-change" is underway in Anbar Province, news registers at top levels of Pentagon and White House.

Nov. 4, 2006: Abu Alwani tribe joins the Awakening, a major breakthrough. Other tribes contact the Awakening to request meetings.

Nov. 20, 2006: Awakening representatives hold meetings with Gov. Maamoun, the Iraqi Deputy PM, the MOD, and CF/ISF officials.

Nov. 23, 2006: Sheik Jassim of the Abu Soda warned by AQ to take down checkpoints and stop working with CF or be killed.

Nov. 25, 2006: AQ attacks Abu Soda tribe; AQ's national commander believed to be planner, delivers speech from mosque prior to attack commencing. Battle of Sufiyah.

December 6, 2006: Deaths of Travis Patriquin, Megan McClung, Vincent Pomante.

January–February 2007: AQ largely cleared from Ramadi area by Iraqi Security Forces and U.S. Army and Marines. Awakening concept begins spreading to other provinces, inspiring Sons of Iraq program.

© 2011 Jeffrey L. Ward
Adapted from Author Maps and Interviews

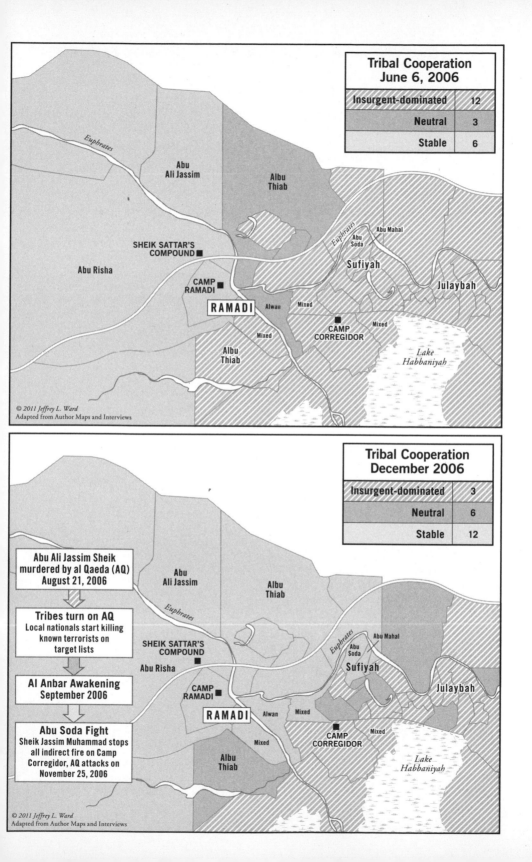

Tribal Cooperation
June 6, 2006

Insurgent-dominated	12
Neutral	3
Stable	6

Euphrates

Abu
Ali Jassim

Albu
Thiab

Euphrates

Abu Mahal

Abu
Soda

SHEIK SATTAR'S
COMPOUND ■

Sufiyah

Julaybah

Abu Risha

CAMP
RAMADI ■

RAMADI

Alwan

Mixed

Mixed

CAMP
CORREGIDOR

Mixed

Mixed

Albu
Thiab

*Lake
Habbaniyah*

© 2011 Jeffrey L. Ward
Adapted from Author Maps and Interviews

Tribal Cooperation
December 2006

Insurgent-dominated	3
Neutral	6
Stable	12

Abu Ali Jassim Sheik
murdered by al Qaeda (AQ)
August 21, 2006

Abu
Ali Jassim

Albu
Thiab

Euphrates

Tribes turn on AQ
Local nationals start killing
known terrorists on
target lists

Euphrates

Abu Mahal

Abu
Soda

SHEIK SATTAR'S
COMPOUND ■

Abu Risha

Sufiyah

Julaybah

Al Anbar Awakening
September 2006

CAMP
RAMADI ■

RAMADI

Alwan

Mixed

Abu Soda Fight
Sheik Jassim Muhammad stops
all indirect fire on Camp
Corregidor, AQ attacks on
November 25, 2006

CAMP
CORREGIDOR

Mixed

Mixed

Albu
Thiab

*Lake
Habbaniyah*

© 2011 Jeffrey L. Ward
Adapted from Author Maps and Interviews

CHAPTER 9

★

THE MEN ON THE WALL

P atriquin and his colleagues were building a new city.

As his brigade and the newly rejuvenated Iraqi police began slowly retaking the neighborhoods of Ramadi block by block, Patriquin was diving into and coordinating important pieces of the brigade's civil affairs programs.

As the brigade's civil affairs officer, as well as its tribal affairs officer, Patriquin was a firm believer in the idea of "using money as a weapons system."

When population centers were cleared and held by coalition forces, he believed, you had to turn on the spigot of contracts and money, humanitarian and reconstruction projects, to get essential services back in operation, including sewers, water, electricity, trash removal, and—especially important in Ramadi—rubble removal, as many buildings downtown had been pulverized by the fighting. Much of the local reconstruction aid doled out by the Americans came from the Commander's Emergency Response Program (CERP), a flexible discretionary fund managed by local U.S. commanders across Iraq.

In July 2006, the brigade liberated the Ramadi General Hospital, which had been an insurgent command post and combat medical treatment center. Patriquin and his colleagues successfully restarted the building as the major public hospital for the whole province, got the medical staff to come back, and supplied the facility with fuel, oil, and medicine. Patriquin enjoyed the commanding view of the city from the hospital's upper floors, but still had to watch out for snipers taking potshots at the windows.

Patriquin constantly urged the brigade's civil affairs teams to seek out local businessmen and businesswomen in Ramadi who could do something, anything, to bring jobs back to the city. In the following months, Patriquin and his fellow soldiers and marines in the brigade's civil affairs teams spent millions of dollars to restart the Ramadi power grid, reopen the water supply, reopen the schools, build playgrounds and ball fields, open civic centers, distribute blankets, sugar, school uniforms and schoolbooks, and get sanitation trucks moving, public buses operating, roads cleared, and local government stood up. Much of the contracting work was done through the sheiks, who often provided the work crews. The efforts sometimes stalled or fell victim to corruption, fraud, or inefficiency. But much was accomplished, and Patriquin took great pride in the successes they enjoyed.

One summer day in 2006, while traveling by convoy to the besieged, battle-scarred fortress of the Government Center, Patriquin noticed something he'd never seen before—children playing on the streets of Ramadi.

"Maybe that's a good sign," he thought.

One day, a colleague poked his head over Patriquin's cubicle and asked him how he was doing.

"Hey, man," a delighted Patriquin announced, "I'm leading a tribal revolt against al-Qaeda along the Euphrates!"

For the Americans, the tide seemed to be turning away from complete disaster, but soldiers and marines were still fighting and dying alongside Iraqi security forces in Ramadi, and the insurgency was striking back at the coalition and its new tribal allies with an urgent lethality.

In one of many such examples, on September 29, 2006, an insurgent tossed a grenade onto a roof where a twenty-five-year-old Navy SEAL, Master-at-Arms Second Class Michael Anthony Monsoor, was stationed along with several other SEALs and Iraqi army soldiers. Monsoor absorbed the grenade blast to protect his comrades and died of his wounds, earning him the Medal of Honor.

In a brazen, broad-daylight show of force in mid-October, squads of armed insurgents briefly paraded up and down a downtown Ramadi boulevard on motorcycles and in vehicles, creating startling video footage broadcast around the world, giving the impression that the insurgency was still in control of the city.

In a series of comments he made to his fellow soldiers, marines, and interpreters in the summer and fall of 2006, Patriquin outlined his thinking on the revolution he was helping engineer, a campaign he thought could turn the battle around in Ramadi. "Working with the tribes to build up the police force is not about making tribal militias. To fight a counterinsurgency you have to connect with the local people. That's exactly what we're doing. What else is going to work?

"We are not going to win these people over by just kicking in their doors and arresting them. We're not going to win by trying to empower a government in Baghdad that has no power, or a governor of Anbar that has no power. The way we're going to win is by building bonds and talking to the people. And whether we like it or not, whether it's democratic or not, the people in charge are the sheiks. We're not going to get anywhere if we ignore the sheiks.

"If you want to stabilize the city, if you want to stabilize the country, you're going to need to cut the crap on all this idealism [of trying to work only through Iraqi government institutions from the top down] and start pushing the right buttons with the sheiks."

At this moment in time, to many observers, Iraq seemed to be condemned to an eternal maelstrom of large-scale chaos, violence, and disintegration. The Americans might be trapped there for decades to come. But Patriquin was one of the first Americans to fully grasp a new and potentially game-changing reality.

"Sattar is the key to Ramadi," he argued. "Nothing will work in Ramadi without him. This guy is huge, huge. This guy is absolutely the center of gravity for us.

"Maybe he's the key to all of western Iraq. If he succeeds here, it could change everything. He is the key. Sattar is the key to reaching peace with the Sunnis. And that's the key to bring peace to the region, and for us to leave Iraq.

"This," Patriquin said to a colleague, *"is our way out."*

In late September, Patriquin's brigade got the unhappy news that they wouldn't be going home when they thought they would. Their tour was going to be extended by forty days, until February 2007.

At this point in his life, explained Captain Patriquin to an acquaintance, he had two goals in life: "I want to win. And I want to go home."

"Look," Sheik Sattar confided to Patriquin one day, "we've got guys coming to us who are on your wanted lists."

Sattar held a computer memory stick in his hand.

It contained a key that would open a door, a door through which peace might come to Anbar.

And it was a door through which the Americans might eventually leave Iraq.

The stick contained a list of the names of more than a thousand Sunni men who were ready to join the rebellion against al-Qaeda in Iraq and enlist in the Iraqi police force. The word was spreading quickly, especially in the rural districts of northern and western Ramadi, that the time had come to join the police. It was now an honorable thing to do, a way to wear a gun, put on a blue uniform, get a paycheck, put food on the table, and even gain respect in the community. Sheik Sattar was spreading the word, and other sheiks were joining him.

The ranks of the Iraqi police were swelling, and if the trend continued at this pace, the police could soon create a tipping point in combat and intelligence power against al-Qaeda.

But a number of the men on the list had, until almost that moment, been the blood enemies of the Americans. They had belonged to, or freelanced for, nationalist insurgent groups like the 1920 Revolution Brigades, or even for al-Qaeda in Iraq and its affiliates.

These Iraqis had American blood on their hands.

A number of these men had planted IEDs, fired mortars and RPGs against coalition troops, and had killed and wounded scores of Americans, including people Patriquin knew and loved. Some of the potential recruits were on U.S. target lists as wanted men. Sattar knew that some of the names on the list would pop up as red flags on various databases of suspected insurgents wanted by American and Iraqi military and intelligence units.

Suddenly, it seemed, these men were ready to switch sides and fight alongside U.S. forces. Sattar wanted to get them a "pass" to be let into the police. This way, they'd more or less be under Iraqi government control, they'd get regular paychecks to support their families, and they could restore some semblance of law and order to their local neighborhoods. Anbar province might have a future.

"They're against al-Qaeda," Sattar assured Patriquin. "They believe in what we're doing. They want to help us. They're giving us a lot of good information through the police, to find out where arms caches are, and where the top, top fish [terrorists] are. We think that we can get a lot out of them."

As an example, Sattar brought up the name of one known insurgent lieutenant who was ready to "flip," saying, "Look, this guy is really good. We can use him.

"If we don't trust them, there's no way we're going to do it," Sattar promised Patriquin. "But if these guys are coming to us and they show a certain level of remorse, or they can demonstrate they'll be of help to us, then we want you to take them into the police. I swear on my family's name, if there's one of these people that's bad, it's on my head. You can throw me in jail."

Then Sattar dropped the heart of the matter on the table, a dilemma that could affect the course of the war in this pivotal province: "We want to make sure that you Americans don't go after them."

Patriquin and his colleagues agonized over the fact that the blood of their friends was on the hands of some of the potential Iraqi recruits. But Patriquin realized before most other Americans that if they didn't open the doors of the Iraqi police wide enough to include former insurgent gunmen and bombers, they would be repeating the same vicious cycle of stalemate in Anbar they'd been condemned to for the last three years.

As Patriquin put it, "If everyone who has thrown a rock or laid an IED against American forces is excluded from the police, there will be very few military-aged males to recruit from in Ramadi."

"Look," Patriquin explained to his colleagues in the brigade, "I think we should totally use these people and not go after them, even though they've got blood on their hands. Obviously they have to be monitored, but you know what, if they turn, and if Sattar and the tribal leaders think we can trust them, these guys would be an asset."

This was an extraordinary moment in the history of the Iraq War.

A junior American officer was conducting informal, de facto amnesty negotiations with a critical Iraqi power broker, someone who in retrospect probably would have been dealt with on these matters by a general or at least a brigade commander. In fact, these talks were so potentially volatile and historic that in the context of the Iraq War, they were roughly almost comparable, for example, to those held by Henry Kissinger with the North Vietnamese at the height of the Vietnam War.

But in a reversal of command roles, Patriquin, only a captain, was talking grand strategy with Sheik Sattar one-on-one, while his army boss, Lieutenant Colonel Jim Lechner, the number-two man in the brigade, was on the other side of the room with Sattar's brother, Ahmed, dealing with more mundane operational issues.

Both Lechner and his boss, brigade commander Colonel Sean MacFarland, sensed that Patriquin was the key to Sattar's heart, and they were happy to let the young captain run with him. "That was something the tribes liked about Patriquin," recalled the interpreter Sterling Jensen, who was in the room for many of these meetings. "They could speak freely with him and they wouldn't get in trouble for it. It was a trust issue. Patriquin was there at a time when there wasn't trust and at a very difficult time. They felt they could talk to him."

Captain Patriquin assured Sattar, "Everybody can make mistakes."

"If they come up hot on our biometric scanners as having spent time at Abu Ghraib, we're not going to automatically send them to jail," he continued. "We'll still honestly consider them for positions with the Iraqi police. As long as it was something that happened a while ago, as long as it isn't something we have recent reporting on, it's okay. We're just happy to have them join the police."

It was exactly what the sheik wanted to hear.

Patriquin explained the simple, brutal logic behind his promise: "In this situation, everybody has blood on their hands."

Soon, Patriquin and Sattar were reviewing even more sensitive and potentially explosive lists.

They were names taken from the American "Most Wanted" short lists of suspected Iraqi insurgents and their tribal facilitators and sympathizers, who were going to be targeted by U.S. forces to be captured and interrogated, which also meant they might be killed in the process of being apprehended.

Patriquin got the names on the lists from his friends in the "secret world" of local American intelligence and Special Operations groups, a world that included the Joint Special Operations Command; the CIA and its civilian contractors; the Defense Intelligence Agency and National Security Agency; and Navy SEALs and other "special operators" attached to the Defense Department or CIA.

These secret players had quaint nicknames like "OGAs" (other governmental agencies, an acronym usually referring to the CIA), "OCF-I" (other coalition forces in Iraq), "secret squirrels," "they who must not be named," and "super-friends."

Many of the secret operators were based at Shark Base, adjacent to Camp Ramadi, and were engaged in tracking, capturing, or killing top Iraqi insurgents. One of the most secret, and effective, organizations in this landscape was called Task Force 145 (soon changed to Task Force 77), and was said to be instrumental in the capture of Saddam Hussein and the killing of Abu

Musab al-Zarqawi. The task force operated throughout Iraq and was believed by outside observers to include Special Forces team members drawn from the army, navy, air force, and CIA Special Activities Division paramilitary force, as well as the British SAS.

In Ramadi, representatives of the secret units got together once a week for a targeting meeting with officers of Patriquin's brigade, to cross-check human target lists, review significant captures over the last seventy-two to ninety-six hours, and make sure they avoided "target fratricide," or "burning each other's targets." Colonel MacFarland made sure Patriquin attended the targeting meetings, so Patriquin could keep track of the American targeting in light of what he was learning from the tribal sheiks.

Patriquin selected suspected insurgent leaders' names from these lists, copied them by hand into a notebook, and quietly discussed some of the names with Sheik Sattar.

A highly delicate and potentially quite dangerous discussion would ensue, as Patriquin and Sattar navigated their way through the names. "We're interested in what you know about these guys on our list," Patriquin would tell Sattar. "If we take this guy out of the environment, we think it will have a very detrimental effect on command and control of insurgent operations."

"Hold off on him," Sattar would suggest to the American about one wanted man. "We can get to him. We can reason with him and bring him over to our side." Patriquin had to judge how far he could trust Sattar to make the right call. One American who witnessed these discussions observes that "Sattar became attached to Travis because Travis was a captain, he was likeable, spoke a little Arabic, had a mustache, and was Sattar's sort of mole with the U.S. Special Forces so they wouldn't target people Sattar thought they shouldn't target."

Patriquin would have known what a dangerous game this was,

as it essentially gave Sattar the power of life and death over men on the American target lists, and conferred potentially tremendous power on him to boost his stature, eliminate rivals, and alter the balance of power among tribes.

Upon learning of this scene in 2010, Alfred Ben Connable, a retired marine intelligence major who served in Anbar province in 2004–2006, said, "What a horrible idea. To give targeting lists to an Iraqi to have them vetted for you? There is no Iraqi without a personal agenda. So whenever you talk to an Iraqi about who to kill and who not to kill, who to capture and who not to capture, of course he's going to use the process to try to improve his standing. Or he's going to take folks off the list who he supports, even if objectively they should be on the list. I'm not besmirching his [Patriquin's] reputation, but I wouldn't do it and I certainly wouldn't recommend anybody else do it."

Despite the risks, as the levels of trust between the two men increased, and as the ranks of the police force swelled and "most wanted" insurgents were killed and captured, Patriquin continued his discreet, "back of the envelope" intelligence exchanges with Sattar.

Spearheaded by Lieutenant Colonel Jim Lechner, a man one officer called "a powerhouse who rarely slept," officers in the brigade fought to push the police recruitment campaign forward, despite skepticism among some officers at MEF headquarters in Fallujah and bureaucratic inertia at the Iraqi Ministry of Interior in Baghdad.

For much of the autumn of 2006, Patriquin's life was consumed with police work—getting recruits screened; shipping them back and forth to police academies in Jordan and Baghdad for training; getting them weapons, ammunition, vehicles, uniforms, and badges; and most of all, getting them paid. Progress was painful, grinding, and punctuated by turf squabbles, shouting matches, and the constant threat of corruption and insurgent infiltration of the Iraqi police. But the process was lurching forward.

Captain Scott Kish of the First Battalion, Sixth Marines recalls how the Awakening directly benefited his work inside the city of Ramadi. "The tribal engagement by Travis Patriquin and Colonel Sean MacFarland was critical because it formed an alliance, and it built trust and confidence with local tribal leaders that eventually led to trust and confidence with the local populace. For the locals in the city, it was a combination of this, the daily work of the marines, and the establishment of the police that came from the Awakening. The burgeoning Awakening provided young men for the establishment of police in the different areas of Ramadi, first the more secure rural areas and eventually by October and November we were able to set up a police headquarters in the city. The Awakening and the tribes now had a stake in the fight. The more areas became settled and quiet, the more reconstruction we were able to provide, which meant the more contracts they were able to gain to do the work. The police work also provided members of their tribes with jobs and pay. It started to be a win/win for them and us. The intel gathered by these tribes was critical. The police that worked with the various battalions were from those areas so they knew who were the good guys and bad guys. As this grew, the locals gained more trust in the police and in us. The locals were now taking charge and providing tips without fear of being intimidated."

At one newly established police station in eastern Ramadi, a remarkable scene unfolded, which was soon replicated throughout the city.

Fifteen U.S. Army infantrymen moved into a large house that army engineers had remodeled into a combat-fortified Iraqi police station on the edge of the Malaab, a dangerous, insurgent-infested district.

That night, under the same roof, fifty newly recruited Iraqi policemen checked their weapons, posted sentries, and got under blankets to go to sleep a few yards away from the American soldiers.

Fifteen Americans and fifty Iraqis slept under the same roof as brothers at war.

And a few weeks earlier, a number of the Iraqis would have been trying to kill American GIs.

Indeed, some of them may have done so.

In the midst of a conversation with Patriquin one day, Sattar waved his hand in a burst of exuberance and announced, "I'm going to call you Hisham Abu Risha. Because I love you. Do you know what Hisham means in Arabic?"

"Yes," said Patriquin. "A sharp sword that never makes a mistake, or generous one." He thought its colloquial meanings included "unbeatable," "destroyer of evil," and "pulverizer."

The word "Hisham" derived from the prophet Mohammed's great-grandfather Hashim ibn Abd al-Manaf, who generously nourished pre-Islamic pilgrims to Mecca with crumbled, or pulverized, bread in broth. In fact, Patriquin first acquired this nickname seven years earlier from his Arab instructors at the Defense Language Institute, so Sattar's impulse was either a coincidence or the result of some clever manipulation on Patriquin's part.

"Hisham, you are American, but you are Abu Risha," he told Patriquin. "I consider you a member of my tribe. Hisham Abu Risha. Any harm that comes to you comes to me. You are a member of my tribe and my family."

Soon, Sattar presented Patriquin with a Bedouin outfit, an

Arabic *abaya* headdress with gold trim and a white *dishdasha* robe. "It's yours," Sattar insisted when the captain began to protest. "You'll need it—it's getting cold!"

"After the war," said Sattar, "when your family comes here, you have a house to stay in—my house. You can build a house nearby and take a wife from the tribe."

At first, Patriquin and Jim Lechner figured Sattar was joking.

When they left the meeting, though, the two men thought about it a bit and came to the same conclusion. The sheik wasn't kidding.

"Hey, let's stop here a second," said Patriquin to Captain Andrew Duprey, the brigade's psychological operations officer.

A few dozen feet away, near the entrance of the Camp Ramadi training facility for Iraqi police, were twenty-five young Iraqi police recruits in trademark bright blue shirts. They all seemed really pissed off about something.

Lighting up a cigarette, Patriquin trained one ear sideways to eavesdrop on their conversation, while pretending to chat with his colleague.

Streams of young tribesmen from the rural areas of Anbar province were coming in to sign up for the nascent national police force, which barely existed a few months earlier. But the stress of numbers was taking a toll, and bureaucratic foul-ups and turf battles were plaguing the process as the American and Iraqi administrators struggled to keep up.

Today, these cadets were bitching and moaning to each other about how poorly they thought they were being treated, about the bad food they were being served, about pretty much everything a young recruit could complain about. They were what the U.S.

military called MAMs, or military-aged males, Sunnis in their late teens and twenties, and until now they provided the bulk of the cannon-fodder recruits and frontline fighters for al-Qaeda in Iraq and other insurgent groups. Until now, their prospects in life largely boiled down to working for the insurgents for very good pay, or working for criminal gangs, or being unemployed and watching their families starve.

The cadets were oblivious to the two U.S. officers standing nearby, assuming that they, like almost all Americans, couldn't understand Arabic.

Having captured the gist of their conversation, Patriquin strode over to the group, and in the custom of all such Iraqi encounters, put his hand to his heart and said, *as-salamu alaykum*, or "peace be upon you."

Patriquin introduced himself, apologized for interrupting them, and asked them what they were upset about.

For a moment the cadets appeared dumbfounded at Patriquin's appearance—his bushy Iraqi-style mustache, his humble greeting, and his thick Arabic-by-way-of-St.-Louis accent. But they recovered quickly and launched into their list of grievances, none of which sounded serious to Patriquin.

Presently Patriquin waved his hand and beckoned, "Stop!"

For the next five minutes, Travis Patriquin berated them like a drill sergeant. Using colloquial Iraqi Arabic stylings, he theatrically hectored and lambasted his astonished audience.

"You are all complainers!" he announced to the group, now circled around him.

"You're not supporting your families; you're not supporting your tribes. It's because of you that the terrorists are moving freely across all of al Anbar province!"

Captain Duprey watched the impromptu speech from the edge

of the crowd, and recalls that the Iraqis looked at Patriquin "in absolute awe."

"Here's an American who speaks not only the language," remembers Duprey, "but the slang, too, and he's just chewing them out in a culturally appropriate manner."

The cadets, according to Duprey, were literally stunned, their jaws agape.

Soon, Patriquin switched from ass-chewing mode into an infectious, exuberant, inspirational pep talk, pumping up the police recruits by appealing to their pride in their families, their tribes, and their Iraq.

"What tribe are you from?" Patriquin demanded of one cadet.

"And what tribe are you from?" he asked another.

"I know the sheik of that tribe," Patriquin announced. "He is a personal friend of mine. He would be ashamed to hear you speaking like this.

"You are the men who will stand watch on the wall," Patriquin declared. "You are the defenders of the tribes!

"You are the ones who are the guardians of your tribes!" Patriquin continued.

"It is because of you that the women and the children will be safe from those that wish to take over your nation!

"It is not America that wishes to take over your nation," Patriquin argued. "We as Americans want nothing more than to be able to go home to our loved ones. But before that happens we want to make sure you are safe with your loved ones."

Patriquin was a huge fan of Shakespeare's *Henry V*, and for a few minutes on a patch of dirt in a combat zone six thousand miles from home, the warrior seemed to be channeling the spirit of King Harry delivering his immortal St. Crispin's Day oration.

By the time Patriquin reached the crescendo of his speech,

the Iraqis were applauding and cheering, and as a group, the circle moved in and enveloped the young American officer in a flurry of apologies, man-hugs and man-kisses.

Soon after, the Iraqi army general in charge of overseeing police training told Patriquin, "I don't know what you said to those guys, but their change in attitude is unbelievable."

By the end of October, as the tribal sheiks and Patriquin accelerated their recruiting drives, the streams of Iraqi police applicants was turning into a flood, and so many hundreds of applicants were showing up that some had to be turned away.

At some point in October 2006, Patriquin quietly decided that the time had come for him to confront one of the things he hated most in life.

It was a foul, despicable enemy that had penetrated the minds of hundreds of thousands of American military men and women, sapped their energy, burned up their time and dulled their decisions. It had no limits and it had no mercy. It was everywhere, infecting everything and replicating itself. It was dragging the military that Travis Patriquin loved into a vast swamp of narcolepsy and wasted effort.

It was a beast he had to slay.

Its name was PowerPoint. And it was a piece of computer software.

PowerPoint was a computer program that dated back to the early days of the Apple Macintosh in the 1980s, was greatly expanded and improved upon by Microsoft in the 1990s, and, by the time of the start of the Iraq War, had become the ubiquitous presentation tool of choice for sharp students, teachers, business managers, government bureaucrats, and military officers the world over. It offered a seductive package of features that made slide projectors and overhead acetates obsolete: rich color pie charts, unlimited photos, snappy bullet-point layouts, color coding, all kinds of text and data effects, and even primitive animation. Power-Point presentations could be, to a point, fun and interesting ways of clearly communicating ideas and information.

It seemed every ambitious American manager on the make had his own PowerPoint presentation, and often many of them, on his laptop. And the American military was no exception—it had thousands upon thousands of PowerPoint presentations. Many officers had PowerPoint presentations. The problem was that the vast majority of the presentations were too long, or overstuffed with data, text, and graphics, or poorly written, or often all three. They would bludgeon you into glazed-eye confusion, daydreams, and sleep. And in addition, unlike a concise, check-the-box memo, PowerPoints were often not geared toward making crisp decisions.

The U.S. Army was drowning in redundant meetings, even in this theater of war, and the flagrant overuse and abuse of color-ful, statistics-choked, mind-numbingly dull PowerPoint presenta-tions was driving Patriquin crazy. The officer class of the army was overrun with PowerPoint Rangers—men and women who could work magic with the software and create masterpiece presenta-tions of entertainment and self-promotion. Patriquin would much rather be out on patrol, on a shooting range or a mission, talking to people, getting to know the country, hunting and killing the enemy and making things happen.

But Patriquin wanted to create a presentation he could show his military colleagues that captured his vision for beating the Iraqi insurgency, and he realized he had to make his own Pow-erPoint presentation, something he had tried to resist for years. Later, he learned he'd be meeting with MEF marine staff officers at Fallujah, and he wanted to have something ready by then. And he wanted to make the presentation really clear and concise. "If I'm going to have to make a PowerPoint," he vowed, "I'm going to do it my way."

He wisecracked, "I want to make it so simple, even a general can understand it."

Patriquin's office neighbor at Camp Ramadi, Captain Andrew Duprey, witnessed Patriquin struggle as he grappled with the PowerPoint software. Duprey was amused by the idea that Patriquin was so smart and knew so many languages, but still couldn't figure out the computer program.

Then one day Patriquin excitedly beckoned him over to his computer screen. He was excited.

"Dude, dude!" said Patriquin. "You gotta check this out. You gotta see this—I did the PowerPoint!"

The two men smiled as Patriquin proudly tapped his keyboard and the presentation unfolded.

"This is awesome, isn't it?" Patriquin asked.

"It sure is, Travis."

The eighteen-page document, titled "How to Win the War in al Anbar by CPT Trav," contained no buzzwords, bullet points, or zippy color-coded pie charts. Instead, it featured funny stick figures and tongue-in-cheek captions to make serious points about sheiks, insurgents, the Iraqi police and army, and cultural awareness, from the perspective of "Joe," an average American soldier.

Patriquin's presentation started off as a joke for no particular purpose, kind of a Bronx cheer aimed at all the presentations he'd been forced to suffer through. It was just Travis being Travis. At first he was reluctant to circulate it because he thought it might be misconstrued as insulting the intelligence of his colleagues. But as he gradually showed it around, he heard people laughing at it and enjoying its blunt logic and militantly anti-PowerPoint perspective so much that he began e-mailing it to his friends in the armed forces.

Once Patriquin released it into cyberspace, the document developed a life of its own, and it started replicating and bouncing around secure military servers the world over, eventually entering the Pentagon. At Fort Leavenworth, Kansas, the commanding general of the army's Command and General Staff College at the time, General David Petraeus, a famously adept PowerPoint presenter, found a copy in his in-box, read through the presentation, and thought, "This makes eminent sense."

In a few months, Patriquin's presentation would become one of the most famous and most downloaded PowerPoint presentations in the history of the American military.

CHAPTER 10

A COCKY SON OF A BITCH

"That army captain is out of control!"

The voice on the phone belonged to a marine staff colonel at Marine Expeditionary Force headquarters in Fallujah.

He was talking about Travis Patriquin, and he and several of his colleagues were enraged that Patriquin was aggressively courting Sheik Sattar, a man who at least one senior marine officer thought should be arrested for alleged ongoing smuggling operations.

Fielding the call was Patriquin's colleague and occasional mentor, marine Lieutenant Colonel John Church, who worked alongside Patriquin for the Ready First Combat Team in Ramadi. Church was the officer in charge of the joint civil affairs detachment in support of the brigade.

"Yeah, man," empathized Church to his fellow marine, "he's completely out of control."

Then Church thought, "And thank God he is, because he's making shit happen."

Tensions between Patriquin and other key officers in the RFCT, on one side, and a few staff officers at MEF headquarters, on the other, had been brewing for weeks over how to engage the tribes in Anbar. In October 2006, as Sheik Sattar's Awakening movement was growing, the debate threatened to erupt into full-scale bureaucratic war, and Patriquin and Church were right in the middle of it.

According to one army officer who served in Patriquin's brigade, "We ended up at some points fighting against our higher headquarters harder than we fought against al-Qaeda in Ramadi. That cost us a lot of effort." A brigade translator who was close to the action described the tone of the interoffice fighting as that of "a catfight between little girls."

It wasn't an institutional clash between the marines and the army, or an intellectual difference over conflicting counterinsurgency doctrines. And it wasn't a dispute over the need to engage tribal leaders. Countless marine and army officers had been reaching out to tribal leaders across Iraq since the first days of the invasion, as had CPA people, State Department staff, and CIA officers and other intelligence agents. But the timing and the conditions were such that these efforts rarely gained any major, lasting traction and had little effect on the overall battlefield or on Iraqi politics.

Instead, these marine and army officers were arguing mainly over which sheiks to talk to, and how much power to give them at the expense of the as yet stillborn Iraqi provincial government in Anbar. The marine officers in question were being cautious, reluctant to create what they feared would be a de facto tribal militia that could further destabilize the already extremely dysfunctional politics of Anbar, or create a competing power structure parallel to the fledgling Iraqi government.

"The MEF was trying to work with the 'high-level' sheiks in Jordan," according to Lieutenant Colonel Tony Deane, a key player in the RFCT's first outreach efforts to Sattar. "This never bore fruit, and the locals [Iraqis who stayed in Anbar] felt the sheiks that split to Jordan lost their vote by leaving. The MEF actually were against the forming of the Anbar Awakening. They were convinced the Awakening sheiks, Sattar especially, were criminals."

But American military officers based in Ramadi, led by Patriquin, Lechner, and Deane, were doing everything they could to support the Awakening and help Sattar. At this point Patriquin viewed the provincial government as powerless, and the governor as useless.

Patriquin was increasingly apoplectic at what he saw as stupidity and incompetence on the part of a few marine staffers at MEF who were ignorant of conditions in Ramadi and, as he saw it, were trying to step on and strangle the Awakening in its crib. "This tribal campaign is going great," he told a colleague, "we are working with the tribes to build up the Iraqi police force. It's not about making tribal militias. To fight a counterinsurgency you have to connect with the local people. That's exactly what we're doing."

"Why aren't you supporting the Iraqi police?" an equally frustrated Sheik Sattar complained to Lieutenant Colonel Lechner. "We're bringing out all these guys who want to fight, not for their tribes, but for Iraq. But they're not getting paid."

"The marines don't want it," replied Lechner.

In fact, according to Brigadier General Robert Neller, the MEF's deputy for operations, the marine officers were trying mightily to carefully expedite the process of recruiting, screening, and training the new police cadets through the Iraqi Ministry of the Interior (MOI), otherwise they wouldn't get paid. "You can't just sprinkle fairy dust on people and make them policemen overnight," he explains. It was a very tough bureaucratic process for the MEF to get Iraqi government officials on board with the new program. "We did not want to bring these guys on and not be able to pay them," says Neller. "The only way to get them paid was to get MOI to issue hiring orders."

In defense of those officers at MEF who were skeptical of Sattar, it's important to point out the peak of interoffice tensions lasted for as little as three months, and that most of the MEF was fully behind the Awakening as early as October 2006, or three months later, depending on who you talk to.

Colonel MacFarland maintains that these tensions are "a bit overblown." He recalls, "Everybody was looking at us sideways, accusing us of arming Sunni militias, which was nonsense. What we were doing was bringing tribal members into the Iraqi security forces. There was certainly a surfeit of caution at the MEF level initially about dealing with Sattar. There was true disagreement over who we should be focusing our engagement on, the sheiks in Jordan, or the sheiks that were still around Ramadi. There was concern that we would alienate the sheiks in Jordan if we engaged these lesser sheiks still in Ramadi. There was a lot of healthy back-and-forth. But nobody ever told me, 'No.' They questioned me, they cautioned me, but none of my bosses ever said, 'No, don't do that.' They deserve a lot of credit for that. Those commanders were going against the recommendations of a lot of their own staff in some cases."

But at the time, the slowness of the process infuriated Sattar as well as Patriquin.

"The marines [at MEF headquarters] must be working for al-Qaeda," grumbled Sattar. "Maybe we should be fighting the marines."

Patriquin hit the roof when in September the *Washington Post* published an article by Tom Ricks based on a five-page secret situation analysis written by Colonel Peter Devlin, a military intelligence officer with the MEF.

The newspaper's initial reporting on the document, soon called the "Devlin Report," painted a very pessimistic picture, with Anbar province appearing to be irretrievably lost to al-Qaeda in Iraq. The complete document, which the *Post* published as a follow-up in November, actually was more nuanced and complex than the initial impressions of it, but the thrust of it as summarized by the *Post* was, in retrospect, off target: "The U.S. military is no longer able to defeat a bloody insurgency in western Iraq or counter al-Qaida's rising popularity there, according to newly disclosed details from a classified Marine Corps intelligence report that set off debate in recent months about the military's mission in Anbar province." In Devlin's defense, he completed the report in August 2006, weeks before the official launch of the Awakening by Sattar and his tribal allies.

"What the hell?" Patriquin fumed to a colleague upon reading the first *Washington Post* report on his computer screen. "Did you read that report? It's ridiculous! What the hell does he [Devlin] know about Ramadi? The marines [at MEF headquarters] don't even know what we're doing! They don't even ask us what's going on. When we tell them, they couldn't care less. Now they come out with this report? Police recruits are going way up! We're building police stations!"

Patriquin's close ally Lieutenant Colonel Church of the marines was caught in a tough spot bureaucratically. He commanded a mixed civil affairs detachment of forty marines and thirty soldiers that was attached to the RFCT in Ramadi, reporting to Colonel MacFarland. But Church also reported to his superior officers in the marine civil affairs chain of command at MEF headquarters. And there was one thing Church was increasingly convinced of—by backing Sheik Sattar, Captain Travis Patriquin was on the right track.

When Church had first met Patriquin upon Church's arrival in Ramadi in September 2006, he asked the army captain what his job was.

"I'm the brigade S9," Patriquin replied.

Church was a seasoned forty-three-year-old lieutenant colonel, a prior enlisted Naval Academy graduate who'd served time in Somalia and ten years on active duty before joining the reserves. He'd already spent a tour in Iraq in 2004. But he'd never heard of an S9 before.

"What the hell is an S9?" he asked.

"Key leadership engagement," replied Patriquin.

"How'd you manage that job?"

"Well, sir, I speak Arabic."

"Okay, that makes sense!" said the marine.

"Technically, I guess I should be doing the S5 [civil affairs] stuff, too," Patriquin explained, "but if I do the S5 stuff I can't talk to the Iraqis as much as I should. And that's where I'm going to make my money."

"You're exactly right," said Church, walking into Patriquin's trap.

"Somebody needs to be doing the S5 stuff," suggested Patriquin, "and sir, maybe it's you!"

Soon, Patriquin and Church struck a deal, with the blessing of MacFarland. Church took over many of the civil affairs functions for the brigade, freeing up Patriquin to focus full-time on coordinating and pushing forward American military support for the Awakening. The result, in Church's words, was that Patriquin became "close to the Iraqis in ways we can never imagine."

As Patriquin's work with Sattar and other sheiks was taking off, Church was having conversations with certain marine superiors about the Awakening that took surreal paths. The thrust of the exchanges, he remembers, went along these lines:

"Don't talk to sheiks," came the order. "We want the Iraqi government to work first."

"That's crazy!" thought Church. "It's lunacy. It's ignorance!"

"You know what?" he replied. "There is no Iraqi government out here, there's nothing—there's only sheiks."

The reply: "You've got to enable the government."

Church would counter, "There is no government! You've got a governor who sits on his ass and doesn't do jack. We've got to engage the sheiks."

"You've got to find a sheik that has no blood on his hands," came the reply.

"Are you crazy?" thought Church. "That's ridiculous. What planet are you on? Where in Iraq do you think we're going to find a leader with no blood on his hands?"

"Listen," Church explained, "we're making allies with people we're working with now, and it's the best we can do."

"Do you want progress?" a superior asked him.

"Yes," said Church.

"Then engage the government."

"There is no government."

Church thought, "Who's on first?"

One marine general based at Camp Fallujah said a member of his staff told him, "We don't know where this is going. Sattar is a fraud. This Awakening thing is just tribal militias. We can't support it. It will all blow up."

The squabbling raged in e-mail traffic, as an MEF officer criticized efforts by brigade officers like Patriquin and Church to get someone appointed to the long-vacant post of mayor for the city of Ramadi prior to as yet unscheduled municipal elections, so the people in Ramadi would have somebody, anybody, to turn to other than the U.S. military.

"Well, you'd have thought we'd shot the second coming of Christ," recalls Church.

"You can't do that," declared an e-mail from a marine officer in Fallujah. "The Iraqis have to do it themselves. Haven't you read T. E. Lawrence? 'Do not try to do too much with your own hands. Better the Arabs do it tolerably than that you do it perfectly. It is their war, and you are to help them, not to win it for them.'"

At this, Patriquin exploded in an e-mail response aimed at every marine colonel and lieutenant colonel who was being critical, the essence of which Church describes as: "That's bullshit! We know what's going on. You don't know what you're talking about. Leave us alone."

By fanning the flames of the Awakening, Patriquin saw a real hope, maybe America's only hope, of slowing down or even stopping the violence in western Iraq. He saw a chance of saving the lives of his fellow U.S. soldiers and marines, Iraqi security officers, and civilians who were still being blown up, shot, beheaded, and mortared to death regularly across the province. Patriquin saw a chance of going home the following February when his tour was up, having accomplished his mission, and the possibility of bequeathing a stable, peaceful city to his beloved Iraqi comrades.

For Patriquin to express his passion so bluntly, and to risk ticking off the brass up the chain of command, was not out of character for him. He was like Sam Damon, the hero of his favorite military novel, the Vietnam-era classic *Once an Eagle*, written by the former marine Anton Myrer and considered an essential work on leadership by legions of American military officers.

In the book, Sam Damon, a consummate soldier who treasures the lives of his troops, spans two World Wars contending with his evil nemesis Courtney Massengale, a scheming, maneuvering careerist who squanders the love of his family and the blood of his soldiers in pursuit of personal advancement.

Patriquin probably aspired to be a Sam Damon. He inspired troops who served under him, and impressed his superiors while sometimes pissing them off. He was a man who didn't shy away from staring down a colonel, or accusing a lieutenant colonel of bullshit. It was behavior driven by a confidence Patriquin gained from his years in Special Forces and from leading troops in combat, and by what he saw as the truth, but it hardly guaranteed him a greased path to the top.

"You'd better talk to that army captain," a marine officer admonished Lieutenant Colonel Church by e-mail. "Who does he think he is?"

Church approached Patriquin and said, "Put your arm out."

"What do you mean, sir?"

Church gently slapped the captain's wrist and said, "Don't do that again."

Both men smiled, and Church said, "Let me take care of those guys. They're human. They're not here every day like we are. Remember what happens when you pick a fight with a pig. You and the pig get muddy—and the pig enjoys it."

Patriquin poured his anger out to Church, explaining, "I get so frustrated, sir! These guys have no clue. They ask such stupid questions."

"You're right," said Church. "I know you're right and you know you're right, but you're pissing people off that we need to work with. You need to be right but less righteous. You're beating your head against walls you don't need to. You need to pick your fights better. Look, you're doing the right thing—you're all over it—but I'm telling you from experience that you're getting frustrated because you're putting your whole heart and soul into this thing."

Church said, "You remind me of this young captain I knew. He was real outspoken and passionate, and used to get into intellectual fights and never back down."

Patriquin asked, "Oh yeah? Who's that?"

"Me," said the marine, "ten years ago."

Tensions were getting so heated that Church was afraid the Awakening was in danger of being derailed or shut down. In late October he decided the time had come to get himself and Patriquin across a table from his direct superiors at Marine Fourth Civil Affairs Group at MEF headquarters. These marines were being more open and supportive than some of their colleagues on the MEF staff, and Church hoped that they'd convince their bosses further up the MEF chain of command to let the Awakening bloom.

Church feared that if they came across as too soft it could be a disastrous meeting, so he encouraged Patriquin to come on as strong as possible. Politically, as a marine himself, Church figured he couldn't argue the Awakening's case too aggressively, for fear of being marked a bureaucratic traitor by those marines opposed to empowering Sattar. He told Patriquin: "I want to show my bosses I have this dynamic, passionate captain who is laying the foundation for great things to happen, if you give us time, like security, so we in civil affairs can get on with the business of building hospitals, schools, roads, businesses, and infrastructure. If we can get my higher-ups to understand this they will support it more robustly—but you've got to impress them.

"Be passionate and be blunt—that's what captains do. As an army officer you'll be able to say things I can't. Be straight up, lay it on the line, and don't worry about it."

Patriquin resisted, asking, "Why do we have to do this? This is a waste of time!"

He was afraid of being pulled away from his crucial work in Ramadi for three days, and he was not looking forward to hitting a brick wall of intransigence. "Hey, you gotta trust me on this," urged Church, "it will allow us to set the tone for Colonel MacFarland. There's a bigger picture here, you need to sell this perspective—so we can control our own destiny."

Eventually, Patriquin relented, "Hey, no problem, sir, glad to do it." The officers assembled a dog and pony show for the marines, and painstakingly rehearsed it, preparing defenses and counterarguments.

As they prepared, Patriquin planned to come on strong by saying, in effect, "There are leaders of Ramadi [sheiks in Jordan being courted by MEF marine staff] who are no longer in Ramadi. Hey—screw them! Screw those guys. They're not here when it counts. Sheik Sattar is. At least he's here. That makes him more credible. I'm going to engage the leaders that are here because they're here. They're not perfect but they're here, and we're going to go with that.

"Personal relationships are critical in Iraq—I'm working with Sheik Sattar because I believe he will emerge as a 'sheik of sheiks' locally. I'm an army captain, my colonel is an army colonel. We're going to do it the army way, we're going to do what we need to do and we need you to support us. It's going to pay off in the long run." His tone would be clear: "We're not going to take direction from you."

At the meeting, Patriquin was "tremendous," according to Church, who recalls the thrust of his colleague's comments as respectful but blunt. Another RFCT officer at the meeting, Captain Aaron Dixon, recalls, "I remember Travis being very frustrated with the fact that it seemed like they were fumbling around the idea of tribal engagement without a flashlight and that every time we tried to tell them that we believed we were on the edge of something great, the 'volume on our microphones' was turned down."

After the meeting, Patriquin expressed anger at some of the questions he was asked, and he wasn't sure what the upshot of the showdown was going to be. He asked Church, "Sir, why don't your marines get it? Why don't they understand?"

But Church was delighted at Patriquin's performance and figured they might have hit a home run. In the end, Church recalls, "It was received exactly the way we wanted. We showed them we knew what we were doing. That's exactly what we hoped for, and that's exactly what happened. The meeting bought us some time and credibility."

They earned precious breathing room for the Awakening.

Back at Camp Ramadi, Church told his friend, a man he would later name his firstborn son after: "The reason I like working with you, Travis, is you are cantankerous, outspoken, profane, and very passionate about what you believe in."

Another marine officer shared a vivid impression of Patriquin with John Church.

"That captain is a cocky son of a bitch," he said.

"But he knows what he's talking about."

Patriquin worked with U.S. intelligence operatives at Shark Base to try to counter the enemy's highly effective rapid-response propaganda machinery.

The insurgents were young, highly computer-savvy masters of the Internet, of everything from blogs to online video distribution. Propaganda and psychological warfare were outside of Patriquin's job description, but he was infuriated by the military's glacially bureaucratic pace of approvals for such messages. Agencies like the CIA, however, could not only move faster, they could skirt the ironclad rules of truthfulness the military laid down for any message broadcast to Iraqis.

"We need to have a blog presence, an online voice," said Patriquin to a colleague, "and that voice needs to give the other side— our side, the side of the people."

Working with his U.S. intelligence contact and a trusted Arabic speaker, Patriquin launched a blog in Arabic that took the voice of a mythical student at al Anbar University. American forces were able to "seed" the blogger's URL around Ramadi, in part by typing it into computers at Internet cafés they raided or otherwise visited, and the intelligence agencies were able to track Internet traffic to the site.

At first, the mythical blogger was somewhat negative toward U.S. troops. As readership of the blog grew, the tone of the blog entries gradually evolved to an anti–al-Qaeda tone, and reinforced messages the Americans wanted to circulate among Ramadi citizens, especially young computer-savvy men.

Before long, U.S. forces had an effective clandestine propaganda tool operating online, in the form of a widely read popular blog—written by a character Travis Patriquin dreamed up in his head.

By late October and early November 2006, Patriquin was riding a whirlwind of action, doing deals with sub-sheiks in one district, promising construction contracts to sheiks in another, trading a new Iraqi police station in one spot for fifty new tribal police recruits in another.

With the marine civil affairs unit, Patriquin organized humanitarian convoys by the Shia-dominated Iraqi army to deliver supplies of sugar, rice, tea, and blankets into Sunni neighborhoods, a move that sharply improved the image of the Iraqi army units around Ramadi among the people.

He was going "outside the wire" and off the American base of Camp Ramadi very often by now, crisscrossing the battle zones of the city, shuttling to dinner at sheiks' houses, speaking colloquial Iraqi Arabic with them, quoting Koranic parables, eating massive amounts of goat meat with his hands, and drinking oceans of sweet Iraqi tea. One sheik, Dahir Sahar al-Duaywi of the Abu Ali Jassim tribe, later told *Time* magazine correspondent Bobby Ghosh of traveling through dangerous sections of Ramadi with Patriquin in his car disguised in a dishdasha to deflect attention.

And Patriquin was described by one colleague as "practically living" at Sheik Sattar's house.

Senior officers of both the Ready First Combat Team and the MEF in Fallujah agreed that Sattar and the Awakening had to be brought into the provincial government, and Governor Maamoun had to be persuaded to enter a give-and-take with Sattar.

By most accounts the two men hated each other, and one attempted reconciliation meeting at a ceremonial dinner degenerated into a shouting match. But the Americans kept trying to broker a marriage, and gradually the two men grudgingly started to cooperate. The Provincial Council was enlarged to include seven

Awakening members, and Sattar was appointed provincial senior terrorism advisor.

Major Niel Smith, the brigade operations officer, recalled the domino effect generated by the Awakening: "One by one, the tribes approach the SAA council and us and ask to join. We wholeheartedly accept, and when a tribe joins, an IP base is created in their area, supported by CF. The U.S. units in the area provide backup and support to the tribal fighters when attacked by AQIZ. By November, most of the area north and west of Ramadi had been secured by tribal forces backed by U.S. and Iraqi army heavy units. The main bases to the west of Ramadi received virtually no indirect fire attacks from October forward. Attacks on coalition forces in these areas drop to zero, and many caches are revealed. As each tribe comes on line, it adds to the Iraqi police recruits, and civil affairs projects are targeted to those areas." The result, wrote Smith: "Tribal engagement allowed what four years of combat operations by U.S. forces had been unable to accomplish."

"When the sheiks start inviting us to dinner," Patriquin predicted to Jim Lechner, "then we'll know we're winning." Toward the end of their brief tour in Tal Afar, the two were having lunch or dinner as the guests of Iraqis several times a week.

By November 2006, the same thing was happening to the two American officers in Ramadi.

At about the same time, the CIA station chief in Ramadi did something that helped jump-start American support for the Awakening.

He sent a cable to his bosses at the agency's headquarters in Langley, Virginia, alerting them to the news that a real change seemed to be under way in the capital of Anbar province.

According to Colonel MacFarland, "The CIA cable served as a wake-up call to the big U.S. government that what was going on in Ramadi was a tectonic shift, a really decisive development. Up to that point, everybody was buying into the line that we were nibbling around the edge of the problem, that we didn't really have a game change under way. But that cable was really important. I can't overestimate the impact of it. It was just as important in the intelligence community as the briefings that Jim Soriano [the State Department officer based in Anbar province] was giving to his superiors and the positive impact they had within the executive branch. Those two tracks are what suddenly changed the attitude in Baghdad and Fallujah and Washington, D.C., about what was happening in Ramadi, not so much what I was saying. It was what those two independent observers were reporting."

On November 18, Patriquin told Sterling Jensen he was hearing that top officials in Washington, D.C., were learning about the Sunni tribal initiative he was spearheading. "People in the Pentagon are starting to see what's going on," he told Jensen, "the Joint Chiefs of Staff and even the president are being briefed about this!"

One day in mid-December, according to Bob Woodward's book *The War Within*, Jim Soriano of the State Department was face-to-face across a secure video link with President George Bush and Secretary of State Condoleezza Rice in the White House Situation Room, telling them "things are beginning to turn" in Anbar province. President Bush, who was in the midst of deciding whether to "surge" additional tens of thousands of troops to Iraq, was thrilled at the news.

As Patriquin and Lechner's tribal outreach efforts intensified, the brigade applied simultaneous pressure on al-Qaeda with aggressive combat operations across much of the city of Ramadi, fighting their way into insurgent neighborhoods and launching combat outposts.

In November a major breakthrough came when the full Abu Alwani tribe was persuaded to "flip" to the coalition side by Governor Maamoun, himself a member of the tribe, and Sheik Sattar. A police station was soon stood up and the tribe began working with the First Battalion, Sixth Marines, led by Lieutenant Colonel William Jurney. That month, a whopping 400-plus recruits were welcomed into the Iraqi police, and Sattar received approval to field a SWAT-style 750-man paramilitary Emergency Response Unit to be attached to the Iraqi police command.

Things were happening so fast that Captain Patriquin sometimes despaired that he had little time to catch his breath, fill out his meeting reports, and get things down on paper so the rest of the brigade could know what he was up to. According to his colleague Majd Alghabra, he was also very worried that after he and his brigade left Ramadi, the success they began might not be followed up on by the next brigade.

Patriquin had only one bodyguard, a battered armored Humvee he scrounged from the Camp Ramadi motor pool, and a laptop. That was it.

He was a one-man show. His biggest problem was that he had no office staff. He was so busy meeting with sheiks that he sometimes missed office meetings and was unavailable for the brigade staff. He was hard-pressed to write anything down; he just didn't have the time.

Patriquin repeatedly begged his bosses for more resources, for at least a single staff assistant, even part-time, to help him organize briefings and paperwork.

"I am only one man," he pleaded, "can I get an NCO [noncommissioned officer] to help me, can I get someone, anyone, in the shop to help me?"

But his bosses turned him down. There were no resources to spare.

The American destiny in Iraq in part boiled down to a vast three-dimensional map Patriquin carried around in his brain, crowded with Ramadi's tribes and sub-tribes, sheiks, police chiefs, and political bosses, names, family relationships, faces, and roads, overlaid with locations of American military outposts, insurgent attacks, and "no go" zones.

The mosaic was incredibly complex and it changed on a daily, even hourly basis.

It was an impossibly intricate maze, but it symbolized a map of how America might extricate itself from Iraq.

And the only place the map existed was inside Travis Patriquin's head.

His office colleague Captain Andrew Duprey, noticing how upset Patriquin was, asked, "Dude, what's wrong?"

"If I get killed," Patriquin mused to a colleague, "they are fucked, because there's nobody to back me up."

His enthusiasm for the mission never flagged, though, and he cheered his fellow American soldiers on with the thought that they were really making a difference. On November 23 he sent an e-mail to his friend Lieutenant Brian Braithwaite, commander of Third Platoon, B Company, 1-36 Infantry attached to 1-37 Armor, a team of forty mechanized infantry soldiers patrolling the still hotly contested area of the Second Officers District in south Ramadi: "You and your boys are on the sharpest end, and that's a tough job. I'm doing all I can to keep you safe by trying to turn tribes and convert nationalist insurgents to our side, but it's hard in your area because the leadership has all fled, so the people are kind of 'feral.' But I'm working on it, I promise you.

"You and your men are at the front of my mind always. You're the reason the rest of us are here. Thanks for what you're doing, and I send every reporter I can to you when they ask me who I think is the best LT out there pounding the street, fighting, and getting to know the people.

"The changes in Ramadi, while not always visible from your Bradley in the dark of night when you're scanning your sector and watching over your men, are amazing."

Patriquin concluded, "God's plan is unknown to us, but there is a plan, I believe that with all my being, and we're all a part of it."

CHAPTER 11

THE TURNING POINT

✪

"What's the worst-case scenario for what's going on right now?"

All eyes were on Travis Patriquin as he pondered the question asked by the brigade's executive officer, Lieutenant Colonel Pete Lee. They and some thirty officers were stuffed into the conference room at Camp Ramadi for the weekly brigade targeting planning meeting they called the "BUB," or battle update brief, on Monday, November 13.

"Boss, the worst thing to have happen," Patriquin replied, "would be if al-Qaeda starts targeting these critical leaders, and either Sheik Sattar gets killed, or Sheik Jassim of the Abu Sodas gets killed." The Abu Soda tribe in Sufiyah was quickly becoming a pivotal potential "swing" group in the strategic tribal calculus of Anbar province, a domino that could set off major, unforeseen chain reactions.

"We will lose the momentum if we lose Jassim," he continued. "We will absolutely lose momentum in Sufiyah. That is a critical point in the fight."

"What can we do to prevent that?" asked Lee.

"Sir, we'll make sure these guys have got phones," said Patriquin, "so if they feel threatened or they're attacked, they can call us."

Patriquin knew that Sheik Jassim was now highly exposed to attack by al-Qaeda fighters garrisoned just a mile or two to the east. Paying a visit to Jassim to pledge his support and the backing of the U.S. military if the Sunni chieftain needed it, Patriquin gave him a prized Thuraya satellite phone, a super-lightweight device favored in Iraq by terrorists for its reliability and untraceability (unless the GPS feature was switched on), and by the U.S. military for special situations like these, as there was no reliable cell-phone service in much of Iraq.

"If you have any tips," Patriquin told Jassim, "or if you ever feel threatened, or if you ever need to contact us, here's my phone number."

There were at least two men who saw the turning point coming.

One of them was Travis Patriquin.

The other was the supreme commander of al-Qaeda in Iraq, an Egyptian-born master bomber and arch-terrorist named Abu Ayyub al-Masri.

One of the key turning points in the Iraq War occurred in a nine-hour battle that started at about one p.m. on November 25, 2006, in the district called Sufiyah, located on a peninsula that juts north into the Euphrates, a strip of farmland and houses the Americans called Sharks Fin.

It was a battle started by one Iraqi farmer who decided to defy the overlords of al-Qaeda.

Travis Patriquin was convinced, as this confrontation drew near, that nothing less than the life or death of the Awakening was hanging in the balance.

By the end of October 2006, thanks to the increasing popularity of Sheik Sattar's Awakening movement, and the Ready First Combat Team's two-pronged strategy of aggressive but highly precise combat operations, coupled with intensive outreach to tribal leaders, a campaign spearheaded by Captain Patriquin, only four tribes remained uncooperative with the U.S. military in the immediate area of Ramadi. By now seven were considered neutral and ten were cooperative, a growing but highly fragile and volatile alliance led by Sheik Sattar.

The ranks of the Iraqi police were starting to swell, and the recruits were patrolling effectively in some districts. In those sections of Ramadi it had, miraculously, become almost peaceful. However, as al-Qaeda's control of the people and the territory of Ramadi slipped, it was striking back with a vengeance, staging attacks on coalition combat outposts and on Iraqi police stations.

One focus of intense hostility remained in the areas around the rural area of Sufiyah, at the eastern edge of the city. East of Ramadi, the U.S. military was still engaging in gun battles every day, through areas called the Malaab, Sanna, Jalayba, and Sufiyah. It was "bandit country." But this might be about to change, as one tribal leader seemed on the verge of "flipping" over to the U.S. and Iraqi government side.

If we grant, as many would be ready to do, that events in Anbar province in the second half of 2006 represent a symbolic "tipping point" or "turning point" in the war, then one of the central moments of the war, a turning point within the turning point, must be the Battle of Sufiyah.

The Sufiyah district straddled the north-south line of drift that separated newly pro-coalition and coalition-leaning tribes to the west of Ramadi and neutral or al-Qaeda—dominated tribes to the east. The battle space within Sufiyah was only some three hundred meters across at its widest point, and the total number of people directly involved in the fight probably numbered fewer than two hundred. But for Iraq and for the American military in this war, the stakes have rarely been higher than they were on this day.

If the insurgents won this battle, the Anbar Awakening would likely have been strangled in its crib, tribal sheiks might have abandoned their embryonic revolt against al-Qaeda, and Anbar province might have stayed locked in a state of Hobbesian, prehistoric collapse for an indefinite period. And without the Awakening, there may not have been the successful "surge" in 2007, and less chance of the major, orderly American withdrawal of combat troops from Iraq that occurred in August 2010.

The man who lit the fuse of the battle was Sheik Jassim Muhammad Saleh al-Suwadawi. He was a former Iraqi air force officer and full-time farmer and community leader who tended a garden of pink roses in his little front yard. The hereditary sheik of Jassim's tribe, the Abu Soda, had fled Iraq, and now Jassim was jockeying to become one of its de facto leaders. Like many Anbari sheiks, he was becoming sick and tired of al-Qaeda's shockingly brutal tactics against local Sunnis, and despondent over the near total collapse of his business and the local economy caused by the continued insurgency.

Compounding Jassim's woes was the unfortunate geographical fact that his neighborhood was caught in the cross fire of an ongoing duel between American and al-Qaeda fighters. A highly skilled mobile al-Qaeda mortar team was commuting by truck from the Abu Bali area into Sufiyah, showering 81mm and 120mm shells upon Camp Corregidor, an American military outpost on the eastern edge of Ramadi, then racing back to safety in insurgent territory to the east.

In fact, Camp Corregidor had been under near continuous

mortar barrages for the past two years. American troops there were reduced to moving around the camp in helmets and full body armor at all times.

"They were knocking the shit out of Camp Corregidor on a daily basis," recalls Major Eric Remoy, the intelligence officer for Patriquin's brigade. "We could never catch these guys in the act, they were just too smart. To give you an idea of how good this mortar team was, we sent a Navy SEAL sniper team into that area to try to kill them. In response to that, the mortar team shot 60mm mortars, which we hadn't seen before, at our sniper team. The mortars landed within about fifty meters of where the SEAL snipers were, and forced us to extract them. Within two hours, the mortar team was firing 120mm mortars at Camp Corregidor—from the same position our snipers withdrew from."

It was al-Qaeda's way, explained Remoy, of saying "Fuck you. We own this ground. You don't."

From Sheik Jassim's point of view, this al-Qaeda team in his own backyard was creating an intolerable situation: they were attracting escalating American artillery counterfire, which was pounding selected "boxes" of his territory, sometimes landing short or long and falling on the property of people in his neighborhood, people he was expected to protect.

When Sheik Sattar and his comrades declared the Awakening on September 14, Sheik Jassim saw an opportunity to change the balance of power in Anbar and drive out al-Qaeda. Jassim was in a highly exposed, vulnerable position geographically—his neighborhood was ringed by the Euphrates River on the north and surrounded by al-Qaeda–dominated districts to the east, south, and west, areas that were essentially no-go zones for the American and Iraqi armies. To slip out to meet with Sattar and other Awakening members, Jassim resorted to swimming hundreds of meters across the Euphrates at night to avoid capture by al-Qaeda patrols.

Patriquin proposed a deal to Sheik Jassim: "If you can stop the al-Qaeda mortars from coming into your district, we'll stop shooting back with our howitzers."

For Jassim, the final outrage was a highly personal one. "On September 28, 2006, one of my brothers and three of my tribesmen were kidnapped," he later explained. "Then I declared open hostilities against the terrorists, and I established checkpoints in my territory."

Sheik Jassim decided to set up four checkpoints on the main roads of Sufiyah to block insurgents, manned by armed young local Sunni men, members of his Abu Soda tribe joined by members of the neighboring Abu Mahal clan, deployed in anti–al-Qaeda tribal patrols, the successors of which the Americans would later call "neighborhood watch groups" and "Sons of Iraq."*

On Sheik Jassim's order, the checkpoints went up.

Over the next months, similar Sunni tribal patrols would spread exponentially through Anbar, into Sunni districts of western Baghdad and then around the capital, and eventually into other sections of the nation, in a shift that would help transform the war in Iraq.

It all started at this moment of the war, in mid-November 2006 in Sufiyah, on a road the Americans called Route Nova. The tribal force began blocking outsiders from driving into Sufiyah. This was one of the first serious Sunni anti–al-Qaeda tribal forces of the war operating outside the Iraqi police or Iraqi army. Some of the young men in the patrols had themselves been al-Qaeda or other insurgent sympathizers or fighters until literally days before.

The lightly armed, un-uniformed Sunni volunteers went out

---

*The previous year, in fact, the CIA initiated an armed neigborhood watch pilot project with one small Ramadi tribe, another precursor of the "Sons of Iraq."

on patrol on foot and in pickup trucks. For two weeks, the al-Qaeda mortar fire stopped. The insurgent mortar teams couldn't get through the roadblocks into Sufiyah.

For the first time in two years, American soldiers could walk around Camp Corregidor without wearing full body armor.

Looking on, Travis Patriquin was thrilled, and hugely impressed. "Man, this guy's legit!" he told a colleague. "Sufiyah is a really, really hot neighborhood. But they're doing exactly what Jassim said they would. They're credible."

"I've only got fifty guys," Sheik Jassim told Patriquin on a satellite phone call in mid-November. "We are facing al-Qaeda by ourselves. We need help. We've got the men, all we need is for you to put up barriers in certain areas, and to get us an Iraqi army and Iraqi police presence out here."

This made good sense to Patriquin, who started getting the wheels in motion to fulfill Jassim's requests.

But now things started happening at a much faster velocity than anybody expected.

Abu Ayyub al-Masri, the commander of al-Qaeda in Iraq, decided it was time to kill the Anbar Awakening.

The anti–al-Qaeda revolt was getting out of hand, making sudden, strong headway with the tribes in west Ramadi and tempting the tribes elsewhere in Anbar to consider joining.

Al-Masri was so concerned about the threat posed to al-Qaeda that he decided to travel to the insurgent stronghold of the Abu Bali district, a five-minute drive east of Sufiyah, to personally take charge of an operation to crush the Awakening—by buying off, terrorizing, or killing Sheik Jassim.

Abu Ayyub al-Masri had killed many people before. Legions of Iraqi men, women, and children had died in attacks by his hand or under his supervision.

Earlier that year, he claimed to have personally cut the heads off two kidnapped, tortured American privates of the 101st Airborne Division, Thomas Tucker and Kristian Menchaca, after they were dragged by a pickup truck at high speed across the back roads of the Sunni "Triangle of Death" before being set on fire. It was supposedly in retaliation for the gang rape of Abeer Qasim Hamza, a fourteen-year-old Iraqi woman, and the murder-incineration of her and her entire family at the hands of U.S. soldiers from the same unit, but this justification may have been applied retroactively.

Now, by neutralizing a pivotal Iraqi tribal leader, he could kill an entire movement.

Al-Masri's high-pitched voice and giggling manner belied the fact that he was the most wanted and talented terrorist in Iraq, following the death in a U.S. air strike five months earlier of his boss, Abu Musab al-Zarqawi.

An explosives expert who supervised networks of suicide bombers and car-bomb factories, al-Masri masterminded a clandestine superhighway that channeled floods of foreign fighters and suicide bombers into Iraq from Syria and beyond, four thousand of whom, he proudly claimed, had died fighting the occupiers.

Al-Masri's jihadist pedigree dated to 1982, when he became a disciple of Ayman al-Zawahiri, the Egyptian doctor who later cofounded al-Qaeda with Osama bin Laden. Al-Masri graduated from bin Laden's elite al Farouq training complex in Afghanistan in 1999–2000, where he met al-Zarqawi, and established one of the first insurgent cells in Baghdad soon after the U.S. invasion. Since the killing by U.S. forces of the famously thuggish al-Zarqawi, al-Masri was waging a national campaign of negotiation and outreach to the many Iraqi insurgent factions that floated in and out of alliance with his loose terrorist umbrella amalgamation known as al-Qaeda in Iraq, or al-Qaeda in Mesopotamia, among other names.

Col. Sean MacFarland, Sheik Sattar abu Risha, founder of the Awakening movement of Iraq, and Cpt. Travis Patriquin (*left to right*). The partnership of these three men and their colleagues symbolized a turning point in the Iraq War that saved thousands of lives, dealt a major blow to al-Qaeda and allowed the United States to begin withdrawing many of its combat forces from Iraq.

Lt. Patriquin at Bagram Air Base, Afghanistan, early 2002. After September 11, 2001, he hustled his way from the sidelines into the first wave of American troops to strike back at al-Qaeda.

Patriquin (*third from left*) meeting Joint Chiefs of Staff Vice Chairman Admiral Edmund Giambastiani (*second from left*) with other officers of his brigade in Tal Afar, Iraq, early 2006. The expression on Patriquin's face is typical of his often skeptical attitude toward military brass.

Patriquin in Iraq, 2006. In the words of one Iraqi, the Iraqi people "absolutely adored Travis." His mustache and his knowledge of colloquial street Arabic helped him fit in. But what stunned people was the degree to which Patriquin, an Arabic linguist, respected and loved Arab culture. He had a plan for victory in Iraq that he was determined to put into action. "I want to win," he said.

An Iraqi Police Emergency Response Unit in Ramadi. Patriquin thought that recruiting thousands of new Iraqi Police was crucial to shifting the order of battle against al-Qaeda. At a key moment, CIA agents stepped in to help.

Patriquin at his desk at Camp Ramadi. "I am leading a tribal revolt against al-Qaeda along the Euphrates," he announced. He was only a captain, but was doing the negotiating work of a general or top diplomat. At his desk, Patriquin created complex tribal maps of the province that contained the earliest designs of a successful U.S. withdrawal from Iraq.

Patriquin with brigade interpreter Sterling Jensen. The two shared a love for Middle Eastern culture, and found themselves inside a remarkable moment in history.

Patriquin and his brigade deputy commanding officer Lt. Col. Jim Lechner, along with an interpreter at left, as guests at an Iraqi tribal sheik's house. The war in al Anbar province was turned around on the battlefield, and in scenes like this, as American officers negotiated with Iraqis over countless cups of chai tea and thousands of cigarettes. Patriquin was a master of these talks.

A mosque in downtown Ramadi. Patriquin knew Arabic verses of the Koran and thought that Islam could be used to great advantage by the Americans. But there was one thing about Islam that especially angered him— when people who didn't know what they were talking about criticized the religion.

Col. Sean MacFarland with Iraqi Police. Some of his superiors worried that MacFarland was "going rogue" by talking to insurgents and standing up an unauthorized tribal militia.

U.S. tank opens fire in Ramadi, 2006. The success of the Awakening was impossible without aggressive combat operations by thousands of soldiers and marines.

Patriquin in Iraq, 2006.

All photos this page courtesy of Amy Patriquin

Sheik Sattar with Major Megan McClung, U.S. Marine Corps. The triathlete and Naval Academy graduate worked with Patriquin to tell the world the great news of was happening in Ramadi: The war was beginning to turn around.

Sheik Sattar and Iraqi police at the Martyr Hisham abu Risha Iraqi Police Station celebrate victory in battle over al-Qaeda in 2007.

Travis Patriquin's triumph: on the Euphrates weeks before his brigade's joint victory with Sunni tribesmen against al-Qaeda at the Battle of Sufiyah, the "turning point inside the turning point" of a crucial phase of the Iraq War. He did not have long to live, but Patriquin already saw his dream beginning to come true.

But the outreach campaign was not going well, and a large Anbari section of the 1920 Revolution Brigades was cracking off from the main group and joining Sattar's Awakening movement. Elsewhere in Iraq, isolated, scattered skirmishes and gun battles were being reported between various insurgent gangs and al-Qaeda forces, often triggered by al-Qaeda's attempts to impose extremely radicalized versions of Islamic law.

In mid-November 2006, Abu Ayyub al-Masri secretly arrived in the Abu Bali area east of Ramadi and called a meeting of his senior fighters there, according to intelligence later pieced together by U.S. analysts. Insurgents still had freedom of movement around wide areas of Anbar, but this was being threatened by the Awakening and by what was happening in the Sufiyah district.

A few miles southeast of Sheik Jassim's house, al-Masri sent a message from his temporary command post to Sheik Jassim with a simple, chilling order: "Take the checkpoints down within seventy-two hours or we will kill you and everyone in your tribe." This was standard procedure for al-Qaeda in Iraq; instead of killing a target of influence right away, they'd usually start with a warning delivered in person or in a "night letter" delivered to the doorstep.

"On the 24th of November I negotiated with some of the chieftains in al-Qaeda to try to avert mayhem," recalled Sheik Jassim. "They negotiated with me to lay down my arms, and they offered me as much as 1 billion Iraqi dinars [about US$900,000]. At the time, they had already decided beforehand that if I couldn't turn an agreement with them right then and there, they would kidnap me and do away with me. They had prepared seventeen vehicles loaded with men and weapons to kidnap me. The meeting took place at Sheik Hamid Jabour's house. I wanted to delay the confrontation with them to a later time when I could better equip myself with men and matériel, but I kind of sensed they were up to no good. I had five armed men with me, and we pulled out of the meeting."

The same day, al-Qaeda fighters killed a member of the neighboring Abu Mahal tribe, which included Sheik Jassim's cousins. Enraged, the sheik called his al-Qaeda contacts and announced, "Look, you've opened another wound. You've just killed one of my tribesmen from the Abu Mahal. We've just agreed that there will be no killing. Therefore, no agreement, no peace with you, period!"

For some reason these warnings and conversations were not passed on to the U.S. military, and Jassim's checkpoints stayed up as the clock ticked to the zero hour declared by the al-Qaeda boss, al-Masri.

Patriquin's satellite phone rang soon after one p.m. the afternoon of Friday, November 25.

"We're under attack!" exclaimed Sheik Jassim. "I've got my men here, we're establishing defensive positions and we're going to fight these guys off. The fight is going on now. We need American help!"

Patriquin assured Jassim he'd do what he could, hung up, and called Sheik Sattar and his deputies for more information, asking, "What do you know?" The reply: "The Abu Sodas are under attack, their people are getting killed. Al-Qaeda is going through houses and massacring them. They really need your help up there."

At an Iraqi army outpost on the north bank of the Euphrates River, soldiers spotted a small flotilla of boats streaming away from Sufiyah, stuffed with panicked civilians, who reported a rampage by irahabi, or terrorists, across the river.

The news flashed to the Tactical Operations Center, or "TOC," at Camp Ramadi, where senior U.S. officers of the brigade quickly gathered with Patriquin to take positions around computerized battle stations around the large room. Three giant TV-computer screens, nicknamed "Bubbavisions," dominated the wall, which projected battle maps and live video feeds.

Patriquin's boss, Colonel MacFarland, was away on leave, so decision-making authority passed collectively to the group of senior officers Patriquin was soon huddling with, and to Lieutenant Colonel Chuck Ferry at Camp Corregidor, the closest U.S. outpost to Sufiyah. Ferry and his translator were also getting frantic calls from Sheik Jassim, pleading for assistance.

Patriquin had "seen this movie" before. He well remembered the story of what happened a year ago when the tribes last tried to turn against al-Qaeda. Sheiks were assassinated, the Americans did nothing, the revolt was crushed, and al-Qaeda was triumphant. "We can't let this happen again," Patriquin thought.

He reviewed the options with his fellow officers. "This is critically important." Patriquin announced, "If we lose the Abu Soda, we lose the Awakening. We have got to help the Abu Sodas. This is the absolute worst-case scenario if we lose Sheik Jassim. If we lose him, we will lose the momentum. This is where we've got to make a stand."

Patriquin's colleagues agreed.

Captain Patriquin called Jassim back with an urgent recommendation: "Call Chuck Ferry at Camp Corregidor." Jassim got through to him at about three p.m., then braced himself for the attack. He was badly outnumbered and outgunned.

When al-Qaeda launched the assault, Jassim could muster only seventeen men, equipped with Motorola radios, AK-47s, and thirty or forty rounds of ammunition per piece. The sheik and his men faced a synchronized surprise assault by a large force of al-Qaeda fighters, all of them wearing masks and colored headdresses. U.S. military analysts estimated the force to number from

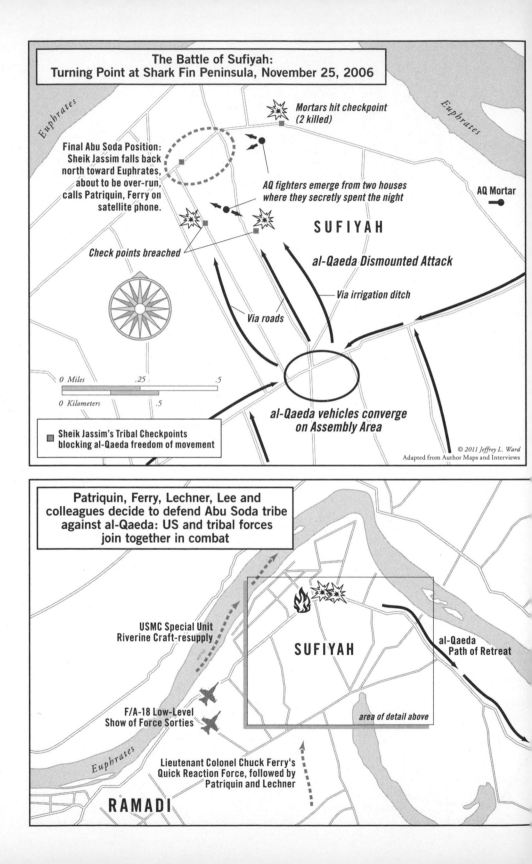

The Battle of Sufiyah:
Turning Point at Shark Fin Peninsula, November 25, 2006

Euphrates

Euphrates

Mortars hit checkpoint
(2 killed)

Final Abu Soda Position:
Sheik Jassim falls back
north toward Euphrates,
about to be over-run,
calls Patriquin, Ferry on
satellite phone.

AQ fighters emerge from two houses
where they secretly spent the night

AQ Mortar

Check points breached

SUFIYAH

al-Qaeda Dismounted Attack

Via irrigation ditch

Via roads

0 Miles   .25   .5

0 Kilometers   .5

*al-Qaeda vehicles converge
on Assembly Area*

■ Sheik Jassim's Tribal Checkpoints
blocking al-Qaeda freedom of movement

© 2011 Jeffrey L. Ward
Adapted from Author Maps and Interviews

Patriquin, Ferry, Lechner, Lee and
colleagues decide to defend Abu Soda tribe
against al-Qaeda: US and tribal forces
join together in combat

USMC Special Unit
Riverine Craft-resupply

SUFIYAH

al-Qaeda
Path of Retreat

F/A-18 Low-Level
Show of Force Sorties

area of detail above

Euphrates

Lieutenant Colonel Chuck Ferry's
Quick Reaction Force, followed by
Patriquin and Lechner

RAMADI

(map opposite) In November 2006 the supreme commander of al-Qaeda in Iraq, master terrorist Abu Ayyub Al Masri, entered the Ramadi area to personally take charge of a major operation to kill the Awakening. The target was Sheik Jassim of the Abu Soda tribe in the Sufiyah district. al-Qaeda's plan was to stage a lightning surprise attack to sweep and clear the Shark Fin Peninsula, using squads of light infantry armed with small arms, mortars, grenades and RPGs, in a classic use of combined arms, fire and movement. Additionally, al-Qaeda fighters would apply the "scorched earth" tactic of incinerating everything along their lines of attack. Sheik Jassim was in a remote location largely surrounded by insurgent strongholds, and he and his tribal fighters were outnumbered by at least 3 to 1.

—

(map below) When the attack started, Captain Travis Patriquin instantly realized that the fate of the Awakening was at stake, and possibly the course of the war in Anbar Province. He and his colleagues, including Lieutenant Colonels Chuck Ferry, Jim Lechner, Pete Lee, Joe Harrington and Majors Andy Shoffner, Eric Remoy, Andy Gainey and Niel Smith, made a spontaneous decision to attempt a counterattack and rescue.

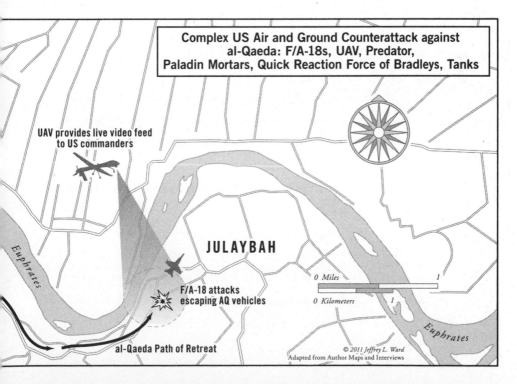

Complex US Air and Ground Counterattack against al-Qaeda: F/A-18s, UAV, Predator, Paladin Mortars, Quick Reaction Force of Bradleys, Tanks

UAV provides live video feed to US commanders

Euphrates

JULAYBAH

F/A-18 attacks escaping AQ vehicles

0 Miles   1

0 Kilometers   1

al-Qaeda Path of Retreat

Euphrates

© 2011 Jeffrey L. Ward
Adapted from Author Maps and Interviews

fifty to a hundred, armed with RPGs, mortars, knives, grenades, and machine guns.

But to Sheik Jassim, it felt like he was being attacked by 850 men.

Al-Qaeda pickup trucks raced in from four directions and converged at an assembly point in an open field south of the village of Sufiyah.

Dozens of fighters dismounted and began sweeping north on foot through the palm groves toward Sufiyah. They traveled in three parallel formations, hopscotching in echelons toward Sheik Jassim's compound, firing AK-47s, rocket-propelled grenades, and mortars in close coordination, pausing to burn down houses, shoot up electrical generators, and summarily shoot old men, women, children, and livestock.

Near the banks of the Euphrates, an al-Qaeda mortar squad set up a post, opened fire, adjusted their aim, and started "walking in rounds" toward Jassim's easternmost checkpoint. Soon they scored a direct hit, killing two of Jassim's men.

In the middle of the village of Sufiyah, hidden al-Qaeda fighters popped out of two houses they had secretly stayed in overnight and opened fire on anything that moved.

For al-Qaeda in Iraq, this was a large and well-coordinated battlefield maneuver. They and other insurgent groups were staging increasingly complex attacks, using suicide-vest explosives and enormous truck bombs carrying thousands of tons of explosives, assaults that sometimes involved multiple detonations and follow-on attacks. But what was notable about this attack was that it was a classic use of combined arms, fire and movement, using "boots on the ground" and small arms as the spearhead.

Sheik Jassim linked up by radio with seven volunteer snipers from the allied Abu Mahal clan to the east, who raced over to join in the fight by opening fire laterally on the enemy columns marching northward.

One of the few advantages held by the Abu Soda and Abu Mahal tribesmen was that they were locals. They knew every back alley and fence in Sufiyah. Thanks to their efforts the insurgents were losing time, repeatedly pausing their attack to evacuate their dead and wounded.

"We used rooftops and ground emplacements, and we picked them off," recalled Sheik Jassim. "We knew who they were because they were wearing masks. Our faces were open. We used maneuver to our advantage. Whenever we got pushed back, we pulled back. Whenever the force was overwhelming, we pulled back to other more secure places."

But Jassim's forces, running low on ammunition, were retreating north toward the Euphrates, where they would be trapped with their backs to the river.

It was getting dark, and the battery on his satellite phone was running out.

Inside his post at Camp Corregidor a few kilometers southwest of the attack, Lieutenant Colonel Chuck Ferry could hear the sounds of the battle raging at Sufiyah.

An experienced combat veteran of tours in Mogadishu, Afghanistan, and Iraq, Ferry's instinct was to go up there and fight. However, there was no plan in place for a rescue operation of this kind. This was all new. In fact, there had never been a major case of combat cooperation between Sunni tribes and the U.S. military before in the history of the Iraq War, other than the joint operations between U.S. troops and Sunni tribesmen that occurred the year before in the city of Al Qaim.

Ferry and his fellow American officers would have to improvise on the spot.

Until now, the brigade had been gearing up for a major surprise combat offensive to clear al-Qaeda strongpoints downtown
in the city of Ramadi, which was supposed to begin in two days,
spearheaded by Lieutenant Colonel Ferry's battalion.

Now they'd have to ditch that operation and throw everything
into helping the Abu Soda.

Ferry considered the difficulty of fighting his way north along
Route Apple to try to reach the Abu Soda tribe. He didn't know the
area very well and it was assumed to be heavily infested with al-
Qaeda fighters and ambush points. He could only attempt a rescue
with a huge amount of combat power.

Ferry struggled briefly with the idea of launching a rescue, as it
would completely upend Colonel MacFarland's planned offensive
in the city, and MacFarland was outside Iraq at the moment. "I'm
changing his plan while he's gone," Ferry worried. But he knew
MacFarland well enough to believe he would approve, and the U.S.
Army leaves wide latitude for commanders to take the initiative.

Ferry also worried that this might be some kind of baited
ambush, as he didn't know much about the Sufiyah area, and almost
nothing about the Abu Soda tribe. His battalion had arrived in
Ramadi only a few weeks earlier. But he figured since al-Qaeda was
killing civilians, he had to try and stop it.

Over the radio, he told his colleagues in the TOC at Camp
Ramadi, "I am launching a counterattack force from Camp Corregidor going north to relieve him." Not knowing how fast he could
get to Jassim, Ferry called in close air support, including two
F/A-18 Hornets and a Predator drone armed with Hellfire missiles,
all under his direct control.

The officers of the Ready First Combat Team made the quick
decision to do something very new in the Iraq War—to launch a
joint combat operation between U.S. forces and Sunni tribes.

Ferry figured it might take as long as two or three hours to fight their way up. "Screw it," thought Ferry. "We're going to go up there and help this guy." He began assembling a "quick reaction force" rescue convoy of about 120 soldiers traveling in M1 tanks, Humvees, and Bradley armored fighting vehicles. "On numerous occasions during the fight into Jassim's position," remembers Ferry, "we moved on foot while the vehicles remained on the road in order to clear houses and protect the tanks while they moved through obstacles."

Through the afternoon, multiple pieces of the American military machine were coming together spontaneously and with zero prior planning to rescue the Abu Sodas, and with them the Anbar Awakening.

The pieces included U.S. infantry, heavy artillery, tanks and Bradleys; army and Joint Special Operations Command (JSOC) unmanned aerial surveillance vehicles armed with cameras and bombs; JSOC helicopters, Marine attack aircraft, and Navy SEALs. Three high-tech Tactical Operations Centers were patched in, at Camp Corregidor, Camp Ramadi, and the adjacent Joint Special Operations base. Even marine gunboats would jump into the fight, making it a land, air, and sea operation.

Captain Patriquin was shuttling between the Camp Ramadi TOC and the adjacent intelligence analysis center, glued to his phone in constant conversation with Jassim, Sattar, and other sheiks, trying to manage the flow of information to different pieces of the U.S. military.

An unmanned "Shadow" UAV (unmanned aerial vehicle) was now hovering over the battle area, providing a live video feed of the landscape. And as he watched the al-Qaeda attack unfold in real time, Patriquin was in despair. It looked like Sheik Jassim was doomed.

"We're coming, we're coming, hang on, we're coming!" Patriquin exclaimed in Arabic to Jassim repeatedly by phone through the battle.

The UAV video feed revealed al-Qaeda fighters converging toward the periphery of Sheik Jassim's compound, firing AK-47s and mortars. Jassim and his men fell back north toward the river. The insurgents set Jassim's house on fire, as they were doing with other houses in Sufiyah.

It was about four p.m. when the guns-blazing images of al-Qaeda fighters on the giant screens came into the same frame as pockets of Abu Soda fighters, and someone in the Camp Ramadi TOC announced, "There's a ton of shit going on and we can't really tell what's going on and who's who!"

Darkness was falling and Sheik Jassim and his men dug into a final stand almost with their backs to the Euphrates. Their only lucky break was that it was a good defensive position, an embankment elevated up to about rooftop level, and it afforded his men an open field of fire on the advancing al-Qaeda fighters.

But from the TOC, the figures on the screen were blending together into a chaotic melee. There was no way to distinguish friend from foe. From the air, the bad guys and the good guys all looked pretty much the same. The Americans couldn't attack the insurgents from the air, for fear of killing now friendly tribal fighters.

Patriquin asked Sheik Jassim to describe his exact location and the positions of his tribesmen, but there was no way to tell in the chaos. The Americans were powerless to prevent Jassim and his men from being massacred before their eyes on live TV.

The Sunni tribal fighters were on the verge of being overrun. "The coalition forces were asking me for the exact location of the enemy, but when the enemy penetrated my area, everything was intermingled," recalled Jassim. "In military terms, when everything is intermingled, there is no specific target, so the battle is lost."

Then Travis Patriquin had a brainstorm.

"Hey," he exclaimed in Arabic over the Thuraya, "have your men take out white rags and wave them over your heads! Any pieces of cloth, wave them over your heads! We've got observation in the air, so we can start to figure out where the hell you guys are and direct our fire and support."

This was the kind of logic that Patriquin's colleagues would describe as "pure Trav." His intellectual trademark in the army was thinking in a way that captured the simplest, most effective solution to a problem, expressed in a way that would be understood by the most junior private or a four-star general.

"War is not always that complicated," thought Patriquin, and sometimes the solutions were of such a "duh"-level simplicity that he would jokingly express them in the voice of a mythical "knuckle-dragging Bubba" soldier, or even the maniacal, snickering voice of *South Park*'s Cartman.

It is not known if Patriquin heard of this particular idea before or made it up on the spot, but it emerged spontaneously from his mind today, and it was brilliant.

Sheik Jassim passed on Patriquin's instructions to his fighters.

On the UAV feed, the American officers saw white handkerchiefs popping up and being waved all across the battle area, along with headgear, shirts, and towels.

Now that they could see where the battle lines were, Marine Corps F/A-18 fighter jets called in by Lieutenant Colonel Ferry could perform low-level "show of force" sorties or "dry fire gun runs" over the al-Qaeda positions, without opening fire. The lines were still too close together and intermixed in spots to open fire, but flying at less than one thousand feet, the jets made a hell of a lot of noise, and it was hoped this would intimidate the insurgents, convince them that an air attack was imminent, and scare them off, or at least slow their momentum.

The brigade had eight large self-propelled Paladin howitzer artillery pieces, both at Camp Ramadi, twelve kilometers west of Sufiyah, and closer in at Lake Habbaniyah. Each piece was crewed by a nine-man team and all were commanded by army Lieutenant Colonel Joe Harrington.

The Paladins were the size of a tank and very precise in their ability both to pinpoint the source of hostile fire at long ranges and to lock onto it with radar. From the Camp Ramadi TOC, Harrington ordered the Paladins to pump out smoke rounds and nearly a hundred 155mm high-explosive rounds in the fields around the al-Qaeda attackers, to slow their advance.

The presumably stunned al-Qaeda fighters, who had no reason to expect the Americans to jump into the battle, much less this fast and this big, showed signs of confusion, and their advance slowed. In some spots they were breaking off contact. The dramatic demonstration of American presence, and firepower, seemed to be working.

Sheik Jassim noticed that as soon as the American jets screamed overhead, the al-Qaeda advance began to collapse.

Meanwhile, Ferry and his relief column were hitting major problems on their journey north to the battle zone. "The road march was about six or seven kilometers," remembered Ferry, "all through IED-infested insurgent-held territory."

Al-Qaeda fighters had blockaded the route.

Ferry recalled, "We came across something I've never seen in Iraq or Afghanistan: palm trees cut down and thrown across the road, interlaced with IEDs, which I was very surprised to see. I had the tanks use high-explosive rounds to basically blow away the trees, obstacles, and IEDs to make a path. And then my infantrymen, fighting on foot, cleared the pathway in front of the tanks," one of which was hit by an IED but not disabled.

Halfway up toward Sufiyah, said Ferry, "We had several insurgent vehicles come flying down the road at us, and we destroyed those with tank and small-arms fire."

It was now totally dark and Ferry couldn't figure out where Sheik Jassim was, so he had his interpreter explain to the sheik how to use the GPS feature on his Thuraya phone. Soon Jassim reported that they were still under heavy attack but that the Americans were getting so close he thought he could hear them. The two men agreed for the tribesmen to build a giant signal fire to help the Americans home in on them.

In the brigade TOC, Patriquin and his colleagues watched as the UAV feed revealed a gruesome sight.

Al-Qaeda fighters were withdrawing en masse from the scene into pickup trucks and cars, four of which were dragging dead bodies in the road by ropes and chains. They were the bodies of Abu Soda and Abu Mahal tribesmen, and the insurgents were mutilating them as war trophies to insult and terrorize the tribes.

This was a stupid move, as it allowed the UAV to lock onto their images and track them as they headed east toward their home bases of Julaybah and the Abu Bali peninsula. "For us it was brilliant," recalls Major Eric Remoy, "because it provided clear hostile intent and positive ID." According to Lieutenant Colonel Pete Lee, "As the bad guys retreated, we went after them. We were pretty aggressive in our approach to killing bad guys. We followed the ROE [rules of engagement] very strictly, but if we had positive ID we would go after them pretty damn quickly."

Now there were multiple U.S. aircraft shadowing the al-Qaeda

withdrawal: a Marine Corps F/A-18, the brigade's unarmed reconnaissance Shadow UAV, and an armed Predator UAV under the
control of the Special Operations task force unit at Camp Ramadi.

The Marine F/A-18 pilot followed one set of two vehicles eastward until they were stationary and the area cleared, and got the
green light to engage from Lee and the brigade fire support officer,
Major Andrew Gainey, as well as Lieutenant Colonel Ferry.

At six fifteen p.m. the jet opened fire with its 20mm cannon,
igniting large secondary explosions and destroying the vehicles
and several enemy fighters. The aircraft soon dispatched a third
vehicle, and the Predator destroyed a fourth vehicle farther out
with a Hellfire missile. About fifteen to twenty insurgents died in
these air-to-surface strikes.

At Camp Ramadi, Patriquin and Lieutenant Colonel Jim Lechner prepared a second rescue column to race up to Sufiyah and
reinforce the tribes.

Patriquin knew one of the most urgent needs of the tribesmen
now was more guns and ammunition to replace their stocks emptied in the battle. He and Lechner came up with an off-the-books
solution: They raided their own vault of captured al-Qaeda AK-47
rifles and ammo, piled the goods into a Bradley fighting vehicle,
and set off in the night.

Patriquin was intensely focused on getting face-to-face with
Sheik Jassim and showing him the Americans were there to sup-
port him. He kept repeating his satellite phone mantra to the sheik:
"Hang on—we're coming!"

Thinking forward several days, the U.S. brigade's operations
officer considered the logistics of resupplying Jassim's forces, to follow up on what Patriquin and Lechner could scrounge up tonight.
Major Andy Shoffner faced the difficulties of freely moving relief
columns from Camp Ramadi to Sufiyah without a major combat

operation; they did not yet have reliable freedom of movement through the city.

But the Americans did have "freedom of the seas" up and down the Euphrates River. The marines at Camp Blue Diamond had a Dam Security Unit patrolling the river, consisting of up-armored forty-foot gunboats. So Major Shoffner briefed the marines and they prepared to launch a waterborne three-day cycle of supplies for the beleaguered tribes, including medical supplies and evacuation boats in case ground and air operations were impossible.

At ten thirty p.m., Chuck Ferry managed to zero in on Sheik Jassim's giant signal fire, find the tribal leader, and start to secure the area and treat and evacuate casualties. "It was a very surreal scene," Ferry recalled, "nighttime, smoke, houses on fire, we were in a very dynamic area, lots of men running around heavily armed with guns, and they all looked like insurgents. We couldn't tell friend from foe."

He was still concerned about the possibilities of a trap, or a renegade tribesman opening fire on the Americans.

"Okay, look," Ferry told the sheik, "I'm here to help you—but if any of your men tries anything funny we will shoot them down in a heartbeat. Tell me what the situation is, tell me where the bad guys are, and tell me where your guys are. We'll mark all your men with white tape on their sleeve to ID them as friendly. Give me some of your most trusted men and take me where the enemy is."

Then for the first time in Ramadi, platoons of U.S. Army troops went out on patrol with Sunni tribesmen, to protect Iraqi civilians against terrorist attack.

When Patriquin and Lieutenant Colonel Lechner finally linked up with Sheik Jassim very late that night, Lechner recalled, "The minute we walked in that room, the sheik's face just lit up and you could tell he knew everything was going to be okay. We brought in all the AK-47s and .50-caliber machine guns and a lot of ammo. It was like Christmas morning with all the stuff we brought."

Lieutenant Colonel Ferry ordered in helicopters to insert a U.S. infantry platoon around Sheik Jassim's compound. The choppers evacuated the sheik and his wounded to Camp Corregidor.

The final number of Iraqi casualties of the battle was unclear, but Sheik Jassim reported about seventeen of his tribal fighters and civilians were "martyred," and a U.S. Army analysis found that "data would account for totals of 45–60 AQ fighters killed that day, although the reports varied and were hard to sort out." Such numbers would make it an unusually bloody defeat for the insurgents. There were some U.S. casualties from IEDs and small-arms fire, but no fatalities.

Patriquin, Lechner, Ferry, and their colleagues worked quickly to exploit the success of the Battle of Sufiyah.

"The next day," reported Ferry, "we conducted a helicopter air assault with more combat power back into Sufiyah, and after that we never left." Within forty-eight hours the Americans airdropped leaflets over Sufiyah celebrating the victory, announcing that the Abu Soda had won the fight and al-Qaeda had been defeated.

Sheik Jassim started an information campaign of his own: "I started an education program, trying to educate people to the fact that we were a small band of men who defeated a huge number of men. God granted us the victory because we were in the right and the terrorists were in the wrong. So I was able to bring in many people on my side. Eastern Ramadi has about twelve tribes. Within three months, I was able to enlist many of these tribes into the police fold."

With the victory, Jassim became the paramount leader of his tribe. The word on the street was that Jassim had bought a special chopping machine, into which he would feed terrorists to be chopped to pieces. After the battle, Sheik Sattar proudly referred to Sheik Jassim as the Lion of East Ramadi.

Sattar's Awakening movement gained a sharp burst of new credibility, prestige, and power with the rescue of the Abu Sodas, a wave of momentum that continued through 2007 and early 2008, when the province was largely pacified.

If the Americans had done nothing, or if the rescue had failed and the Abu Soda tribe had been wiped out, it is highly likely that the Awakening movement would have stalled then and there. It may even have completely collapsed at that point in time, and the Sunni tribes of Anbar could have written off any further cooperation with the U.S. military, this time for good.

But with victory, the game-changing impact of the battle was almost immediate. "We established a patrol base in Sufiyah as a base of operations to expand out and start working to kill or capture al-Qaeda," reported Lieutenant Colonel Ferry, "and to recruit other sheiks and tribes. That started a series of events that slowly one by one flipped all the tribes in eastern Ramadi. There was still a lot of combat and casualties to come, but that was kind of the starting point of the turnaround. We had a constant fight against IEDs and small arms for another six weeks until we beat it down."

Reflecting on the battle, Colonel MacFarland agreed: "After the fight, the Abu Sodas said, 'Okay, we're ready now to stand up and join with the coalition to fight al-Qaeda. We're not going to be intimidated anymore.' The other Sufiyah tribes began to flip to our side as well, and that enabled us to establish a permanent presence up there."

"In the broader context of things, the battle represented the cresting of the hill in our efforts to achieve irreversible momentum versus AQ in Ramadi," wrote Major Eric Remoy. "To my recollection, the attack against the tribes in the Sofia was the last concerted effort by AQ to mount a counterattack to our offensive operations in Ramadi during the tenure of the Ready First Combat Team. The direct involvement by AAM [al-Qaeda chieftain Abu Ayyub al-Masri] highlights the importance that AQ placed on this fight, and the operational impact that Ramadi posed to AQ strategic efforts in Iraq."

"We kicked al-Qaeda's ass in its own backyard," was how Major Joe Harrington put it.

"Right then and there," explained Sheik Abdul Rahman al-Janabi of the Abu Mahal tribe, "the barrier of fear was broken in all of Ramadi, so open warfare against the terrorists took place."

Later, General George Casey, the commander of U.S. forces in Iraq, chose November 28, 2006, as the date marking the moment the "kinetic phase of operations" in Ramadi was finished.

For Colonel MacFarland, the critical point of the battle was Travis Patriquin's brainstorm when the tribe was about to be overrun and he told Sheik Jassim, in Arabic, how to identify themselves. "With that we were able to break the back of the attack and the enemy began to withdraw. We were able to pursue them and wipe out a lot of al-Qaeda fighters in the process. It was his linguistic ability and his quick, out-of-the-box thinking that saved the day for the Abu Sodas.

"It was Travis's idea."

CHAPTER 12

A SOLDIER'S DREAM

★

"I always dream about Ramadi," said Patriquin as he puffed on a cigar.

One day while relaxing with the interpreter Sa'ad Mohammed, Captain Patriquin told his friend of a dream he was having over and over.

It was a vivid, recurring vision of what the city would look like when the insurgents were gone, the violence had stopped, and the war was over.

"I dream the city will be safe. I'll go outside the wire without a vest and helmet and I'll never carry my rifle when I go and see people."

The rubble and ruins of the city would blossom with peace, and with the fruit of scores of dozens of civil affairs projects Patriquin and his colleagues had helped the Iraqis start up.

Restaurants and factories would reopen, schools would fill up with children in smart uniforms, the markets would bustle with shoppers, and the resorts around Lake Habbaniyah would teem with families from Baghdad on vacation.

"I dream that when things settle down here, one day I will take my wife and my kids to Iraq," Patriquin explained to Mohammed. "We'll stay here for at least a month, and we'll stay at Sheik Sattar's house. I'll take them all around Ramadi. I'll show them, yeah, there's a police station I built, there's a hospital I built. Oh, yeah, over there is where I got hit with an IED, and that's where my friend got killed.

"I know my family and my country will be proud. I want to take my wife and kids here to show them what their dad has done for the American people and the Iraqi people, so they can be proud of me."

Mohammed recalls, "This was all his specific soldier's dream, to bring his wife and children over and show them every single mission he had done."

Enthused by Patriquin's vision, Mohammed implored him, "If you come back to Ramadi with your family, even if you don't have time to come visit me in Baghdad, send me your pictures! I want to see you walking the streets of Ramadi in civilian clothes!"

"I want to show them everything," continued Patriquin.

"I want to come back here, so I can relive all my memories, and remember what I've done."

On December 2 and 3, Patriquin and Lechner met with Sattar, his brother, Ahmed, and several other sheiks to review the ongoing Iraqi police recruiting drives, which had become a roaring success in terms of numbers.

Over the next eight weeks, nearly two thousand fresh recruits would join the Iraqi police force and its Emergency Response Units in Ramadi and elsewhere in Anbar province, giving the coalition the rough equivalent of three extra battalions of armed men. Before the Anbar Awakening, only nine of the twenty-one tribes in Ramadi were cooperative or neutral to coalition forces. By now it had doubled to eighteen.

The joint Sunni-American victory at the Battle of Sufiyah gave both groups a burst of optimism, and it solidified Sattar's ascendant position among the sheiks.

Patriquin saw that the sheiks were increasingly confident in the strength and quality of the police, and they were delighted with the help that the Americans were giving. One of the sheiks' only complaints was that they wanted the Americans to design a system that could process two or three times the number of recruits each day, which was initially capped at 125. Patriquin wrote in his report of the meetings that the sheiks were ready and eager to provide "as many recruits as we are willing to take."

A source of constant concern for Patriquin and his colleagues was that the new Iraqi policemen be supervised by the proper Iraqi government chain of command, and not by sheiks. If sheiks issued orders to Iraqi police, they would essentially be a tribal militia, and the experiment could be summarily canceled by MEF headquarters and Iraqi government officials in Baghdad.

Sheik Ahmed took pains to reassure Lechner and Patriquin that this wouldn't happen, as Patriquin reported: "He stated emphatically that the sheiks have no business giving orders to the rank-and-file soldiers, and that SAA [the Awakening] held daily consultations with General Khalil, General Hamid, and other officers from Ministry of Interior and Ministry of Defense, and that is who they wanted to deal with on a strategic level, and there has never been any desire for the SAA to direct day-to-day Iraqi police operations."

Patriquin thought about how different the current situation was versus a year earlier, when the abortive Anbar People's Council (APC) was launched, and then quickly crushed in an orgy of bloodletting by al-Qaeda. He wrote, "One of the many reasons the People's Committee [sic] failed was that the members were attempting to fight al-Qaeda and coalition forces at the same time, as well as the fact that the security situation and cooperation between the local groups and CF were nonexistent compared to what exists today."

During the talks with Sattar and the other sheiks, Patriquin jotted down notes he would later expand into his official reports of the meetings. Excerpts from his reports trace the psychological shift that was occurring among the population, and outline the grand vision Sattar was forming for spreading the Awakening far beyond the city of Ramadi to reach across Iraq.

Patriquin wrote: "Having been given a viable political alternative to joining the 'Shi'a'-dominated national government [the Iraqi army], young men have embraced the Iraqi police as the way to serve their families, their country, and their tribes which is in line with Arab idealism and doesn't compromise their belief system. They still believe they are fighting a foreign invader, they've just transferred their energy against al-Qaeda instead of us, viewing us more as an ally than an enemy. Having fought us for years, they respect our military prowess, and are now very happy that we're all on the same side.

"Sattar demonstrated this by spinning around on the floor and looking at us over his shoulder, patting it and stating that now coalition forces sit on the shoulder of SAA, helping them, a reference to the Islamic angel that sits on the right shoulder of all devout Muslims, instead of in front of them, fighting them at the same time as al-Qaeda.

"Sattar spoke of a time when the police could stroll to work after prayer, purchase food in markets along the way, and everyone was peaceful. He also feels very strongly that Ramadi needs to be made an example for the rest of Anbar, and the fall of Ramadi into terrorist control was one of the things that toppled Anbar as a whole. He said that people look to their capital, and Ramadi has long been in the hearts of the people of Anbar, and when it fell, they felt the entire province needed to follow.

"SAA has plans for Iraq that go something like this: SAA calms down Ramadi, which in turn convinces the rest of Anbar that there is hope, and turns the rest of Anbar away from accepting terrorism. Then, reacting to the Anbar example, the other predominately Sunni provinces turn towards the philosophy of the SAA. After the provinces of Salah al Din, Ninewah, Anbar, and Diyala are successfully coopted to the side of SAA, SAA will leverage the considerable Sunni-Shi'a tribal ties to engage the Shi'a tribes in the South."

Patriquin concluded, "Once this has been accomplished foreign elements will realize that they cannot make inroads into society anymore, and the only remaining elements that cause problems will be the [Shiite militias] Badr Corps and JAM. These problems, of course, will be trickier to solve, and will probably involve a large movement by ISF forces against the Shi'a militias in Baghdad. Once this is accomplished, Iraq will be united again, and strong and unstoppable in the Middle East. Ultimately, the goal of SAA is one united Iraq strong enough to stand up to Iran. Iraqi unification has long been a goal of the SAA, as well as an end to sectarian violence."

It was all a grand vision of the future that Patriquin fervently shared.

Travis Patriquin looked like a happy, excited man on Wednesday, December 6, 2006, because on that day, he was going to help tell the world about the turnaround that was happening in his patch of Iraq.

He and his colleagues were going to escort two national reporters around Ramadi, Oliver North of Fox News and his TV crew, and Sarah Childress, a reporter for *Newsweek*, and her photographer, Alvaro Ybarra. Patriquin felt that there was a huge, historic story developing in Ramadi, and that a turning point in the war was under way that Americans must know about. And by now, it seemed that almost everyone at Marine Expeditionary Force headquarters in Fallujah was fully behind Sattar's Awakening, and giving Patriquin's brigade all the help they could give.

"It's good they're here," Patriquin said of the reporters to Sergeant Domenico Carbone, a driver in the personal security detail assigned to his convoy that day. "It's very important that they're here. They'll get to see that the sheiks are a key element to our success here. They're the key to winning everything. If we get on their side, and they're good people, they can work with us and we can work with them. They've got all the power. If we work with them, they can definitely help us win everything. *We can actually win this whole thing.*"

Patriquin's twenty-two-year-old gunner and good friend Specialist Vincent J. Pomante seemed in an exuberant mood, too. While waiting at Sheik Sattar's compound for Childress's visit with Sheik Sattar to conclude, Pomante let Sattar's young son Sattam sit in the driver's seat of Patriquin's Humvee and play with operating the radio. The boy was only nine years old but was already developing a commanding presence and movie-star charisma like his father, and as the youth declared "Radio Check! Radio Check!" into the handheld microphone, Pomante was consumed with laughter.

There was another soldier who seemed to be in very high spirits that day, too. Her name was Megan Malia Leilani McClung. She was a thirty-four-year-old Hawaii-born and California-raised U.S. Marine Corps major, a graduate of the U.S. Naval Academy at Annapolis, Maryland; the daughter of a marine officer who saw combat in Vietnam during the Tet Offensive; and the granddaughter of a U.S. Navy pilot and a U.S. Army veteran of World War II.

A dedicated runner, McClung had competed in seven Ironman Triathlons and had recently completed a master's degree in criminology from Boston University online, and for the past few weeks was serving as the new PAO, or public affairs officer, for the Ready First Combat Team in Ramadi. She was in the final month of a yearlong deployment to Iraq. She was running the brigade's media "embed" program, in which visiting reporters were absorbed directly into frontline combat units, as they had been since the war began. She was a highly enthusiastic proponent of the embed process, and she supervised the program with great energy and efficiency.

As a relatively rare female American officer traveling around Ramadi, McClung was developing friendships with local women and the wives of sheiks, and she learned that many of them had a shared desire: they'd love to have some hand and face cream. McClung enlisted the help of her mother and father in Washington State, who were emptying local store shelves of the items and packing a giant care package for her to share with the Iraqi women.

Patriquin and McClung had not known each other for long, but they were soul mates in a shared, intensely passionate belief— the world had to know about what was going on in Ramadi. The Iraq War was turning around. "Before we leave here," McClung promised her friends, "we will make al Anbar a safer place."

Despite the negative impact of the controversial Marine Corps "Devlin Report," coverage of which seemed to declare the war was lost in Anbar, other observers were beginning to entertain different conclusions, including a small but growing number of reporters.

On September 29, 2006, Colonel Sean MacFarland in Ramadi held a video-link press conference with reporters at the Pentagon briefing room, including representatives of the Associated Press, NBC News, ABC News, Fox News, and Reuters. MacFarland told them, "Well, I think we've actually tipped. Attacks are down 25 percent over the past couple of months, and coalition forces, together with the Iraqi security forces, have steadily increased their presence inside of the city. The Iraqi police recruiting has soared tenfold, and Iraqi army readiness has improved to the point where Iraqi army battalions are now assuming the lead in portions of the city and its suburbs. Public works projects are now beginning to bring real improvements in quality of life. Water and power projects are moving forward. And by February, we will have more than doubled both basic services. Even more encouraging has been the surge in interest among local leaders in cooperating with the coalition and the Iraqi security forces in the fight against al-Qaeda."

Reporters had heard this kind of happy talk on Iraq from countless American spokesmen before, but this was starting to feel different. On October 29, 2006, the *Times* (of London) published a balanced and quite positive piece by the respected correspondent Martin Fletcher titled "Fighting Back: The City Determined Not to Become al-Qaeda's Capital." Fletcher reported that "something remarkable has been happening in Ramadi," and "the outcome could have far-reaching consequences." Fletcher conducted what he described as the first face-to-face interview of Sheik Sattar with a Western journalist, and quoted a local Iraqi security official as saying, "Right now almost all the tribes are fighting the terrorists—the women, the children and even the dogs are fighting them."

Fletcher remembers his surprise at what he saw in Ramadi. "I was expecting to find a story of how grim and violent the place was. But to my astonishment I found it was in the throes of a power struggle, with the Sunni tribal leaders signing up hundreds of their followers to join the police, which was at that time a reviled institution among Sunnis because it was mainly Shia. The Sunni tribal leaders were fighting a terrific power battle against the al-Qaeda terrorists who had moved into Ramadi a couple of years earlier and imposed a reign of terror. The tribal leaders had made common cause with the American military, which was a complete reversal. It was pure luck, I just happened to be the first person [reporter] on the spot. It was a small team involved in forging this alliance, and Colonel MacFarland was the leader. But the guy who was doing the talking and the wooing of the sheiks over what he described as thousands of cups of tea and hundreds of cigarettes was Travis Patriquin."

The article was a symbolic breakthrough for Patriquin's brigade, and more media outlets were contacting Major Megan McClung for information on what was going on and to arrange visits to the combat zone.

McClung was the perfect officer for the job, according to her former marine boss, Lieutenant Colonel Bryan Salas, who described McClung as "a fireball, probably one of the most effective Public Affairs Officers I've ever seen. She could charm anybody out of their socks." Her colleague Lieutenant Colonel John Church said, "She could not just simply enter a room. She bounced and bounded in, ready to meet anyone and anything with an optimistic tenacity that intimidated some, but inspired many. She was a runner who would pound her body for 26 miles, only to be smiling and laughing for the last .2, egging on her fellow runners with taunts of good sportsmanship. She was an inspiration to everyone she met, energetic, almost frantic at times. She had only two speeds: high speed or off. She was a woman, strong and beautiful."

Church told the story of an admiring local Iraqi man who

shared his feelings about the redheaded McClung. "I would like to marry her," the man declared. "She is amazing. Her hair is like fire, and she is like fire. I would like to marry her, but I don't think I could control her." Church noted, "This was a very wise man."

On the afternoon of December 6, after dropping off Ollie North and his crew at Camp Blue Diamond for lunch and preparing to join Patriquin and Lechner in escorting the *Newsweek* duo in a convoy to Combat Outpost Falcon in south-central Ramadi, the five-foot-four marine major did something that struck one of the drivers, army Sergeant Domenico Carbone, as really odd coming from a person who was three levels above him in rank in the chain of command.

In the spirit of a kid sister or a small child, Major McClung jumped up onto Sergeant Carbone's back, laughing. "A major doesn't do that," recalls Carbone. "They're not like that. We'd never spoken to each other before. For her to do that was very unexpected."

For the twenty-five-year-old reporter Sarah Childress, this was her first time "outside the wire" in a full-scale combat zone. She'd embedded to Iraq once before, in June and July, to the northern city of Kirkuk, but it was nowhere near as dangerous as Ramadi, and she'd actually stayed in a hotel on the U.S. base there. She explains her *Newsweek* assignment on December 6, 2006: "I was just gathering string for a magazine piece. I was there to write two stories, one about the Awakening and another about the MIT [joint U.S.-Iraqi Military Transition Teams]. It was part of a bigger story people in DC were working on."

The convoy moved along a road the Americans called Route Sunset and was coming within sight of their destination, Combat Outpost Falcon, a few hundred meters away. They were close to a fortified American combat outpost of 250 soldiers, but until they got there they were in al-Qaeda–contested territory. This stretch of road should have been secure—it was closed to civilian traffic and watched over by U.S. soldiers in a Bradley Fighting Vehicle twenty-four hours a day.

But there was at least one gap in their coverage. Civilian foot traffic was allowed to cross the road twice a day. There was a school nearby, and schoolchildren crossed the dusty street on their way to and from home. The Americans didn't want to disrupt the lives of the children by forcing them and other civilians to walk around a longer route every day, and this opened up just enough of a window to allow an insurgent disguised as a youth or as an escorting parent to infiltrate a group crossing the road and quickly bury an improvised explosive device without being spotted.

Patriquin's convoy had five vehicles, including a lead Humvee and a second Humvee driven by Sergeant Carbone that contained Lieutenant Colonel Jim Lechner, his interpreter, Sterling Jensen, and *Newsweek*'s Sarah Childress inside. The next Humvee in line, the third one, contained Captain Patriquin, Major McClung, Specialist Vincent Pomante manning the gunner's swivel turret atop the vehicle, and their driver.

In the second Humvee, Jim Lechner caught a glimpse of something metallic in the road ahead, a possible telltale sign of a buried improvised explosive device.

"There's a plate in the road," Lechner said, "move left!"

As his Humvee swerved safely around the spot, the officer called into the radio frequency that connected him to the rest of the convoy, "Go LEFT! . . . Go . . ."

These were split-second observations and reactions—the vehicles passed over any given spot in only two- or three-second intervals—and the terrible calculus of this moment did not allow the driver of Patriquin's Humvee to react fast enough.

When Patriquin's vehicle passed over the spot, an improvised explosive device detonated directly under the fuel tank of the Humvee, pushing the tank up toward the passenger compartment and triggering an enormous explosion and fire.

The Humvee was engulfed in flames, and Patriquin, Pomante, and McClung were killed.

Travis Patriquin either escaped through or was blown out of the front window of the vehicle, and he died facing down in the road. Megan McClung died inside the vehicle, and a mortally wounded Vincent Pomante was pushed out of his position atop the Humvee, which rolled about a hundred feet before hitting a closed fruit stand on the side of Route Sunset.

McClung was the first female marine officer to be killed in Iraq, the first female graduate of the United States Naval Academy to be killed in action since the school was founded in 1845, and the highest-ranking female U.S. military officer to die in the Iraq War. McClung was the sixty-ninth U.S. servicewoman to be killed in the war. She was buried thirteen days later with full military honors at Arlington National Cemetery. Pomante was buried at his hometown of Westerville, Ohio, after a service in which the congregation sang "Onward, Christian Soldiers" and "On Eagles' Wings."

After the explosion, the driver escaped their vehicle, and according to witnesses, he jumped into the second vehicle in the convoy while slapping at flames covering his arm and screaming, "I'm on fire! I'm on fire!" Sarah Childress helped pour water on him to extinguish the fire, and Lechner ordered him taken to a first aid station at Combat Outpost Falcon.

Major Bajema was inside his command post at the operations center at COP Falcon when he heard the explosion. He threw on his helmet and protective vest, grabbed a couple of soldiers, and ran out to the site.

"Everyone was in complete shock," recalls Bajema. "Lechner was assessing the situation. He informed me that we had three killed in action. He had good control of the site, but it was a dangerous situation all the way around. The ammunition inside the Humvee was exploding and rounds were being cooked off as the Humvee burned. I scaled off the area with one tank and two Bradleys and twenty soldiers looking at windows and rooftops. I told First Sergeant Luis Duran to hook up a pressure washer to a Humvee and put the fire out, and he and three or four other soldiers put their lives at risk fighting the fire from five feet away as .50-caliber rounds of ammunition were cooking off."

The personnel in the convoy were evacuated as Bajema and his troops proceeded to recover the three KIA soldiers' remains and secure the site. "Then we started getting attacked with small-arms fire and hand grenades from some of the rooftops three or four houses away," remembers Bajema, "and cars pulled up from five hundred feet away starting to take pictures and videotaping the scene. The Bradley engaged and destroyed two of these vehicles."

By now, an American unmanned aerial vehicle was ten thousand feet overhead surveying the scene, and Bajema got word from the brigade Tactical Operations Center that two withdrawing vehicles that had been the source of enemy fire were being tracked to an enormous house in a nearby neighborhood. The compound belonged to a doctor—either a willing insurgent collaborator or coerced into being one—who set up a makeshift medical clinic for insurgents inside his home, complete with a homemade operating room. Bajema took command of two tanks and drove them two miles to the doctor's enormous house and walled compound.

"We pushed part of the wall down with a tank," says Bajema.

"Then we started taking machine-gun fire from inside the house. It's not very smart to take on a tank with machine guns; in fact, it's probably the dumbest thing you can do. We opened up with tank rounds into the house, which started a fire, then we destroyed two vehicles in the driveway."

Bajema ordered an infantry platoon pulled away from recovery duty at the IED site to assault the compound, and as Colonel Sean MacFarland and his brigade staff watched the UAV feed on the jumbo TV at Camp Ramadi, about fifty civilians were detained, including women, children, and about twenty-five military-aged males from Ramadi, Fallujah, and Baghdad. Seven weapons were found. It turned out that the whole group was part of a wedding party earlier that day, and when they heard of the nearby strike on the American convoy, the men spontaneously decided to join in and attack Americans as targets of opportunity. They probably were not connected to the IED attack.

From his house a few miles west of COP Falcon, Sheik Sattar could see smoke rising from the attack site. An American officer who told Sattar of the death of his friend Travis Patriquin describes the sheik as being stunned, devastated, and quietly weeping.

Sattar soon mobilized his entire tribal and police network to focus on one urgent objective: find out who killed Patriquin and his colleagues. A rumor quickly spread that Sattar downed a fifth of Jack Daniel's and vowed that the streets would run red with the blood of the killers.

"I don't know why," Sattar was later heard to say, "for some reason when I make good friends with Americans, they become my brother, and then they die. I don't have luck with friends. So I don't want any more American friends."

"But they want to continue the mission of Captain Patriquin," interjected brigade interpreter Sa'ad Mohammed.

"Don't think anybody's going to replace Captain Patriquin," Sattar countered. "No one is going to replace Captain Patriquin, just as no one could replace [Lieutenant] Colonel McLaughlin. Even if someone could, I'm not going to be close to them."

He explained, "I don't want them to die."

For Sergeant Domenico Carbone, the lead driver of the convoy, his emotions of shock and fury extended not only to the enemy but to whatever "higher-ups" in the Pentagon dreamed up the media embed program. "I feel it was an absolute waste of lives and a waste of fucking time, taking reporters around just to get some action. I didn't like it from the beginning and none of my guys did. The media shouldn't be there. There was no actual mission, it was a fantasy mission. And people got killed. I have nothing personal against the *Newsweek* reporter. I want to thank her because she helped the wounded driver by putting water on his arm and comforting him, but the simple fact is I don't think she should have been there to begin with. It's our higher-ups' fault for inviting them out to ride around with us. All the media needs to know is what we fucking tell them."

Carbone recalls that after the attack, his fellow soldiers were crying, furious, and having "a tug-of-war with each other trying to calm each other down." He had to restrain himself from storming into the Camp Ramadi operations center and screaming at his commanders, "What the fuck were we doing out there? There was no point!" Carbone says, "A lot of my guys were not doing well after that incident. Luckily we did not have a lot of time left in Iraq at that point."

However, it is pure speculation, but for their part, Patriquin and McClung and Pomante died in pursuit of a mission that they all probably felt highly committed to and supportive of, the mission of letting America and the world know about the positive transformation that was occurring in Anbar province. The American people had until then been accustomed to a relentless barrage of bad news from Iraq. Public support for the war was in a long, steep decline, and there seemed to be no way out.

Finally there was a huge, potential "good news" story coming out of Iraq.

As Patriquin put it, "We can actually win this whole thing."

At the same time that the three American soldiers' bodies were being taken away from the attack site on Route Sunset, a man's singing voice could be heard drifting across the rooftops and alleyways of south-central Ramadi. The sound came from a mosque, and it was the sound of the muezzin chanting the Muslim afternoon call to prayer:

> *God is great,*
> *God is great,*
> *There is no God but God,*
> *And I bear witness that Muhammad is his prophet.*
> *Make haste toward prayer,*
> *Come to the true success,*
> *God is great,*
> *God is great,*
> *There is no God but God.*

Late that afternoon, when Captain Andrew Duprey heard his office mate and good friend Patriquin had been killed, he rushed to join the farewell honor guard as the soldiers' remains were flown out.

"I ran across Camp Ramadi in the dark, tripped five times, and sprinted down to where the Hero Flight was going to be," Duprey remembers. "I got there early and fifty folks lined up. We got into a formation and I was in the first rank. We stood there and waited, and finally the helicopter started coming in, and the bodies were brought out to the helicopter flight line from the aid station by a Humvee ambulance and then the pallbearers would bring them out into the helicopter. Right before the aircraft arrived, the order was given to about face, so we wouldn't get hit with sand and gravel kicked up by rotor blades. They gave the order to about face and I turned around and there were hundreds and hundreds of people standing in formation. That was the largest Hero Flight I have ever, ever seen."

"How many people are here?" Duprey asked a colleague.

"I don't know," came the reply, "I lost count at around a thousand."

The memorial service for Patriquin, Pomante, and McClung was held a few days later at Camp Ramadi. The large hall was packed with American military, intelligence, and civilian personnel.

As was customary, the fallen marine and soldiers were symbolized by a display facing the audience, featuring three giant portraits of the three warriors, placed next to stands on which rested their weapons, medals, helmets, boots, and dog tags.

In a scene that was extremely rare, if not unheard of, in the Iraq War to date, a sizable delegation of Iraqi sheiks and security officers filed into the assembly, and took up the position of honor in the very first row of the service, sitting alongside Sean MacFarland and Jim Lechner.

The Iraqi guests included three of the central figures of the al Anbar Awakening: Sheik Sattar, Sheik Hamid al-Hayes, and Tariq Yusif Mohammad al-Thiyabi, the Awakening's military planner and soon-to-be Anbar provincial police chief. Other Iraqi notables included Sheik Jassim of the Abu Soda tribe, Sheik Muhammed of the Abu Shaban tribe, other sheiks, Ramadi's police chief, Colonel Khalil Ibrahim, and a detachment of uniformed Iraqi police officers.

A few Americans who were not fully aware of the magnitude of Patriquin's partnership with the Iraqis were surprised, and even resentful that the Iraqis sat down at the head of the assembly, as they were invited to do.

"What the fuck are they doing here?" muttered one American. "I can't believe those assholes are here."

Another voice snapped, "You obviously don't get it. Those are the people they died for! They were so loved by those sheiks that they're coming here to pay their respects."

Eulogies were given and music was played, including patriotic songs and the theme from the movie *Braveheart*, and a symbolic unanswered roll call was given for the fallen soldiers and marine.

Colonel MacFarland declared in his funeral oration for Patriquin, "When the history of this conflict is written, his contributions will loom very large. And I will personally do all I can to make sure he receives the credit and recognition that he deserves. Because not only did Travis deeply believe in the Ready First Combat Team mission, he was the architect of one of the central and perhaps the decisive aspect."

In a moment described by Captain Duprey as "one of the most touching scenes I've ever seen in my life," Sheik Sattar and all the Iraqi guests lined up to face the displays and pray, say farewell, and in the case of the Iraqi police officers, snap off British-style bent-knee military salutes to the fallen soldiers' giant photographs.

Following the Islamic funeral custom, Sheik Sattar wiped his face in sorrow, held up his hands, and said a prayer, the traditional form of which concludes, "O Allah, admit him to Paradise and protect him from the torment of the grave and the torment of

Hell-fire; make his grave spacious and fill it with light." Then he bent over to grasp the dog tags of Patriquin, Pomante, and McClung, as all the Iraqis and Americans did.

Patriquin's body was flown to the United States for burial with full military honors at a cemetery near his boyhood home of Salem in Dent County, Missouri. His family and friends laid him to rest, accompanied by representatives of the Pawnee Nation, who offered songs and gifts for his three young children. Patriquin's decorations included a Bronze Star, a posthumous Bronze Star and Purple Heart, an Army Commendation Medal, a Joint Service Achievement Medal, an Army Achievement Medal, the Good Conduct Medal, and his prized Combat Infantryman's Badge.

After the service, a child came up to Patriquin's army buddies Tommy Olsowy and Shawn Nickell and noticed Olsowy's Special Forces, Airborne, and Ranger tabs. "Wow!" said the boy. "Was Travis a Ranger, too?"

The two men looked at each other, remembering Patriquin's repeated bad luck with injuries that forced him out of Ranger School.

"Yeah, Trav was a Ranger," said Nickell, and the child walked off.

"Hey," said Olsowy to his friend, "he's more of a Ranger than you and I will ever be."

Within forty hours of the death of Patriquin and his colleagues, a twenty-year-old relative of Sheik Sattar walked into Sattar's house and told him he knew who killed the Americans. He lived in the area of the attack and said he happened to see the three young men who planted the IED. They were locals, and he knew their names. Sattar relayed the information to Lechner, who passed word to the Iraqi police, who spent days running down the lead and pinpointing the suspects' locations in a neighborhood along the banks of the Euphrates.

Lieutenant Colonel Lechner met with the Iraqi police commander for the area, Lieutenant Colonel Sallam Alwani, who the Americans considered so effective they called him the Iraqi Chuck Norris.

"This is the house they're in," said one of Sallam's officers, pointing to a spot on a satellite map.

"How do you know that?" asked Lechner.

"I went to high school with these guys," the policeman replied. "Two days ago I went over and had tea with them. They showed me the video they made of the attack."

Late in the cool, misty evening of December 19, 2006, Jim Lechner told his interpreter Sterling Jensen and fourteen soldiers in the brigade's military police security detail that they were going on a night mission. To prevent any possibility of a security leak, he had kept the operation and its objective completely secret until then. He explains, "I didn't want some American unit to blow into the neighborhood, hit the wrong house, and have these guys escape. I wanted to run this personally because I didn't want it to get screwed up."

At two in the morning of December 20, the American soldiers, joined by Colonel Sallam and eight of his Iraqi policemen, set off from a U.S. Marine Corps outpost toward the target neighborhood a kilometer away. Rather than risk a noisy entry by vehicle, they marched in pitch darkness on foot into the neighborhood, which felt old and almost medieval to Lechner. In addition to the three suspects in the IED attack, they had a list of seven other suspects believed to be insurgents close by, so they hoped to raid five or six houses in total.

As they approached the first house, believed to contain two brothers in the IED team, Lechner knew that the slightest bit of noise or a barking dog could alert the neighborhood, blow the operation, and possibly trap the raiders in a firefight in hostile territory, so complete silence was essential. "Typically Americans will break a door down, and not even knock," he explains. "This time, I wanted a smooth, low-impact entry, with no doors broken down. I had the Americans sealing off the alleyway, forming a perimeter. One Iraqi policeman just hopped over the wall, opened the gate, lifted one of the doors off its hinges, and five policemen, one American soldier, my interpreter and I went right into the bedroom with a flashlight."

Five people were asleep in the room, a mother, a father, and three others, including one suspected member of the IED team, a twenty-year-old man. An Iraqi policeman identified him. The flashlight shone on his face as he lifted his head and peered out from under his blanket.

Seconds later, the stunned suspect was in an alley, bound in flex-cuffs with guns pointed at him as a voice demanded, "Where is your brother?" The suspect blurted, "My brother's not here. I'll take you to him, I'll take you right to him! He's two doors down." Soon the two brothers were both prisoners, as well as the third member of the IED team.

Lechner was face-to-face with three men whom he suspected of killing his colleagues and very nearly killing him, and it would have been easy to put bullets in their heads. "I was considering all the options that night," he explains. "But I ruled out executing them on the spot—I wanted to take them down hard, and legally. I was dead-set on using the Iraqi police, and building a packet of evidence and statements that would hold up in the judicial system."

The operation proceeded like clockwork, as house after house was raided and suspects were snatched out of bed, dragged out, and flex-cuffed. They were moving so quickly that Lechner was worried one of his soldiers might be accidentally left behind.

The interpreter Sterling Jensen was practically giddy with tension, adrenaline, and euphoria over the fact that they had captured all three suspects in the killings of his friends. He remembers, "At first I was amazed at how easy it was. Then I thought, 'This is stupid, this is crazy! They look like teenagers. I could hang out with them in a café in Syria.' One of the guys I could tell was kind of mentally deranged, but the other was a student with acne on his face. These weren't terrorists. They did it for the money." Lechner agrees that the suspects looked like "a classic IED team, unemployed young men recruited by al-Qaeda for money."

Lechner recalls, "We missed the insurgent cell leader and any foreign fighters, but we captured eight guys, including all three of the guys we were looking for, the guys who actually built and emplaced the IED and took part in the attack. We walked them in their bare feet through a dump. I didn't feel sorry for them for a minute. We dragged them into an Iraqi police station, where they were held for a few weeks, before being shipped to Baghdad. I was torn between being happy to get them and frustration over the fact that the best thing I could hope for would be ten years in jail, and there's a chance they could be released after a year or two in an amnesty."

Later that day, when Lechner returned to Camp Ramadi, his staff gave him a cake for his fortieth birthday, and a big USO troop came by to perform for the troops. One of the featured players was the country music star Keni Thomas, who had served with Lechner in the Seventy-fifth Ranger Regiment during the Battle of Mogadishu in 1993.

It was a good day for Lechner.

EPILOGUE

A SOLDIER'S LEGACY

Much as Travis Patriquin hoped and dreamed, the Anbar Awakening changed the course of the Iraq War.

And Patriquin himself can be considered a key figure among many others in helping to shape the history of the conflict.

If Travis Patriquin had never been born, it is entirely possible that the Awakening would have occurred on the same trajectory that it did. But an equally convincing speculation is that he was the key person at an absolutely critical time and place of the war, and without him, events might have taken a different course.

Travis Patriquin was the principal driving force inside the Ready First Combat Team in mobilizing U.S. military support for the Awakening in the critical period of its formation in September through December 2006. The Awakening was a largely Iraqi creation authored by Sheik Sattar and many of his countrymen, but without the guidance and support of the U.S. military, including its combat power, the movement had little chance of succeeding.

The Awakening directly led to many of the conditions for the success of the U.S. troop surge in 2007, conditions that, along with a cease-fire by Shiite militias and improved coalition counterinsurgency tactics, led to sustained, dramatic reductions in violence in Iraq from the end of 2007 onward. The post-Awakening Iraq is still massively dysfunctional and plagued by sporadic terrorism, terrible poverty, and chronic political paralysis, and theoretically it might at any time quickly unravel back to 2006 levels of violence, or even worse. But it is a much different nation today than it was in 2006, and a large part of the reason is the Awakening.

History is a hall of mirrors, a wilderness of entangled and often unfathomable causes and effects, unproveable "turning points," counterfactuals and what-ifs. As the author and counterinsurgency expert Bing West noted, "Iraq was a kaleidoscope. Turn it one way and you think you see the pattern. Then along comes some unexpected event and the pattern dissolves." Until late 2006, the pattern of the Iraq War seemed to lead inexorably to absolute chaos. Then the Awakening came along and dissolved the pattern, or so it seemed.

But several strong possibilities appear. Without Sheik Sattar and his tribal allies stepping forward and declaring war on al-Qaeda in al Anbar, you obviously have no Awakening. And without Patriquin, MacFarland, Lechner, Tony Deane, Pat Fagan, Teddy Gates, Bill Jurney, and thousands of soldiers and marines and key U.S. intelligence people to support Sattar and the Iraqi police, you probably have no successful Awakening, either. "I'd say 20 percent of the credit for the change in Ramadi could be taken by U.S. forces," said U.S. Army Lieutenant Nathan Strickland in 2008. "The vast majority of the turnaround is due to the sheiks." But even if the 20 percent estimate is correct, it is still an absolutely critical factor. The sheiks could not have succeeded in throwing off the yoke of al-Qaeda without the work of American soldiers and marines.

Captain Travis Patriquin can be thought of, symbolically at least, as a key link in this chain of Iraqi history, and representative of many Americans who helped Iraq pull itself back from the final abyss of total civil war toward a different future, and a better one. Through an accident of history, Patriquin was placed unusually close to the absolute center of the action, wound up as a key cog in the machine, and by most accounts played his role brilliantly.

Patriquin was obviously a striking and highly unusual personality. He can be thought of as a special, specific archetype of a very American kind of soldier and citizen on the world stage, maybe the kind of soldier we should hear about and know about more, whose most powerful assets are his inspiring personality, his genuine interest in and love of cultures other than his own, and his ability to connect with people through humility, respect, deference, compassion, laughter, and relentless optimism.

Patriquin can also be seen as representative of the countless thousands of members of the American military who toil away every day at lonely sentry posts, on distant ships and submarines, keeping the peace and risking their lives in battle, negotiating with local leaders, building schools, huddling over computers, swabbing decks, fixing equipment, and pushing through paperwork in forgotten outposts in godforsaken spots all around the world. They do it in invisible anonymity—their fellow Americans rarely, if ever, get to see them in action. But if they could, they might feel even prouder to be Americans.

In the months after Travis Patriquin's death, the Awakening, backed by the American military, completed the expulsion of al-Qaeda from most of the province and directly triggered major ripple effects in other parts of Iraq that ushered in a new era of Sunni Iraqi engagement in Iraqi politics.

The Awakening was a great turning point in the Iraq War, a

watershed event that opened up new hopes and possibilities. It marked a turn driven by Iraq's Sunni population from unrestricted civil war, widespread insurgent domination, and profound U.S. despair in the bloodbaths of 2003–2006 to a supremely fragile, still violent, but nonetheless transformed Iraqi military environment, where for periods in 2008 and 2009 U.S. troops actually walked freely without helmets and body armor in Ramadi and patrolled much of Baghdad jointly with local Sunni forces modeled on the Awakening, as the Shiite-dominated Iraqi government slowly, grudgingly absorbed portions of the Sunni forces into the security forces.

The Awakening was a critical factor in creating a new security landscape that saved untold thousands of Iraqi and American lives, and helped allow the United States military to withdraw many of its combat troops in the summer of 2010.

In a series of skirmishes and battles in Ramadi from December 2006 to March 2007, U.S. and Iraqi forces completed the liberation of almost all of the provincial capital city of Ramadi and the areas around it. In January 2007 the first Ramadi Reconstruction Conference was held. A mayor for the city of Ramadi was finally appointed and municipal services and businesses started trickling back to the devastated city, including a number of civil affairs projects engineered by Patriquin and his colleagues.

The last big tribal domino in Ramadi fell in early February 2007, when leaders of the formerly al-Qaeda–dominated and influential Abu Fahd tribe declared they were joining Sattar's Anbar Salvation Council. That month, Colonel Sean MacFarland and his Ready First Combat Team rotated out of Iraq and were replaced by a combat team built around the army's First Brigade of the Third Armored Division, commanded by Colonel John Charlton, which continued vigorous tribal engagement through 2007 and into 2008, building on the work done by Patriquin and his brigade. MacFarland was later promoted to brigadier general.

On March 13, 2007, Shiite prime minister Nouri al-Maliki paid a surprise visit by helicopter to Ramadi's Camp Blue Diamond U.S. Marine Corps base, where he met with Governor Maamoun, Sheik Sattar, and a large delegation of Sunni tribal leaders in a striking public show of unity. With U.S. diplomats and military officers acting as ardent "marriage counselors," Governor Maamoun and Sheik Sattar were led to increased, if highly grudging, cooperation, and Awakening figures were absorbed into the Anbar government and Provincial Council. Companies controlled by Sattar and his brother, Ahmed, performed one of the first big job-creating projects in the city: rubble removal in the battle-pulverized districts around the Government Center.

A symbolic triumph occurred in late March 2007, when Iraqi police forces, largely comprised of members recruited by the Awakening, and backed up by American and Iraqi troops, moved down every street in the Qatana district and killed some of the last insurgents dug into the city's downtown, while U.S. Marines provided overwatch from the Seventeenth Street and Qatana joint security stations.

At the climax of the battle, U.S. Marines were amazed to see a small, lone figure in a flowing white robe running up and down Route Michigan clutching a Dragunov sniper rifle, yelling victory cheers and taunting the insurgents. It was Sheik Sattar.

Sattar's military advisor, Tariq Yusif Mohammad al-Thiyabi, recalled to a U.S. Marine Corps historian, "As a military person, I took cover behind the concrete barriers. I have to declare for history's sake that Sheik Sattar did not want to hide. Knowing that he was wearing a white robe, and it made him conspicuous from a long distance, I told him to take cover behind the concrete barrier.

He said, 'No.' He remained standing. He said, 'I will stand and fight.' Colonel [Thaddeus] McWhorter [USMC] contacted me. He was pleading with me to pull Sheik Sattar out because the danger was escalating and Sheik Sattar had become a symbol for all of Anbar. They were afraid that something would happen to him, and it would cause a great downfall to Anbar. I used all my means to pull Sheik Sattar out of danger so he wouldn't get hurt."

Also as Travis Patriquin hoped, the religious character of Ramadi transformed from an environment where al-Qaeda firebrand clerics dominated the mosques to a much more moderate, tolerant, more authentic version of conservative Islam. Patriquin's colleague and former brigade interpreter Sterling Jensen saw this as a pivotal change. He wrote, "A scarcely mentioned reason for the Awakening's rapid success in Ramadi and in the rest of Anbar was that the heads of the Sunni Endowment and Muslim Scholars in Anbar believed in Sheik Abdul Sattar's initiative to rid the province of extremism. Once they were given protection by the Iraqi police, a handful of these leading clerics moderated religious speeches in mosques, issued fatwas against working for al-Qaeda, encouraged young men to join the ISF [Iraqi security forces], and gave moral and religious support to the Awakening movement. The Awakening would not have survived without the support of these religious leaders."

Sheik Sattar led the Anbar Awakening through the summer of 2007, becoming the most powerful man in the province and a nationally prominent figure in Iraq. Autonomous Sunni "Awakening Councils" formed in other provinces—Diyala, Salahadin, and Baghdad—and Sattar met with top government officials in Baghdad and received delegations from across the country. The name of Sattar's movement was changed, to Mutammar Sahwat al-Iraq, or the Iraqi Awakening. And while the Awakening Councils that formed outside Anbar were inspired by Sattar's Awakening, most in fact did not take orders from him.

Continuing his habit of saying things that Americans loved to hear, Sattar declared to one journalist, "I swear to God, if we have good weapons, if we have good vehicles, if we have good support, I can fight al-Qaeda all the way to Afghanistan." Bing West once asked Sheik Sattar why the Awakening hadn't happened years ago and prevented the slaughter of countless Iraqis and Americans. "We Sunnis had to convince ourselves," Sattar explained. "You Americans couldn't do it." When he was once asked why the Sunni Awakening happened, he explained simply that the insurgents were "killing innocent people, anyone suspected of opposing them—they brought us nothing but destruction and we finally said, enough is enough." On other occasions, he said, "When we realized that the Americans were our friends, we said we'll stick with them. You point a gun at our friends the Americans, at any American soldiers, and you're pointing a gun at us." "When we realized that the Americans were not our enemies and they are here to help us, that was our real Awakening." "When the Americans came, we thought they were the enemy. The Awakening came when we realized the Americans were our friends."

In February 2007 General George Casey was replaced by General David Petraeus as commander of U.S. forces in Iraq, and that month Petraeus paid a visit to Ramadi, where he was astonished to see the magnitude of the apparent turnaround under way. At an upbeat briefing given by Colonel Sean MacFarland, Petraeus declared, "I'm so happy I could kiss you guys." A marine general reportedly interjected a highly out-of-synch comment about Sheik Sattar being "a small fish—don't worry, we're working with the big fish [exiled sheiks in Jordan]." Petraeus countered by saying unequivocally "We've got to support this—let's support what's going on here now," a comment that energized his new command.

Petraeus and his deputy, Raymond Odierno, the commanding general of Multinational Forces–Iraq, quickly instituted a series of new counterinsurgency measures, including a U.S. military program based on the example of Anbar that paid Sunni tribesmen and former insurgents in a number of Sunni districts in Baghdad and rural Sunni areas to side with U.S. military forces and patrol their neighborhoods. The new force, which briefly carried the faintly comical, Kiwanis Club–style American names of "concerned local citizens" and "neighborhood watch groups," and was later called the Sons of Iraq program, eventually had ninety thousand Iraqi men across Iraq on the American military payroll, including in previous insurgent hotbeds in Baghdad and south and west of the capital. Former nationalist insurgents and even al-Qaeda foot soldiers stopped killing American troops and started joint patrols and security operations with them.

The Awakening of Iraq can be thought of as the exhaustion point and epic opinion shift of the Sunni population against al-Qaeda and in favor of the Americans as temporary allies to defend against both al-Qaeda, and Iranian domination through the Shiite-dominated central government in Baghdad.

The Awakening had early, important sparks in Al Qaim and Ramadi in 2005, but did not begin in earnest until the summer of 2006, when Sheik Sattar and a handful of other tribal leaders decided to risk their lives by openly declaring war on al-Qaeda. This opinion shift helped enable the "surge" of early 2007 to succeed. The Sons of Iraq program was an outgrowth of Sunni anti–al-Qaeda sentiment capitalized on by the Awakening movement, but it was not a part of the Awakening organization, which was confined largely to Ramadi, and the Sons of Iraq never reported to Sattar. One big difference between the two was that in Anbar, tribal fighters were recruited directly into the Iraqi police and were paid and ostensibly supervised by the Iraqi government's Ministry of the Interior. The Sons of Iraq program was run and paid for by the U.S. military, in the hope that the fighters would eventually be absorbed into the Iraqi security forces.

By the end of 2007, after some terrible months, violence in Iraq was experiencing a sharp plunge that endured through 2010. The main reasons for the drop were the combined effects of the Awakening, the Sons of Iraq, the surge, the standing down of the al-Sadr Shiite militia, and new counterinsurgency tactics and technologies instituted by Petraeus and Odierno. U.S. military fatalities plunged from 904 in 2007 to 314 in 2008, and down to 149 in 2009 and 60 in 2010.

The Shiite-dominated Iraqi government was intensely wary of the Sons of Iraq program; in some cases they actively tried to stop it and dragged their feet on absorbing Sunni volunteers into the Iraqi security forces. Government officials felt many of the volunteers were criminals, killers, and former outright local al-Qaeda leaders, and feared them infiltrating the army and police.

In late 2006, President George W. Bush, overruling objections from some of his military and civilian advisors, ordered an extra five combat brigades totaling thirty thousand troops to be "surged" into Iraq in a major gamble to improve security, especially in the Baghdad area. On hearing of the plan, Sheik Sattar was perplexed. "What are you doing that for?" he asked American military officers. "What's the usefulness of having more American troops? That's not the issue! Get the Iraqi police the support they need. There are so many people who want to join the police. Get that moving faster. Don't spend your time bringing more Americans in. Bless their heart, we'll fight with them and use their weapons but they don't know what they're doing. They're not useful here."

"The success in al Anbar wasn't the result of the troop surge," argues Patriquin's colleague Captain Michael Murphy. "The surge worked because of a fundamental Iraqi policy change at the grassroots level that started in al Anbar. It paved the way for what could fundamentally be a significant turning point in Iraq. It's a chicken-and-egg situation. The chicken was the al Anbar Awakening. The egg was the troop surge."

"The tribes didn't flip because they liked us," says Army Major Niel Smith, who also served with Patriquin. "They flipped for two reasons: they were fed up with al-Qaeda and they saw the Awakening movement becoming the big kid on the block. When Travis was killed, things had already been set in motion to the point that they could not easily have been reversed. The rest of us could finish what he had started. If he had been killed four or five months earlier, it may not have happened."

In September 2007, when journalist Martin Fletcher returned to Ramadi and again interviewed Sheik Sattar, nearly a year after his first visit, the Awakening movement in Anbar was already fracturing under the weight of severe intertribal rivalries and personality clashes. The Awakening's cofounder Sheik Hamid al-Hayes was already peeling away from the group, and Sheik Hatem Suleiman, scion of the powerful Dulaimi Confederation and a habitual harsh critic of Sattar, was intensifying his ongoing war of words against Sattar, whom he called a "Disney character" created by the Americans. Sattar had just returned from a conference with Prime Minister Maliki in Baghdad, during which the two discussed how to encourage reconciliation between the Shia and Sunni populations.

Fletcher recalls his last visit with Sattar: "A convoy of Humvees took my photographer and me out to his compound. It was heavily fortified, the land all around was razed, an American tank was parked outside. The Iraqi police were all around, there was a watchtower, barbed wire, and floodlights. This was a guy who had survived numerous assassination attempts and was probably al-Qaeda's number-one target. It was late afternoon. We sat outside on white plastic chairs. It was blazing hot, and I was served hot chai and really strong coffee. Sattar was dressed in pristine white robes, he was chain-smoking and playing with his prayer beads. He remembered me. He joked about how his grandfather fought the British after the First World War."

Sattar was in a wistful mood, and told Fletcher the era of violence in Iraq was over. "In place of every improvised explosive device," he said, "we will plant a flower."

Fletcher then asked Sattar about a man he remembered from his visit in 2006, a strapping army soldier named Captain Travis Patriquin.

Sattar's face became solemn as he said, "He was an extraordinary man who played a very, very important role. He was my brother. He spoke Arabic and he looked like an Arab man. He was very humble and friendly. He used to play around here with the kids and my son. My oldest son here knows him well. When he came at the start of the Awakening, we needed someone like Captain Patriquin. He was always helping me. He helped us with weapons and ammunition and equipment to fight the terrorists. There were people who needed help, who were in trouble, and Captain Patriquin went there and brought them food and whatever they needed. On another occasion there was an attack when al-Qaeda was targeting women and children. He actually defended these women and children against the terrorists. This was a true battle. Captain Patriquin was extraordinary. He really was very, very important in building rapport between the U.S. and the sheiks. We lost a person who was very dear to us."

Speaking about the risk of his own assassination, Sattar said, "Allah gives you your first day, and he gives you your last."

On September 8, 2007, Sheik Sattar fulfilled one of his greatest ambitions—he met with President George W. Bush and other top American officials at an American air base in Anbar, the head of a delegation that included the Anbar governor and other sheiks. As he posed for pictures with a delighted Bush, Sattar struck the pose of a dashing young Arab potentate, a man of action, and a man of destiny.

Ten days later, Sattar was killed by a bomb planted by al-Qaeda operatives in his own backyard. One of Sattar's bodyguards was arrested and confessed that al-Qaeda had bribed him to betray Sattar and allow the bomb to be planted. The Awakening did not die with Sattar, however, and his brother, Ahmed, stepped in to assume leadership of the movement into 2011.

Both the Sunni Awakening and the surge shared two goals: to reduce the level of violence in Iraq, and to reengage Sunnis in the national political dialogue in a way that would create durable national political institutions. The first has happened; but the second hasn't yet. The "breathing space" and reductions in violence resulting from the Awakening and the surge have not yet led to sustained national reconciliation. Iraqi politics is still bedeviled and polarized by sectarian factions that dominate government ministries and block legislative progress.

The city of Ramadi is still plagued by occasional bombings, inadequate city services, and stalled reconstruction projects, but many businesses and schools are operating, much of the water system and power grids have been restored, Iraqi police are on patrol, and the American military has withdrawn to Camp Ramadi in a greatly reduced and strictly "advise-and-assist" role. The days of prehistoric anarchy in Anbar province seem to be over, at least for now, and the city is in some ways light-years away from where it was in 2006. Many of the civil affairs projects started by Travis Patriquin and his colleagues have come to fruition.

General David Petraeus, the American most credited with orchestrating a security turnaround in Iraq in 2007, sees the Awakening as a watershed moment in the war, and Travis Patriquin as a key figure in making the Awakening possible. "I was very impressed by Patriquin's stick-figure PowerPoint when I read it in the fall of 2006, and by a memo he wrote that summer called 'The View of Ramadi from Camp Ramadi,'" Petraeus recalls. "Patriquin's whole concept was eminently sensible. We came in later with the surge, and I often note that the most important surge was not a surge in forces, it was a surge of ideas. It was the focus on the human terrain, which is the decisive terrain. It was the focus on securing the people by living with them. Promoting reconciliation was a key element, as was relentlessly going after the irreconcilables. It's tragic that Patriquin was killed, having helped Colonel MacFarland develop the initiatives that ultimately led to the true Awakening. The reason I went to Ramadi for my very first trip in February 2007 was to see this. It was the kind of initiative that had real promise. It was what we needed to do."

For General Petraeus, the Awakening came at an extremely important time, as he was under great pressure to deliver fast political and security progress in Iraq. "The Awakening was hugely important," he argues. "It was a major element in reengaging the Sunni population of Iraq in the new Iraq. Until that time a substantial portion of the Sunnis felt they had no future in their country. Their incentives lay more in opposing the new Iraq rather than supporting it. And it also helped produce the dramatic improvement in the security situation, and to do it frankly in relatively short order, although it didn't seem that fast at the time for those of us living through it. I had several different clocks running. And arguably the most important clock was the one that was running on Capitol Hill. I knew I had to go back for a series of congressional hearings in September 2007. The fact is if we had not been able to show demonstrable improvement in the security situation, I'm not sure we would have had the opportunity to continue the effort as we were able to do. So in that sense the Awakening was hugely important as well. We had to work up from the bottom even before we could reach down from the top. If we didn't get something going, we were going to run out of time. The Washington clock would expire."

Petraeus concludes that "the effects of the Awakening enabled a much more rapid turnaround than ever would have been possible had it not taken place. When you combine that with taking away sanctuaries and safe havens from al-Qaeda–Iraq, convincing the Sadr militia to stand down, improvements in Iraqi security forces, and governance starting again, you have all these pieces reinforcing each other. This is not over by any means. There still is al-Qaeda in Iraq, though its top leaders have been taken out. There still are militia extremists. There is still a competition for political and economic power. But we went from over 220 attacks per day as late as June 2007 to less than twenty attacks per day in early 2010."

The Awakening party scored impressive gains in Anbar's 2009 provincial elections, and managed to finally unseat the Islamic Party of Iraq from domination of the provincial government, by ousting Governor Maamoun and replacing him with an Awakening-supported candidate for governor, Qassem Mohammad al-Fahdawi. In December 2009, he was nearly killed in a suicide bombing at the entrance to the Provincial Government Center in

Ramadi, an attack that killed twenty-four people, blew off the governor's arm, and confined him to a wheelchair.

In Iraq's 2010 parliamentary elections, however, Awakening candidates were trounced in Anbar, as the party suffered from widespread disappointment at the slow pace of reconstruction, lack of security, and alleged rampant corruption in the province. The Awakening turned into "an enterprise for deals and contracts," complained one Ramadi sheik. "Anbar is splintered; the tribes are splintered." Anas Ahmed, a twenty-two-year-old resident of the city, quipped, "One gang leaves and another one comes in." Rasoul Mohammed Salman, a twenty-three-year-old university student, complained, "The city is a cake that's shared among the leaders of the Awakening and the tribal leaders at the expense of the powerless citizens. We don't know when the next car bomb will explode or the next roadside bomb will go off."

Despite the failures and limitations of the Awakening, it remains a critical moment both in Iraqi history and in the American experience in Iraq. Other than Afghanistan, the global amalgamation of terrorists that calls itself "al-Qaeda" had never before or since captured and held as significant a strategic prize as Anbar province; and the Islamic caliphate it created there, complete with parades, checkpoints, taxes, sharia courts, sharia law, control of the mosques, and even shadow government ministries, proved so offensive and terrorizing to the local Muslim Arab population, and so disruptive to society, that local leaders overthrew the false caliphate and ran al-Qaeda, for the most part, out of town, with the crucial help of American combat power. For the Sunnis of Iraq, the Awakening was a step back from oblivion. For the Americans, it was one of several doors that allowed them to hope to leave Iraq with some hope of a semblance of order and honor.

Historical skirmishes have broken out among some Americans

over who deserves credit for "enabling" the Awakening. In a six-hundred-plus-page U.S. Marine Corps oral history collection on the Awakening published in late 2009 (a collection in which Travis Patriquin's name appears exactly once, and in passing), a few marine officers who were based at MEF headquarters in Fallujah in 2004–2008 seem to take issue at least implicitly with the historical narrative that gives a huge degree of credit, quite naturally, to the Ready First Combat Team, which itself included about a thousand marines. The RFCT, after all, was the unit that was there in the critical period of 2006 when the Awakening took off; they were the people doing the fighting, the dying, and the tribal engagement with Sattar and his allies.

The argument against giving maximum or sole credit to the RFCT is an interesting, provocative, and sometimes somewhat strained one. It seems to suppose that since Anbar province was a marine area of operations since 2004, all positive developments that occurred there were the result of enlightened leadership from the very top down, and a consistent tribal engagement policy from the top generals, over several years.

For example, Marine Lieutenant General John F. Kelly argues in the introduction to the collection that "no single personality was the key in Anbar, no shiny new field manual the reason why, and no 'surge' or single unit made it happen. It was a combination of many factors, not the least of which—perhaps the most important—was the consistent command philosophy that drove operations in Anbar from March 2004 forward. Each MNF-W [Multinational Force–West] commander and the troops under him continued to build upon the work of all those who came before."

A related argument about the Awakening, and one that could have much validity, was made by the former marine intelligence officer Major Ben Connable: "It's a process, not an event. It is not something that happened overnight. It is not something that was created by an American unit, or a series of American units. It was not something we did. It is something that happened over time, that we helped set the conditions for, and so you've got to understand that counterinsurgency operations take time. There is no miracle cure, no surprise negotiation with the right guy that's going to turn the whole thing around. That happens only in very, very few cases, and I would argue even in those cases [that] the social conditions have to be right for that to occur."

Some Americans place the beginning of the Awakening not with Sattar in the summer of 2006 but with the aborted Anbar People's Council the year before, or with the revolt in Al Qaim in 2005 and the forming of the Sunni Desert Protectors tribal paramilitary force there. Others place it at the many talks held between Anbar sheiks in Jordan and elsewhere with soldiers, marines, State Department, and CIA people going back to 2004. Some CIA officials have privately asserted that that agency's very extensive work in Anbar province, and especially its frequent contacts with Sheik Sattar, was the critical piece. They all may be right.

But one can also argue that the partnership between Sattar and Travis Patriquin and his colleagues was the critical driving force at the critical moment of the Awakening.

The strongest voices in favor of this point of view are the military officers who served with Patriquin, many of whom see him as the key American personality who helped the Iraqis launch the Awakening at the moment of its birth, from the bottom up.

"Travis figured out before anyone else did that while we were trying to force the government to stand up and take control, the government couldn't do it unless the sheiks allowed their tribes to support the government," maintains U.S. Marine Corps Lieutenant Colonel Mark Bramwell, then a civil affairs officer in Ramadi.

"It's amazing how all the good ideas come from the guys at the point end of the spear, not the generals at the top. Travis made a critical impact. He turned the corner. It shut down the insurgency and it forced the generals to then comply with success."

Lieutenant Colonel Miccioto Johnson, U.S. Army, a Ready First Combat Team battalion commander, said of Patriquin: "He started it. He was the one that made them understand that the Americans were human, that we're not all infidels, because he was able to directly relate to them and spoke the language. He was the first American voice who led Sattar to think, 'I can trust these guys, I can work with them.' He was the first to show them the Americans were here for their best interests. He facilitated them trusting us."

Captain Pat Fagan, who worked closely with Patriquin and Sattar, sees it this way: "Travis saw a way forward when everybody else saw nothing but doom and gloom. I thought maybe he was a bit too optimistic. I thought, this guy doesn't know what the reality on the ground is. It turned out he knew better than all the rest of us. He realized the Iraqi people are the key to this fight. No amount of guns and bombs is going to win this war. We're going to win by co-opting the people to fight against the extremists. He believed that if we could divorce the people from the insurgents we could win. I thought it was pretty stunning to see that kind of vision put into action. Without his hard work, this whole opportunity would have been missed. People keep talking about 'the surge' and 'the marine model' when talking about the turnaround in al Anbar. It is a lie. The tribal sheiks, with the support of a few ingenious battalion and brigade level leaders, chiefly Trav Patriquin and Colonel Sean MacFarland, got this effort off the ground despite a lack of support from the Marine Division Headquarters. The tribal sheiks and the Ready First Brigade Combat Team took a big chance, and the Awakening has since blossomed into a tremendous success.

Travis Patriquin's efforts and vision should be mandatory study for all ground combat and civil affairs officers."

"I cannot stress enough the role that Travis played in Ramadi," says Army Captain Chad Pillai, another RFCT battalion tribal affairs officer. "I can tell you his impact was immense. Ramadi went from a war-torn city with everyone hating the Americans to a city on the verge of change and a new wave of hope on the horizon. Travis and others successfully worked with a few sheiks and helped promote their cause, which led to the current situation where the tribes turned to support the Americans and fight to defeat al-Qaeda. It was Travis's constant engagement with them that made that possible. Who was Travis? We joked that he was the Lawrence of Arabia of Iraq. In reality, he was so much more than simply Lawrence of Arabia. He was an individual that we would need ten thousand more of in order to end this war and bring about peace. Travis was a true Warrior Diplomat and a Warrior Scholar. He demonstrated that battles could be won without firing a shot and that talking and listening could have an impact."

Robert Gates, the U.S. secretary of defense, paid tribute to Patriquin in a speech he gave to the Association of the United States Army in 2007: "He did not have a chance to see his ideas and efforts bear fruit, but no doubt would have been proud to have seen what the hard work, courage and ingenuity of the soldiers had started: a city liberated, al-Qaeda uprooted and reeling, and the tide turned, at least in this one important battle, in a conflict that will determine the future of the Middle East for decades to come."

Former Iraqi Air Force Major General Najim Abed Al-Jabouri, who worked closely with Patriquin as the mayor of Tal Afar, offers a stirring tribute to the impact of Patriquin and his colleagues: "What MacFarland and Patriquin did in Tal Afar and Ramadi, and later General Petraeus did this in parts of Baghdad, was they integrated the Americans with the Iraqi people. That's how Iraqis came to know what the true nature of the military was. They saw soldiers who had good feelings toward Iraqis, not soldiers who wanted to kill them.

"What MacFarland and Patriquin did was a really amazing accomplishment," Najim says. "If it wasn't for these steps that Petraeus took advantage of, it doesn't matter if you sent 200,000 or 300,000 more troops in Iraq, it wouldn't have made any difference. That's the key that you've got to understand. You focus on the people, not just the enemy. The problem the Americans had was they were focusing just on the enemy. They didn't care about the people who were living amidst the enemy. That's the key. There was a balance between focusing on the enemy and the people.

"There isn't anyone inside or outside of Iraq in 2006 who would have imagined that you could get al-Qaeda out of Ramadi," says the former mayor. "And that's why Patriquin, McMaster, MacFarland and Petraeus deserve to have statues built for them. It's true! Can you imagine how much Iraqi and American blood was spilled in Ramadi trying to fight without anything achieved? No one imagined that al-Qaeda could be expelled from Ramadi. They did it without a really big battle. They did it with their minds and their influence on the people. After they gained the trust of the people, it seemed very simple."

Najim concludes: "Americans haven't appreciated the value of what McMaster, MacFarland, Patriquin and Petraeus have done. It was a miracle, an absolute miracle. America hasn't learned the lesson it should have: We need people like Patriquin in the American military, not just for Iraq, but for all the Middle East, Afghanistan, Pakistan, and elsewhere. People who are principled and who can win the hearts and minds of the people with their culture and their minds, not their weapons."

According to Patriquin's commander, Sean MacFarland, "It all kind of comes back to Sattar, and Sattar reaching out to the brigade, and especially to Travis. A lot of people had meetings with Sattar and they think because they met with him, therefore they helped create the Awakening. Well, listen, having meetings with Sattar was not exceptional. Now one of the guys who deserves a lot of the credit for this whole thing is then Lieutenant Colonel Tony Deane. He is probably as important as Travis in many ways. He was initially the guy cultivating Sattar, with his civil-military affairs officer, Captain Pat Fagan. Those three guys, Travis, Tony and Pat, plus Jim Lechner, deserve a lot of credit for cultivating Sattar, probably the most credit. And Jim Lechner really delivered the goods to make Sattar believe we were as good as our word.

"Travis grew to mythical stature among the tribes. He played a very decisive role when the tribes were attacked by al-Qaeda, and this is what caused all of Anbar province to flip over to our side. When he was killed and I talked to sheiks from all around Ramadi, east, west, north, south, it didn't matter, their eyes would all brim with tears whenever you mentioned his name. They just adored him.

"What it really boils down to is there's a personality aspect to this that matters. And Travis was a central personality. Travis was my main link to Sattar. He wasn't my only link, but it was Travis who really gained Sattar's affection, and personalized our relationship with Sattar. And the personalization of that relationship was what was critical and allowed it to endure some pretty tough days."

MacFarland concludes, "I really don't know that the Awakening would have happened had it not been for Travis and Sattar meeting each other. Sometimes history turns on personalities and little meetings like that. Sometimes it's having the right people at the right place at the right time.

"Travis and Sattar were two men of destiny who happened to meet at the right place at the right time. And the rest is history."

In September 2010, Ramadi's mayor, Latif Eyada, declared of Patriquin, "He was a hero." When asked why, he replied, "He gave us our freedom."

On the west side of Ramadi, in the province of Anbar, in the Republic of Iraq, there is a neighborhood called Tameen that once was under the control of al-Qaeda.

It is home to an Iraqi police station that was built in early 2007, upon the ruins of a former Ba'ath party building.

It is an all-purpose police station, and its two hundred and thirty officers handle all kinds of things, from security patrols and burglaries to domestic violence, traffic duties, and lost dogs.

The building is called Martyr Hisham Abu Risha Police Station, named after Travis Patriquin, using the Arabic tribal name Sheik Sattar gave him. A few weeks after Patriquin's death, Sattar directed that the station be named in honor of a man he called his brother.

"We named this police station after Captain Patriquin because he played a very strong role in helping the tribes," explained Colonel Jabar Hamid Ajaj, the station's commander. "He was hoping our district would have a police station and everyone could start living normal lives. He had a very big role in our success against the terrorists and in uniting the tribes and the sheiks. I am very proud of this name for our station."

It is the only Iraqi building named after an American.

On the wall of the Martyr Hisham Abu Risha Police Station there hangs a photo of Travis Patriquin, a man who loved his family, loved the army, and loved the United States.

He was a man who loved Iraq.

SOURCE NOTES

There are four main research sources for this book: Travis Patriquin's own writings; U.S. military documents; author interviews; and other people's writings that have appeared in books, the media, or online.

Patriquin's thoughts and dialogue are all based directly on his writings, his e-mails and online postings, and statements he made at the time to his colleagues or family, to which I sometimes made very minor edits for grammar or clarity.

Military ranks are as of 2006. Most of the information in this book, unless otherwise indicated below, is from interviews the author conducted in 2007–2011 by phone, e-mail, skype, or in person. The source of dialogue in scenes involving Travis Patriquin and Iraqis is usually one or more of the Arabic-speaking interpreters who were in the room with him at the time, primarily Majd Alghabra, Sterling Jensen, Sa'ad Mohammed, or Atheer Agoubi. Whenever possible, the dialogue was also checked with others who were in the room at the time.

When Arabic names are translated to English, confusion often reigns. The name of Sheik Sattar, for example, has been rendered in press reports and military documents as Sittar abu-Risha; Sattar al-Buzayi, Abdul Sattar Abu Risha, and Abd Sittar Bezea Ftikhan. His tribe has been spelled abu Risha, Abouricha, and Rishawi. The tribe of Sattar's onetime ally Hamid al-Hayes is variously spelled Abu Diab, Thiab, and Ziab. The name of a key Ramadi sheik who was killed in August 2006 is often expressed in press and military reporting as Sheik Ali Jassim, when a more accurate version is Sheik Khaled A'rak (or Khalid Arrak) Ehtami Al-A'layawi'a of the Abu Ali Jassim tribe. While I've tried to be consistent and accurate with English renditions of Arabic names, I'm afraid this book does not help bring clarity to the situation.

A very valuable resource for background on the Awakening is the U.S. Marine Corps's two-volume oral history project *al Anbar Awakening* (referred to in notes below as "Marine Corps Oral History"), edited by Colonel Gary W. Montgomery and Timothy S. McWilliams, published in 2009 by the Marine Corps University Press in Quantico, Virginia, and available online. One volume is devoted to the U.S. military perspective, largely focused on marines, and the other volume is a fascinating series of oral histories of Iraqis.

Two notable books have been published about events in Ramadi: *The Sheriff of Ramadi: Navy SEALS and the Winning of al Anbar* by Dick Couch (Naval Institute Press, 2008) and *A Chance in Hell: The Men Who Triumphed Over Iraq's Deadliest City and Turned the Tide of War* by *USA Today* correspondent Jim Michaels (St. Martin's Press, 2010).

Author Interviews

Amy Patriquin, Gary Patriquin, Daniel Patriquin, Karrie Patriquin Zamora, Amy Pomante, Vincent Pomante, Jr., Karen Pomante,

Mike McClung, David Petraeus, Peter Chiarelli, George Casey, Sean MacFarland, Jim Lechner, Latif Eyada, Martin Fletcher, Andrew Duprey, Amy Forsythe, Chuck Ferry, Atheer Agoubi, Tony Deane, Shawn Nickell, Teddy Gates, Chad Pillai, Sarah Childress, Dave Grossman, Peter Mansoor, Roger Crombie, Pat Fagan, Jon-Paul Hart, Mark Lovejoy, Sterling Jensen, Louis Lartigue, Edward Goldner, Mark Bramwell, Billie Hensley, Scott Kish, Ricky Phelps, Ryan McDermott, Olsowy, Rusty Thomason, Ron Clark, Paul Weyrauch, Jimmy Vaughan, Rory Mauldin, Jeremy Sandor, Pete Lee, Anthony Passero, Paul Bremer, John Gronski, Dave Osborne, Brian Braithwaite, Will Bardenwerper, Ken Baker, Eric Remoy, Philip Mayberry, Andy Shoffner, Miccioto Johnson, Domenico Carbone, Andrew Gainey, Mike Bajema, Floyd Sheldon, Niel Smith, Paul Woods, Russ Wagner, Justin Corder, Mike Murphy, Aaron Dixon, Serge Franjie, Austin Long, Hikmet Sulaiman, Dan Walrath, Bill Jurney, Daniel Zappa, Kevin Collett, Jim Soriano, Brian Adamson, Butch Bowman, Gary Kidder, Najim Abed Al-Jabouri, Vincent Tedesco, Travis Stork, Gary Patton, Doug Overdeer, Edward Sullivan, Thaddeus McWhorter, Miguel Aguirre, Andy Griffith, Timothy Sebenick, Alton Lippe, Christopher Holston, Ken Zurcher, Howard Gregory, Matthew Van Wagenen, David Bradley, Joseph Harrington, Ron Thebau, John Tien, Andrew Slack, Ben Connable, David Pyle, Bryan Salas, Adel Abouhana, Chris Holton, Thomas Hollis, David Raugh, Tim McWilliams, Gary Montgomery, John Church, Jassim Muhammad Saleh al-Suwadawi, Jabar Hamid Ajaj, Adam McLaughlin, Sean Bolling, Terrence Finneran, Robert Neller, John Allen, Chris Hogan, Luiz Alicia-Rivera, Mike Williams, John Spencer. Some people interviewed requested anonymity, mostly people working in the U.S. intelligence and military Special Operations fields.

Materials Written by Travis Patriquin

Personal e-mails by Patriquin to his friends and family members, courtesy Amy Patriquin and friends and colleagues of Travis Patriquin.

Patriquin's personal papers, courtesy Amy Patriquin.

Operation Anaconda After-Action Report for SOT-A Team Alpha 506, U.S. Special Forces Command, March 2002.

Bilat Reports (meeting reports) filed by Patriquin on encounters with Iraqi sheiks, military and government officials, and citizens, October 2006–December 2006.

Online postings under name "travisquin" on lightfighter.net, April 19, 2005–November 21, 2006, courtesy lightfighter.net and Amy Patriquin.

"The View of Ramadi from Camp Ramadi," briefing paper for Ready First Combat Team (RFCT) brigade staff, Captain Travis Patriquin, June 4, 2006.

"Red on Red Violence and How to Make It Work for Us," briefing paper for RFCT brigade staff, June 4, 2006.

"How to Win the War in Al Anbar (by CPT Trav)," PowerPoint briefing for RFCT colleagues, MEF staff, and other audiences, October 2006.

"Ocam's [sic] Razor and the Ba'ath Party Threat to Tal Afar and Iraq as a Whole," draft working paper for RFCT staff, circa early 2006.

"Using Occam's Razor to Connect the Dots: The Ba'ath Party and the Insurgency in Tal Afar," *Military Review* (January–February 2007).

Videotape of brigade media training interview with Patriquin, early 2006.

U.S. Military Materials

U.S. Army personnel records pertaining to the career of Travis Patriquin, courtesy Amy Patriquin.

Ready First Combat Team After-Action Report, April 2007, covering experience in Tal Afar and Ramadi in 2006–2007.

Bilat Reports (meeting reports) filed by RFCT officers on encounters with Iraqi sheiks, military and government officials, July 2006–December 2006.

"1st BCT, 1st AD in Ramadi, OIF, 05–07," RFCT PowerPoint briefing, circa May 2007.

"TF 1-77 Steel Tigers O&I [Operations and Intelligence] Brief: Blood on the Axe," September 18, 2007.

"Western Ramadi Security Conference," RFCT PowerPoint briefing, circa September 2007.

"Task Force Duke O&I [Operations and Intelligence] Brief," RFCT PowerPoint briefing, circa December 2006.

"Ramadi Event Timeline," RFCT PowerPoint briefing, circa January 2007.

"Battle of Sufiyah," RFCT PowerPoint historical review, undated.

"Task Force 1st Battalion 37th Armor 'The Bandits' in OIF 05–07," PowerPoint presentation, undated.

"1st Battalion, 35th Armor, After-action Report, Operation Iraqi Freedom, 05–07," undated.

"CENTCOM Call Forward Force & Combat Operations in Ramadi, Operation Iraqi Freedom, 05–07," undated.

"Scheme of Maneuver," PowerPoint map and notes on Battle of Sufiyah prepared for the author on November 1, 2009, by USMC historian Colonel Gary Montgomery based on his battle site survey and interviews with Sheik Jassim and others in Ramadi in February 2009.

Memorandum, December 10, 2006, from Colonel Sean MacFarland to Commander, Army Human Resources Command, recommending award of the Presidential Unit Citation to RFCT "for extraordinary execution of counterinsurgency (COIN) operations and Iraqi Security Forces (ISF) transition in Tal Afar and Ar Ramadi, Iraq, from 14 February, 2006, to 18 February, 2007."

"Shiekh Abd Sittar Bezea Ftikhan," RFCT intelligence briefing, November 12, 2006.

"1st Army—Clear Hold Build," PowerPoint briefing, U.S. Army Combined Arms Center, February 13, 2009.

PowerPoint briefing on 1/137 Battalion's experience in Tal Afar and Ramadi, January 2006–February 2007, undated.

"2/28 BCT Fallen Warrior Memorial, By BG John L. Gronski Commander of 2/28 BCT in Ramadi, Iraq," undated.

"Setting Conditions in Ramadi," paper by BG John F. Gronski, July 2007.

Videotape of memorial service at Camp Ramadi for Travis Patriquin, Megan McClung, Vincent Pomante, December 2006.

Videotape of founding public meeting of the declaration of the Anbar Awakening at Sheik Sattar's compound, September 14, 2006, filmed by Sattar's staff and given to U.S. military, courtesy of Anthony Deane.

Interviews with Roger Crombie, Sean MacFarland, and Anthony Deane, Operational Leadership Experiences, Combat Studies Institute, Fort Leavenworth, Kansas.

Other Sources
Notes of Martin Fletcher interviews of Iraqis and Americans in Ramadi about Travis Patriquin, October 2007, courtesy of Martin Fletcher.

Personal journal of Sterling Jensen, courtesy of Sterling Jensen.

Personal journal of Anthony Passero on Operation Anaconda, courtesy of Anthony Passero.

Sterling Jensen, "News From the Awakening," briefing series published in 2008 by Foundation for Defense of Democracies; accessed at www.defenddemocracy.org.

"Al Qa'ida in Iraq Situation Report," captured al-Qaeda document, from the U.S. Military Academy's Combating Terrorism Center Harmony Database; available at ctc.usma.edu/harmony/harmony _docs.asp.

Iraq coverage of the *New York Times, Washington Post, Wall Street Journal*, Al Jazeera, *USA Today, Guardian, Time, Newsweek*, the *Times* (of London), BBC, Fox News, CNN, *Daily Star, Mother Jones, Los Angeles Times, The Nation, Weekly Standard*, Associated Press, Reuters, *Army Times, Inside the Pentagon, Stars and Stripes, Military Review*, New Yorker, *Christian Science Monitor*, Small Wars Journal blog, NPR.

Adam Geibel, "Operation Anaconda, Shah-i-Khot Valley," *Military Review* (May 2002).

Niel Smith and Sean MacFarland, "Anbar Awakens: The Tipping Point," *Military Review* (March 2008), and Sean MacFarland, "Addendum: Anbar Awakens," *Military Review* (May 2008).

Bing West, *The Strongest Tribe: War, Politics and the End Game in Iraq* (Random House, 2008).

Mitchell Reiss, *Negotiating with Evil: When to Talk to Terrorists* (Open Road Media, 2011).

Bing West, "Counterinsurgency Lessons from Iraq," *Military Review* (March 2009).

Michael Eisenstadt, "Iraq: Tribal Engagement Lessons Learned," *Military Review* (September 2007).

Andrew Lubin, "Ramadi from the Caliphate to Capitalism," *Naval Institute Proceedings*, April 2008.

Michael Visconage, "Turning the Tide in the West," *Marine Corps Gazette*, February 2008.

Dick Couch, "The Lessons of Ramadi," *Naval Institute Proceedings*, October 2008.

Anthony Deane, "Providing Security Force Assistance in an Economy of Force Battle," *Military Review* (January–February 2010).

Mark Cancian, "What Turned the Tide in Anbar?" *Military Review* (September 2009).

Dave Kilcullen, "Anatomy of a Tribal Revolt," August 29, 2007; accessed at www.smallwarsjournal.com.

Tim Dyhouse, "Ramadi: A Tale of Two Cities," *VFW* (Veterans of Foreign Wars magazine, August 2007).

Tim Dyhouse, "Ramadi: Success Rides on the Marines' Shoulders," *VFW* (Veterans of Foreign Wars magazine, September 2007).

Neil Shea, "Ramadi Nights," *Virginia Quarterly Review* (January 2008).

Additional Source Notes

PROLOGUE

Patriquin's meeting Sattar: details and dialogue are from interviews with a Baghdad-born interpreter for the U.S. military who was known to Americans at Camp Ramadi by the nickname "Ricky Martin." He asked me not to use his real name, so I refer to him in this book as Sa'ad Mohammed, which is the only pseudonym used in this book. References to the work of the CIA in this book are primarily from interviews with several U.S. government officials and civilians with firsthand knowledge of the events described. It is important to note that this author has come across no indication of CIA contacts with the late Sheik Sattar's brother and current Awakening leader, Sheik Ahmed abu Risha. **"Travis and I were both Infantry officers":** interview with James Lechner. **"I know sheiks":** interview with Adel Abouhana. **"He had insurgent credentials":** "Marine Corps Oral History." **Sattar background in 2003:** interview with Tom Hollis. **Sattar's detention by Special Forces in 2004:** interview with person with direct knowledge of the operation. **Hart on Patriquin:** interview with Jon-Paul Hart. **Pillai on Patriquin:** interview with Chad Pillai.

CHAPTER I

Afghanistan detail and dialogue; Patriquin's thoughts and statements in the Shah-i-Kot Valley: primary sources are Patriquin's detailed after-action report of his team's experience in Operation Anaconda; his postings on lightfighter.net; his e-mails after the battle to Rory Mauldin and other colleagues; after-action reports and award citation paperwork by Patriquin's Special Forces superiors on the operation, and interviews with Rory Mauldin,

Jeremy Sandor, Roger Crombie, Tony Passero, John Spencer, Amy Patriquin, and David Osborne. Sean Naylor's book *Not a Good Day to Die* provides valuable background on Operation Anaconda.

CHAPTER 2

Patriquin thoughts, quotes, biographical, and personal details in this chapter are from interviews with Patriquin's immediate family members and close friends; statements and e-mails he gave to his family and friends; and his postings on lightfighter.net in 2005 and 2006. **Patriquin's experiences in Jordan and Kuwait:** interviews with Patriquin's travel colleagues Ken Baker and Jeremy Sandor, and with Amy Patriquin. **Bowman on Patriquin:** interview with Clayton "Butch" Bowman. **"I thought he was a bullshit artist":** interview with DLI classmate of Patriquin. **Lippe on Patriquin:** interview with Alton Lippe. **"They're fanatics over there":** interview with close friend of Patriquin.

CHAPTER 3

Patriquin's thoughts and opinions in this chapter are from his memos, meeting reports, and other communications to the Ready First Combat Team staff; from statements and e-mails he gave to his family and friends; and from his postings on lightfighter. net. **"The most fucked-up place on Earth":** Neil Shea, "Ramadi Nights," *Virginia Quarterly Review* (Winter 2008). **"I'm going to lose maybe a hundred soldiers":** interview with Sean MacFarland. **"Ramadi was known for IEDs":** Shea, "Ramadi Nights." **"The sheer scale of violence in Ramadi"; "It's out of control"; "We just go out, lose people":** Todd Pittman, "Insurgents Hamper U.S., Iraqi Forces in Ramadi," Associated Press, May 22, 2006. **"It was** a disaster when al-Qaeda entered"; "The ugliest torture was committed"; "Ramadi became a ghost town": "Marine Corps Oral History." **MacFarland biographical details:** interview with Sean MacFarland. **Deane on MacFarland:** interview with Tony Deane. **MacFarland's mind-set on entering Ramadi:** interview with Sean MacFarland. **Ready First Combat Team composition:** interview with Sean MacFarland; RFCT documents. **American techniques to penetrate insurgent computer networks and phone calls:** Shane Harris, "The Cyberwar Plan," *National Journal*, November 13, 2009. **"It seemed to be an enigma":** George Packer, "The Lesson of Tal Afar: Letter from Iraq," *New Yorker*, April 10, 2006. **Wagner quotes on Patriquin:** interview with Russell Wagner. **"Once he knew he was going to be stuck":** interview with Aaron Dixon. **Lee on Patriquin:** interview with Pete Lee. **Deane on Patriquin:** interview with Tony Deane. **Dixon on Patriquin:** interview with Aaron Dixon. **Bardenwerper on Patriquin:** interview with William Bardenwerper. **"I met with tribal leaders all the time":** interview with Paul Bremer. **MacFarland's impressions of Patriquin; "Travis, you've got to help me out":** interview with Sean MacFarland.

CHAPTER 4

Patriquin's thoughts and quotes in this chapter are directly from his memos, meeting reports, and other communications to the RFCT staff; from statements and e-mails he gave to his family and friends; and from his postings on lightfighter.net. **"We are now amidst the date groves":** Sir Austen Henry Layard, *Discoveries Among the Ruins of Nineveh and Babylon* (New York: Harper & Brothers, 1853), p. 403. **"Patriquin didn't set out to fuck up":** interview with military officer who served in Ramadi in 2006.

CHAPTER 5

"You guys are way too cocky": interview with Sterling Jensen. "My perception was": interview with John Gronski. "The sooner you encourage young men": interview with John Gronski. Sunni tribesmen defending Shiites: Ellen Knickmeyer and Jonathan Finer, "Iraqi Sunnis Battle to Defend Shiites," *Washington Post* Foreign Service, Sunday, August 14, 2005. "My God"; "We were only a brigade": interview with John Gronski. "We never really established security": "Marine Corps Oral History." Events of January 3, 2006: interview with John Gronski. "I'm okay, go check on my boys": interview with Sa'ad Mohammed. "We simply didn't have enough security": interview with John Gronski. "Our methodology was to drop combat outposts": interview with Aaron Dixon.

CHAPTER 6

The main source for dialogue in meetings involving Patriquin in Ramadi in this chapter are interviews with interpreters (primarily Majd Alghabra and Sterling Jensen), military officers who were in the room at the time, and Patriquin's written reports, which periodically included passages of verbatim dialogue. "Fuck the Iraqis"; Patriquin on Iraqi police: interview with member of Patriquin's personal security detail. Ed Sullivan on sheiks and al-Qaeda: interview with Ed Sullivan. Patriquin gathering West's personal effects: interview with Sterling Jensen. Deane's thoughts and quotes on police recruitment: interview with Tony Deane. "I want to fight al-Qaeda with you": interview with Teddy Gates. "Temporary substations": interview with person involved in the process. Recruiting drive in late July; Patriquin and Lechner quotes: interviews with Tony Deane, Sterling Jensen, and Michael Murphy. According to Deane, other officers who were instrumental in building the relationship with Sattar were Captains Sean Frerking and John Cornett. **CIA money for police bonuses:** interviews with three people with direct knowledge of the process. **Evolution of Patriquin-Sattar relationship in July and August 2006:** interview with Majd Alghabra. **Sattar's quotes on Bush; liberating Iraq; and Americans walking the streets:** interview with Serge Franjie, who was an interpreter for Tony Deane's battalion. **Patriquin-Sattar meetings' details and dialogue; Patriquin's conversation with Sunni cleric:** interview with Majd Alghabra.

CHAPTER 7

Details and quotes on TAA activities, including Patriquin detail: RFCT intelligence documents, and interviews with five military, intelligence, and civilian personnel with direct experience in the events. **MacFarland on attack on Jazeera Iraqi police station:** interview with Sean MacFarland. **Teddy Gates comments on Iraqi police:** interview with Teddy Gates. **Patriquin thought the enemy had made a huge mistake:** interview with Sterling Jensen. **Patriquin late August meeting with Sattar and sheiks:** interview with Majd Alghabra. **Raugh, Bergman, Deane meetings with Sattar and sheiks in late August and September 2:** interviews with Tony Deane and Dave Raugh.

CHAPTER 8

Details of September 9, 2006, meeting: interviews with Sean MacFarland, Tony Deane, Majd Alghabra, Atheer Agoubi, and Sterling Jensen. Also, Jensen's contemporaneous journal notes of the meeting, courtesy Sterling Jensen. Note: What MacFarland didn't know as he pondered the "1776 feeling" of the moment was that Travis Patriquin's seventh great-grandfather, John Hart, was actually at Independence Hall in 1776 and signed the Declaration of Independence, as one of five signers from New Jersey who were delegates to the Second Continental Congress. Two years later, Hart lunched with George Washington and hosted his twelve thousand American soldiers to camp out and refresh themselves at his farm, days before the colonials' strategic victory at the Battle of Monmouth, the biggest clash of men in the Revolutionary War. And a man who might have been John Hart's direct ancestor, Edward Hart of Flushing, Queens, then part of the Dutch colony of New Netherland, was in 1657 the lead author of the historic Flushing Remonstrance, a petition for religious freedom. The appeal, considered a precursor to the U.S. Constitution's freedom of religion clause in the Bill of Rights, called for freedom of worship for all Christians and, in a remarkably foresighted passage, declared that "the law of love, peace and liberty" extends to all, including Jews, as well as "Turks and Egyptians"—in other words, Muslims. The records that would prove the speculated genealogical connection were lost in a 1789 fire, but if the theory was true, Edward Hart might have been Patriquin's ninth or tenth great-grandfather or great-granduncle, or otherwise a direct ancestor of Patriquin's. Sources: interview with Gary Patriquin, and interview with and research papers of Alice Smith, descendant of and genealogical researcher of John Hart. **"I think this is awesome!"; "That was the real deal"; "I think so, too"**: interview with Sterling Jensen. **Sattar switched off a major portion of the insurgency**: RFCT intelligence document. **Sattar-MacFarland exchange and MacFarland thoughts on Mohammed Mahmoud Latif**: interview with Sean MacFarland. **Sattar-Patriquin exchange on September 13**: interview with Majd Alghabra. **Details of September 14, 2006, sheiks' meeting and public declaration of Sahwa al Anbar**: videotape of the meeting shot by Sattar's staff and given to Tony Deane. I am grateful to Deane for the recording and to Atheer Agoubi for translating the key dialogue of this meeting for me. **"Sheik Sattar stated that the Sheik Council meeting"**: RFCT Bilat Report, September 15, 2006.

CHAPTER 9

Patriquin encouraged by seeing children on streets of Ramadi: "Ramadi Update," MEF public affairs video shot by USMC Staff Sergeant Amy Forsythe, August 3, 2006; and interview with Amy Forsythe. **Patriquin quotes on tribal strategy and Sattar:** interviews with Majd Alghabra, Sterling Jensen, and Sa'ad Mohammed. **"This is our way out"**: interview with Scott Kish. **"I want to win. And I want to go home"**: interview with Adel Abouhana. **Patriquin-Sattar exchanges on insurgent targets:** interviews with two people closely involved in the process. **"What a horrible idea"**: interview with Alfred Ben Connable. **"The tribal engagement by Travis Patriquin"**: interview with Scott Kish. **Army infantrymen housed with Iraqi policemen:** interview with Daniel Hensley. **Sattar's nicknaming of Patriquin, gifts:** interviews with Majd Alghabra, Domenico Carbone, James Lechner. **Patriquin's oration to Iraqi police recruits and quotes on evolution of Patriquin's PowerPoint:** interview with Andrew Duprey. Additional detail about PowerPoint from Andrew Slack and Sean MacFarland interviews. **Petraeus thought it made "eminent sense"**: interview with David Petraeus.

CHAPTER 10

Patriquin's attitudes toward certain MEF staff officers; Church's thoughts; e-mails, dialogue, and details about preparation for

and holding of meeting at MEF: interview with John Church. Additional detail from interviews with Aaron Dixon and Sterling Jensen. **"We ended up at some points fighting against our higher headquarters":** interview with RFCT officer. **"Catfight between little girls":** interview with RFCT interpreter. **"The MEF was trying to work":** interview with Tony Deane. **"Why aren't you supporting the Iraqi police?"; "The marines don't want it"; "The marines must be working for al-Qaeda"; "Maybe we should be fighting the marines":** interview with RFCT interpreter. **"You can't just sprinkle fairy dust":** interview with Robert Neller. **"Everybody was looking at us sideways":** interview with Sean MacFarland. **Patriquin worked with intelligence operatives on blog:** interview with Patriquin military colleague. **"One by one, the tribes approach the SAA council":** Niel Smith posting on smallwarsjournal.com. **"When the sheiks start inviting us to dinner":** interview with James Lechner. **CIA Ramadi station chief cable on the Awakening:** interview with Sean MacFarland. **"People in the Pentagon are starting to see":** interview with Sterling Jensen. **"I am only one man"; "If I get killed":** interview with Andrew Duprey.

CHAPTER 11

Detail on the Battle of Sufiyah: interviews with the two key Iraqi players in the incident, Sheik Jassim Muhammad Saleh al-Suwadawi and Sheik Abdul Rahman al-Janabi, both from the "Marine Corps Oral History"; and author interviews with Sheik Jassim, James Lechner, Pete Lee, Sterling Jensen, Eric Remoy, Andrew Shoffner, Niel Smith, Andrew Gainey, Joseph Harrington, Chuck Ferry, Majd Alghabra, and Sean MacFarland. Patriquin's dialogue and thoughts are primarily from interviews with Sterling Jensen,

Andrew Slack, and Majd Alghabra. Additional detail came from interviews with, notes of, and maps of U.S. Marine Corps historian Gary Montgomery, who did a battlefield survey of Sufiyah with Sheik Jassim in early 2009; and from RFCT after-action reports. **"If we grant, as many would be ready to do":** this sentence is shamelessly patterned on a sentence written by George Rippey Stewart that appears on page ix of his book *Pickett's Charge: A Microhistory of the Final Attack at Gettysburg, July 3, 1863* (New York: Houghton Mifflin Harcourt, 1991). He wrote: "If we grant— as many would be ready to do—that the Civil War furnishes the great dramatic episode of the history of the United States, and that Gettysburg provides the climax of the war, then the climax of the climax, the central moment of our history, must be Pickett's Charge." **Details, quotes, and report of December 2 and 3 Patriquin and Lechner meetings with Iraqis:** Patriquin Bilat (meeting) Reports, December 2, 3, and 4, 2006.

CHAPTER 12

Patriquin speaking of his dream of returning to Ramadi: interview with Sa'ad Mohammed. **Details of December 6, 2006, and the deaths of Travis Patriquin, Megan McClung, Vincent Pomante, and aftermath:** interviews with Jim Lechner, Sterling Jensen, Mike Bajema, Domenico Carbone, Sarah Childress, Alvaro Ybarra, Sean MacFarland, and various RFCT members. **"It's good they're here":** interview with Domenico Carbone. **Biographical detail on Megan McClung:** interviews with her father, Mike McClung; Bryan Salas; and John Church. **Note on Specialist Vincent J. "VJ" Pomante III:** Pomante was a man who worked very closely with Patriquin as his office assistant, gunner, and de facto bodyguard "outside the wire." He was a six-foot-four, twenty-two-year-old from Westerville,

Ohio, who was described by his friends as a mellow, super-friendly, fun-loving man, and was described by one reporter who spent time with him, Monte Morin of *Stars and Stripes*, as "a big outdoorsman" who "talked a lot about camping, outdoor gear, fishing and sailing," and "one of those rare soldiers you could talk with and forget you were still in Iraq." A friend described Pomante as always in "an awesome mood." According to his colleagues, Patriquin thought the world of Pomante and planned to put him in for promotion to corporal. **IED explosion:** There is some disagreement over the mechanism of the IED that killed Patriquin, McClung, and Pomante. The local U.S. military commander at Combat Outpost Falcon, Major Mike Bajema, explains, "All of the IEDs in my sector were command-wire detonated, since the new jamming equipment installed on the Humvees was able to block radio and cell phone signals to the IEDs. A command-wire IED could be dropped in the road, or more often pushed with a long pole from behind a wall corner, then the super-thin wires walked across the street by anyone—adult, child, we even once observed a donkey who had a spool of wire on its side. After the attack [on Patriquin's vehicle] the IED's copper wires were traced back to the school's rooftop, which the insurgent used for his cover." A different view is held by Jim Lechner, who surveyed the site and concluded that, in his opinion, military investigators came to the wrong conclusion by analyzing the area around the stopping point of the Humvee and not accounting for the fact that the vehicle rolled several dozen meters away from the initial blast site; and by mistaking, in his opinion, unrelated utility wires around that spot for control wires for the IED. The bomb, he concludes, was a pressure-plate device triggered simply by the vehicle's weight upon it. **"I was expecting to find a story":** interview with Martin Fletcher. **"I don't know why":** interview with Sa'ad Mohammed. **Domenico Carbone's thoughts** and quotes: interview with Domenico Carbone. "We can actually win": interview with Majd Alghabra. Singing voice could be heard: interview with Sarah Childress. Details of Camp Ramadi memorial service for Patriquin, McClung, and Pomante: videotape of service, courtesy Patriquin family; interviews with Sterling Jensen, Sean MacFarland, Andrew Duprey, and several other attendees. "What the fuck are they doing here?"; "You obviously don't get it"; "one of the most touching scenes": interview with Andrew Duprey. "Was Travis a Ranger, too?": interview with Tom Olsowy and Shawn Nickell. Details and quotes on the capture of Patriquin's alleged killers: interviews with James Lechner and Sterling Jensen.

EPILOGUE

"Iraq was a kaleidoscope": Bing West, *The Strongest Tribe: War, Politics and the Endgame in Iraq* (New York: Random House, 2009), p. xiv. "I'd say 20 percent of the credit": Todd Pitman, "Sunni Sheiks Join Troops to Fight Insurgency," Associated Press, March 26, 2007. "As a military person": "Marine Corps Oral History." "A scarcely mentioned reason": paper by Najim al-Jabouri and Sterling Jensen, commissioned by the Center for a New American Security and the College of William and Mary for a conference on the Sunni Awakening, in January 2010. Sattar statements on the Awakening, the Americans, and the surge: interviews with Majd Alghabra, Atheer Agoubi, Sterling Jensen, Sa'ad Mohammed. "The success in al Anbar wasn't the result of the troop surge": interview with Michael Murphy. "I'm so happy I could kiss you"; "a small fish": interview with David Petraeus. Petraeus on Patriquin, Ramadi, the Awakening, and the surge: interview with David Petraeus. "A convoy of Humvees"; "In place of every improvised explosive"; "He was an extraordinary man"; "He spoke Arabic"; "Allah gives you your first day": Martin Fletcher's notes of interview with Sheik Sattar, courtesy Martin Fletcher. "No single personality was the key"; "It's a process, not an event": Marine Corps Oral History. "It all kind of comes back to Sattar": interview with Sean MacFarland. "Travis grew to mythical stature"; "I really don't know that the Awakening": interview with Sean MacFarland. "He was a hero": interview with Latif Eyada. "We named this station": Martin Fletcher notes of interview with Colonel Jabar Hamid Ajaj. Details of Martyr Hisham abu Risha Police Station: interview with Colonel Jabar Hamid Ajaj.

ACKNOWLEDGMENTS

I am greatly indebted to the family of Travis Patriquin for their extraordinary support of my work, especially Amy Patriquin, Gary and Connie Patriquin, Dan Patriquin, Karrie Patriquin Zamora, Billie Hensley, and Carmen Pharis; and to the families of Megan McClung and Vincent Pomante.

I want to thank everyone else who helped make this book possible: especially the people I interviewed; my agent, Mel Berger of William Morris Endeavor and his colleague Graham Jainecke; my editor, Brent Howard; my publisher, Kara Welsh; and Jay Barksdale, David Smith and Wayne Furman of the New York Public Library, who gave the book a home as it was being born in the incredible Frederick Lewis Allen Room for Writers.

My own family was a tremendous help to me, and I thank Naomi, Brendan, Marilou, Bill, Kate, Joe, Chizuko, and Shigeo for their inspiration and support.

INDEX

A-10 tank-killing aircraft, 22
ABC News, 248
Abdel Rahman Mosque,
    Ramadi, 142
Abraham, 90
Abu Aetha tribe, 143
Abu Ali Jassim tribe, 143, 204
Abu Alwani tribe, 207
Abu Bali district, 219, 221, 233
Abu Fahd tribe, 140, 268
Abu Ghraib prison, 92
Abu Mahal tribe, 67, 111, 218, 222,
    226–27, 233
Abu Risha tribe, 4, 123
Abu Shaban tribe, 258
Abu Soda tribe, 213, 216, 218, 222,
    227–30, 233, 236, 237, 238
Abu Thiab tribe, 152
AC-130 attack aircraft, 22, 27
ACOG (advanced combat optical
    gun sight), 29
Afghanistan
    al-Qaeda in, 10, 19–21, 23–26, 31,
        35, 38, 40, 43, 220
    Patriquin in, 10, 19–21, 23, 24, 26,
        27, 29–34, 38–43, 59, 73, 74
    Shah-i-Kot Valley, Battle of, 10,
        19–22, 24–35, 38–43
    Tora Bora, Battle of, 24, 43

Agoubi, Atheer, 130–31
AH-64 Apache gunships, 21
Ahmed, Anas, 279
Ajaj, Jabar Hamid, 286
Ajlun, Jordan, 55
Al Janabi tribe, 163
al-Qaeda, in Afghanistan, 10, 19–21,
    23–26, 31, 35, 38, 40, 43, 220
al-Qaeda in Iraq, 8, 92
    Al-A'layawi'a murder and,
        143, 144
    in Al Qaim, 111–12
    attack on Jazeera police station
        and, 143–44
    in Ramadi, 63–71, 98, 100, 109–10,
        113–14, 116–17, 123–27, 129,
        132–35, 139–45
    Sufiyah and, 213–19, 221–23, 226–38
    TAA (Thawar al Anbar) death squads
        and, 139–42
    tribal alliance against, 151–55,
        157–63, 172–76, 213–19, 221–23,
        226–38, 244–45, 248–49, 266,
        267, 269–75, 279
Al Qaim, Iraq, 111–12, 152, 272, 281
al-A'layawi'a, Khaled A'rak
    Ehtami, 143, 144
Alexander the Great, 19, 90
Alford, Dale, 111

Alghabra, Majd, 129–30, 133, 135, 152, 207
Alwani, Sallam, 260
Amariyah, Iraq, 111
Amman, Jordan, 55, 60, 99, 106
Anbar Emergency Council (Anbar Salvation Council), 146, 153, 154, 159, 163, 268
Anbar People's Council (APC), 112, 155, 158, 243–44, 281
Anbar province (*see* Patriquin, Travis; Reconstruction of Ramadi; Sattar abu Risha, Sheik; Tribal engagement policy)
Anbar Provincial Council, 153, 154, 205, 269
al Anbar University, 67
AO Topeka, 71
Apple Macintosh, 184
Aqaba, Jordan, 55
Arab Bulletin, 79
Arab-Israeli War of 1973, 207
Arabian Desert, 48
Arabic language, 10–11, 23, 24, 47–48, 53–57
Armstrong, Karen, 79
al-Assafi, Thamer Ibrahim Tahir, 68
Associated Press, 248
Awakening movement, 112, 139, 153, 158, 159, 160, 162, 163, 179, 192–95, 198, 205–6, 214–17, 221, 229, 237, 243–45, 265–85
Aylwin-Foster, Nigel, 78
al-Aziz, Sabah al-Sattam Effan Fahran al-Shurji, 67, 111

B-2 bombers, 21
B-52 bombers, 21
Ba'athists, 70, 110, 162
Babylon, 90
Badr Corps, 245
Baghdad, Iraq, 63, 66, 90–93, 111, 125, 141, 178, 220, 268, 270, 272
Bagram Air Base, Afghanistan, 23, 30, 41
Bajema, Major, 252–54
Baker, Ken, 48, 56, 58, 60
Baqubah, Iraq, 116
Bardenwerper, Will, 82
Bedouin tribes, 5, 48, 66, 67, 106
Bergman, Chuck, 145
Bethlehem, 56
bin Laden, Osama, 24, 71, 220

Black Hawk Down, 4
Blocking Position Eve, 28, 30
Bowman, Butch, 52
Braithwaite, Brian, 208
Bramwell, Mark, 281–82
Bremer, Paul, 84, 96
British
    in Afghanistan, 19
    in Iraq, 5, 90
British SAS, 177
Bush, George W., 132, 146, 206, 276
    Iraq War and, 91–92
    troop surge and, 273

Camp Blue Diamond, 128, 163, 235, 250, 269
Camp Corregidor, 216–17, 219, 223, 227–29, 236
Camp Fallujah, 71, 99
Camp Hurricane Point, Ramadi, 108
Camp Ramadi, 8, 72, 85, 89, 90, 99, 113, 125, 153, 204, 222, 229, 234, 276–77
Campbell University, 73
Cann, Adam, 114
Carbone, Domenico, 246, 250, 251, 255
Casey, George, 238, 271
Charlton, John, 268
Chechnya fighters, 43
Cheney, Dick, 96
    Iraq War and, 91–92
Chiarelli, Pete, 71
Childress, Sarah, 246, 250–52, 255
Chinook CH-47 helicopters, 25, 27
Christianity, 90
Church, John, 191, 196–202, 249–50
CIA (Central Intelligence Agency), 6, 72, 84, 94, 99, 129, 156, 176, 192, 203, 205–6, 281
CIA Special Activities Division, 177
Civil-Military Operations (CMO) officer, 75
Close air support (CAS), 28
Coalition Provincial Authority (CPA), 84, 192
Colombia, 53
Combat Outpost Falcon, 250, 252
Commander's Emergency Response Program (CERP), 169
Connable, Alfred "Ben," 6, 113, 178, 280–81

COP (combat outpost) concept, 97–98, 108, 116–17, 215
Counterinsurgency, history of, |94, 95, 99
Crombie, Roger, 25, 27, 31, 33, 34, 38, 40
Crusades, 59, 134

Damascus, Syria, 106, 151
Dead Sea, 55, 56, 60
Deane, Anthony, 4, 67, 69, 81, 117–18, 123–27, 135, 146, 160, 162, 192–93, 266, 285
Declaration of Independence, 49
Defense, U.S. Department of, 176
Defense Intelligence Agency (DIA), 72, 176
Defense Language Aptitude Battery, 53
Defense Language Institute, Monterey, California, 10, 47, 50, 53–54, 78–79, 180
Desert Protectors, 111, 281
Devlin, Peter, 195
Devlin Report, 195, 247
Dixon, Aaron, 75–76, 81, 98, 202
Diyala province, 245, 270
Dresden, Germany, 64
al-Duaywi, Dahir Sahar, 204
Dulaimi Confederation, 4, 111
Duprey, Andrew, 9–10, 181, 183, 186, 208, 255–56, 258
Duran, Luis, 253

Eagles Cell, 111
Emergency Response Units, 207, 242
Euphrates River, 16, 64, 72, 89–90, 125, 128, 214, 217–18, 226, 227, 230, 235
Eyada, Latif, 286

F-16 fighter-bombers, 21–22
F-18 fighter-bombers, 21–22, 229, 231, 234
F-18 Hornets, 21–22
Fagan, Pat, 118, 125, 135, 162, 266, 282–83, 285
al-Fahdawi, Qassem Mohammad, 278
Fallujah, Iraq, 8, 15, 65, 69, 71, 92, 97, 116, 125, 135
al Farouq training complex, Afghanistan, 220
Ferry, Chuck, 223, 227–29, 231–37

"Fighting Back: The City Determined Not to Become al-Qaeda's Capital" (Fletcher), 248–49
Fletcher, Martin, 248–49, 274–75
Fort Benning, Georgia, 22, 39, 51
Fort Bragg, North Carolina, 10, 22, 33, 73
Fort Campbell, Kentucky, 48, 55
Fort Chaffee, Arkansas, 52
Fort Leavenworth, Kansas, 187
Fox News, 245, 248
Francis Howell North High School, St. Charles, Missouri, 50
Franks, Tommy, 43
Friedberg, Germany, 75

Gainey, Andrew, 234
Gaoud, Faisal, 152
Garden of Eden, 90
Gates, Robert, 283
Gates, Teddy, 118, 124, 125, 144, 266
Geneva Convention rules, 24
Ghosh, Bobby, 204
Golan Heights, 55
Great Awakening, 10
Green Berets, 52, 53
Gronski, John, 105, 108, 112–15
Gulbuddin, Zia, 27
Gulf States, 5
Gulf War, 21

Haditha, Iraq, 92, 111
Hamas of Iraq, 157, 158
Hamid, General, 243
Hamza, Abeer Qasim, 220
Hamza Brigade, 111
Harrington, Joe, 232, 238
Hart, John, 49
Hart, Jon-Paul, 9
Hassan, Ali, 66
al-Hayes, Hamid, 152, 160, 257, 274
Heinlein, Robert, 50
Hellfire missiles, 228, 234
Henry V, King of England, 184
Henry V (Shakespeare), 183
Himalayan Mountains, 20
Hiroshima, 64
Hit, Iraq, 111
Holden, William, 81
Hollis, Tom, 7
"How to Win the War in al Anbar by CPT Trav," 186–87
Hussein, Saddam, 70, 83, 121
    capture of, 92, 176

Ia Drang, Battle of, 33
Ibrahim, Khalil, 258
IEDs (improvised explosive devices),
    8, 64, 69, 105, 107, 134, 173,
    232–33, 237, 252, 254
Iliad (Homer), 51
Inkblot method, 98, 117
Inquisition, 59
Intelligence, 6–7, 25–26, 72, 111,
    176–79
Iran, 153
Iran-Iraq War, 83, 134
Iraq War, management of, 89–93
Iraqi army, 14, 73, 96, 97, 124, 140, 145,
    162, 204, 219, 248
Iraqi Constitution, 146
Iraqi Islamic Party, 65, 146, 278
Iraqi Ministry of Defense, 243
Iraqi Ministry of the Interior (MOA),
    124, 178, 193–94, 243
Iraqi police, 14–15, 73, 77, 96–98, 106,
    108, 122, 132, 133, 135, 140,
    154–55, 179–84, 205, 207, 215,
    219, 244, 261, 273
    Jazeera station, attack on, 143–44
    Martyr Hisham Abu Risha Police
       Station, Tameen, 286
    Patriquin and, 174–76, 178–79,
       181–84, 243
    Qatana district battle and, 269
    recruitment of, 113–14, 123–29,
       173–76, 178, 193–94, 242, 243,
       248, 249
Irbid, Jordan, 55
Islam, 57–60, 90, 134
Israel, 57
Iwo Jima, 143

Jabour, Hamid, 221
al-Jabouri, Najim Abed, 283–84
Jalayba district, 215
JAM, 245
al-Janabi, Abdul Rahman, 238
Jassem, Zaif, 163
Jazeera police station, attack on, 143–44
Jensen, Sterling, 151–53, 157, 175, 206,
    251, 260, 262, 270
Jerash, Jordan, 55
Jericho, 56
Jerusalem, 56
Jesus Christ, 56, 134
Jesus Prayer, 57
John the Baptist, 56

Johnson, Miccioto, 282
Jordan, 6, 8, 10, 48, 55–59, 78, 125, 178
    Anbar sheiks in exile in, 141, 152, 161,
       192–94, 271
JTJ (Jama'at al-Tawhid wal-Jihad), 70
Judaism, 59, 60, 90
Julaybah district, 233
Jurney, Bill, 266

Kabul, Afghanistan, 23, 43
Kale, Afghanistan, 30
Karbala, Iraq, 93
Kelly, John F., 280
Khalidiyah, Iraq, 111
Khalil, General, 243
Khanjar, Ahmad, 111
Kish, Scott, 179
Kissinger, Henry, 175, 207
Koran, 47, 58, 77, 161
Korean War, 21
Kubaysah, Iraq, 111
Kurdistan, 92
Kuwait, 48, 59, 78

Lake Habaniya, Ramadi, 108, 232, 241
Latif, Mohammad Mahmoud, 157–58
Lawrence, T. E., 47, 49, 79, 198
Lawrence of Arabia (movie), 49
Layard, Austen Henry, 90
Lechner, Jim, 4–5, 13, 105–6, 118,
    125, 128, 132, 135, 175, 178, 181,
    193, 205, 206, 234–36, 242, 243,
    250–53, 257, 259–62, 266, 285
Lee, Pete, 80–81, 213–14, 233, 234
Leonardo da Vinci, 10
Leticia, Colombia, 53
Lewis, Bernard, 79
Lincoln, Abraham, 132
Lippe, Alton, 54
Lovejoy, Mark, 4

M1 Abrams tanks, 65
M203 grenades, 28, 39
Maamoun Sami Rashid, Governor, 65, 99,
    146, 154, 156, 160, 162, 204–5, 207,
    269, 278, 279
MacFarland, Sean, 63–64, 70–72, 96–97,
    106, 116–18, 143–44, 146, 160, 175,
    196, 223, 228, 237, 238, 257, 266,
    268, 269, 282
    background of, 69
    funeral oration for Patriquin by, 258
    on interoffice tensions, 194

Latif, negotiations with, 157–58
Patriquin and, 9, 69, 73, 82, 85,
    98–99, 284–85
press conference about Ramadi,
    247–48
tribal engagement policy and,
    85, 93, 98–99, 126–27, 135,
    151–58, 179
Magnum, P.I. (TV series), 51
al-Mahalawi, Raja Nawaf
    Farhan, 65
Mahdi Army, 93
Malaab district, 108, 180, 215
al-Maliki, Nouri, 269, 274
Man-Portable Signal Intelligence
    system, 30
al-Manaf, Hashim ibn Abd, 180
Mansoor, Pete, 93
Martyr Hisham Abu Risha
    Police Station, Tameen, 286
Marzak, Afghanistan, 30
al-Masri, Abu Ayyub, 214,
    219–22, 238
Mattis, James, 65
Mauldin, Rory, 24, 27, 29–32,
    34–35, 38–41
McClung, Megan Malia Leilani,
    246–47, 249–52, 255, 257, 259
McClure, Doug, 50
McLaughlin, Mike, 15, 108–9, 113–14,
    133, 255
McMaster, H. R., 77, 97, 107, 284
McWhorter, Thaddeus, 270
Mecca, 60, 180
Media embed program, 245–50,
    255–56
Medina, 60
Menchaca, Kristian, 220
Mesopotamia, 5, 90
Miami Vice (TV series), 51
Microsoft, 184
Modern Standard Arabic, 47
Mogadishu, Battle of, 4–5, 262
Mohammed, Sa'ad, 130, 241–42, 254
Mohammed the Prophet, 67, 180
Mojica, Sergeant, 28
Mongols, 90
Monsoor, Michael Anthony, 171
Morse code, 52
Mortar attacks, 8, 25–26, 216–17, 219
Moses, 55
Mount Nebo, Jordan, 55, 60
Multinational Corps—Iraq, 71

Murphy, Mike, 128, 132, 274
Mutammar Sahwat al-Iraq (Iraqi
    Awakening), 270–71
Myrer, Anton, 199

National Security Agency, 72, 176
    Director's Medal, 53
NBC News, 248
Neighborhood watch groups, 218, 272
Neller, Robert, 193–94
Newsweek magazine, 246, 250
Nickell, Shawn, 259
1920 Revolution Brigades, 110–11, 153,
    157, 158, 173, 221
Ninewah province, 245
Nixon, Richard, 49
North, Oliver, 245, 250

Obama, Barack, 183
Odierno, Raymond, 272, 273
Odyssey (Homer), 51
Officer Candidate School,
    Fort Benning, 39
Oil pipeline, Ramadi, 140
Old Testament, 59
Olsowy, Tommy, 259
Once an Eagle (Myrer), 199
Operation Anaconda, 43, 73, 74
Operation Steel Curtain, 111
Osborne, David, 22, 39
Ottomans, 5, 49

Paladin howitzers, 232
Pashto language, 23
Passero, Anthony, 25, 26, 28–29,
    31–35, 38, 40
Patriquin, Amy Alston, 49, 54–57, 91
Patriquin, Danny, 91
Patriquin, Gary, 49–50
Patriquin, Travis
    in Afghanistan, 10, 19–21, 23, 24, 26,
        27, 29–34, 38–43, 59, 73, 74
    Alghabra and, 152
    ancestry of, 49
    Arabic blog written by, 203–4
    as Arabic speaker, 10–11, 47–48,
        53–57, 77–78, 80, 182–83,
        231, 238
    birth of, 49, 50
    burial of, 259
    on center of insurgency, 71
    childhood of, 50
    children of, 49, 55

Patriquin, Travis *(cont.)*
  Church and, 191, 196–202
  death of, 252, 254, 256, 285
  decorations awarded to, 10, 42, 259
  at Defense Language Institute, 10, 47, 50, 53–54
  Devlin Report and, 195
  early military career of, 10, 51–53
  education of, 50, 73
  first marriage of, 50, 54
  full name of, 49
  history of counterinsurgency and, 94, 95
  humanitarian convoys and, 204
  intellect of, 9–10
  interoffice tensions and, 191–92, 198–200
  Iraqi culture and, 77–81
  Jensen and, 151–52
  joins army, 50
  in Jordan, 55–58, 60
  as key figure in Awakening, 265, 267
  knee problems of, 22, 23, 42, 73
  in Latin America, 53
  leadership skills of, 74
  Lechner and, 5
  MacFarland and, 9, 69, 73, 82, 85, 98–99, 284–85
  Mansoor and, 93
  mantras of, 32–33
  Marine Fourth Civil Affairs Group meeting and, 200–2
  marksmanship training and, 76
  media embed program and, 245–46, 255–56
  memorial service for, 257–58
  midcareer switch by, 75–76
  mustache of, 12–13, 131
  nickname of, 180
  at Officer Candidate School, Fort Benning, 39
  as Pashto speaker, 23
  patriotism of, 49
  personality of, 5, 9, 40, 52, 74, 82, 130, 131, 267, 285
  personnel records of, 52
  physical appearance of, 12–13, 81, 131, 182
  police recruits and, 174–76, 178–79, 181–84, 243
  PowerPoint presentations and, 184–87, 277
  at Ranger School, Fort Benning, 22, 259
  reading by, 50, 51, 79
  reconstruction of Ramadi and, 169–70, 241–42
  religion and, 57–60, 134
  Sattar and, 3–5, 8, 9, 11–16, 118, 129–35, 144–45, 151–53, 157–60, 163, 172, 174–78, 180–81, 201–2, 204–5, 254–55, 275–76, 281, 282, 285, 286
  Sufiyah and, 219, 222–23, 229–31, 234–36, 238
  Sunni-Shia relations and, 115
  suspects in death of, 259–62
  TAA (Thawar al Anbar) death squads and, 139–43
  in Tal Afar, 77, 82
  targeting lists and, 176–78
  tribal engagement policy and, 94–95, 105–6, 151–53, 157–60, 163, 171–72, 174–76, 207–9, 213–15, 219, 243–46, 265, 277, 281–85
  tributes to, 281–86
  TV shows and, 50–51
  at Wadi Rum, 47–49
Persian Gulf War, 83
Persians, 90
Petra, Jordan, 55
Petraeus, David, 187, 271–73, 277–78, 283, 284
Pillai, Chad, 9, 283
Pittman, Todd, 66
Plain of Lagash, Iraq, 89
Pomante, Vincent J., 246, 251, 252, 255, 257, 259
Posttraumatic stress disorder (PTSD), 41
PowerPoint presentations, 184–87, 277
Predator drones, 22, 228, 234
Presidential Unit Citation, 93

Qatana district, 269

Rawah, Iraq, 111
Ramadi, Iraq *(see* Patriquin, Travis; Reconstruction of Ramadi; Sattar abu Risha, Sheik; Tribal engagement policy)
Ramadi General Hospital, 67, 170
Ramadi Reconstruction Conference, 268
Rand Corporation, 85
Ranger School, Fort Benning, 22, 259
Raugh, Dave, 145, 146

Reconstruction of Ramadi, 169–70, 179, 241–42, 248–49, 276–77
Remoy, Eric, 217, 233, 237–38
Renaissance, 10
Republican Guard, 92
Reuters, 248
Rice, Condoleezza, 206
Ricks, Tom, 195
River Jordan, 56
Roman Catholic Church, 57
Route Apple, 228
Route Michigan, 105, 269
Route Nova, 218
Route Sunset, 250–52
RPG attacks, 105, 173
Ruble, Britt, 66
Rumsfeld, Donald, 96
    Iraq War and, 91–92, 112

SAA (Sahwa al Anbar) (see Awakening movement)
al-Sadr, Moqtada, 93, 115, 273
St. Louis, Missouri, 49
Salah al Din province, 245, 270
Salas, Bryan, 249
Salman, Rasoul Mohammed, 279
Sandor, Jeremy, 24, 29–30, 31
Sanna district, 215
Satellite phone technology, 42–43
Sattar, Ahmed, 4, 8, 123–27, 133, 160, 175, 242, 276
Sattar, Sattam, 160, 246, 275
Sattar abu Risha, Sheik, 3, 14, 15, 99, 106, 107, 117–18, 139, 192, 193, 195, 198, 213, 222, 229, 237, 242
    al-A'layawi'a murder and, 144
    alliance against al-Qaeda and, 8, 145–47, 151–55, 157–63, 172–76, 215, 244–45, 266, 269–72, 275
    arrest of, 7
    Deane and, 123–27, 146–47
    death of, 276
    Latif, negotiations with, 157–58
    Maamoun and, 204–5
    operations of, 6–7
    Patriquin and, 3–5, 8, 9, 11–16, 118, 129–35, 144–45, 151–53, 157–60, 163, 172, 174–78, 180–81, 201–2, 204–5, 254–55, 275–76, 281, 282, 285, 286
    at Patriquin's memorial service, 257–59
    photographed with Bush, 276

    physical appearance of, 6
    press and, 246, 248, 274–75
    Qatana district battle and, 269–70
    TAA (Thawar al Anbar) and, 142
    targeting lists and, 177–78
    U.S. intelligence and, 6, 7
    U.S. troop surge and, 273–74
Saudi Arabia, 8, 48, 59
Second Officers District, Ramadi, 209
Serkhankel, Afghanistan, 30
Seven Pillars of Wisdom: A Triumph (Lawrence), 47, 49
Shadow UAV (unmanned aerial vehicle), 229, 230, 233, 234
Shah-i-Kot Valley, Battle of, 10, 19–22, 24–35, 38–43
Sharia law, 67
Shark Base, 72, 176, 203
Sharks Fin, 214
Shoffner, Thomas "Andy," 65–66, 234–35
SIGINT (signals intelligence), 52
Smith, Niel, 97, 205, 274
Sofia (see Sufiyah, Iraq)
Somalia, 4–5
Sons of Iraq program, 218, 272–73
Soriano, Jim, 206
Soviets, in Afghanistan, 19
Special Forces Qualification Course (Q Course), 53
Spiegel, Peter, 24–25
Stalingrad, 64
Starship Troopers (Heinlein), 50
State, U.S. Department of, 192, 206, 281
Strickland, Nathan, 266
Sufiyah, Iraq, 122, 213–19, 221–23, 226–38, 243
Suicide bombings, 114, 220, 278–79
Suleiman, Hatem, 274
Sullivan, Ed, 109–10
Sumerians, 89
Sunni tribal sheiks (see Tribal engagement policy)
al-Suwadawi, Jassim Muhammad Saleh, 213–14, 216–23, 226–37
SVBIED (suicide vehicle-borne improvised explosive device), 143
Syria, 106, 151, 153, 161, 220

TAA (Thawar al Anbar) death squads, 139–43
Takfirist, 101

Takur Ghar mountain, 28
Tal Afar, Iraq, 11, 13, 24, 77, 82, 97,
    106, 107, 205, 283
Taliban, 23, 25, 26, 31, 38, 43
Tameen police station, 286
Task Force 77, 176
Task Force 145, 176–77
Tatars, 67
al-Thiyabi, Tariq Yusif Mohammad,
    160, 257, 269–70
Thomas, Keni, 262
Tigris River, 90
Times (of London), 248
Tora Bora, Battle of, 24, 43
Torah, 59
Triangle of Death, 220
Tribal engagement policy, 85, 93–95,
    98–99, 105–6, 126–27, 135,
    151–60, 162, 163, 171–72, 174–76,
    179, 207–9, 213–15, 219, 243–46,
    265, 277, 281–85
Tucker, Thomas, 220
Turks, 90

UH-60 medical evacuation
    helicopter, 40
Ur, 90
Urdu language, 24
U.S. First Battalion, Sixth Marines, 207
U.S. Army First Brigade, Third Armored
    Division, 268
U.S. Army Second Brigade Combat Team,
    Twenty-eighth Infantry Division,
    15, 105, 107–8, 110, 113–16
U.S. Army Third Armored Cavalry
    Regiment, 77, 97
U.S. Army Third Ranger
    Battalion, 4–5
U.S. Army 5th Special Forces Group,
    10, 23, 24, 48, 55
U.S. Army 7th Special Forces Group, 10, 51
U.S. Army 10th Mountain Division,
    23–27, 30, 38, 41, 74
U.S. Army 82nd Airborne
    Division, 22, 23, 73, 74
U.S. Army 101st Airborne Division, 24, 25,
    33, 41, 72, 74, 220

U.S. Army First Brigade, First Armored
    Division, 44, 71, 72
U.S. Army National Guard, 8
U.S. Joint Special Operations Command
    (JSOC), 72, 176, 229
U.S. Marine Expeditionary Force—West
    (MEF), 71, 113, 125, 126, 135, 178,
    191–98, 243
U.S. Marine Fourth Civil Affairs Group,
    200–2
U.S. Navy SEAL Special Operations, 72,
    176, 217, 229
U.S. Ready First Combat Team (RFCT),
    71, 75–77, 93, 107, 108, 114–17,
    126, 127, 191, 213–15, 227–28, 265,
    268, 280, 282
U.S. Special Operations Team Alpha,
    23, 29, 32, 39–41, 51–53, 74
Uzbekistan, 23, 43

Vann, John Paul, 94
Vietnam War, 21, 33, 49, 94, 99,
    161, 175, 247
"View of Ramadi from Camp Ramadi,
    The" (Patriquin), 277
Virginian, The (TV series), 50

Wadi Rum, 47–49, 60
Wagner, Russell, 74
Walrath, Dan, 125
Washington Post, 140, 195
Welch, Richard D., 6
West, Bing, 156, 266
West, Jason, 117
West Bank, 56
WMDs (weapons of mass
    destruction), 92
World War I, 5

Yarmouk University, Jordan, 10, 55
Ybarra, Alvaro, 246

Zamora, Karrie Patriquin, 90
al-Zarqawi, Abu Musab, 111, 116, 140,
    176–77, 220
al-Zawahiri, Ayman, 220
Zilmer, Rick, 71